Function

Robert C. Martin Series

Visit **informit.com/martinseries** for a complete list of available publications.

The **Robert C. Martin Series** is directed at software developers, team-leaders, business analysts, and managers who want to increase their skills and proficiency to the level of a Master Craftsman. The series contains books that guide software professionals in the principles, patterns, and practices of programming, software project management, requirements gathering, design, analysis, testing, and others.

Make sure to connect with us!
informit.com/socialconnect

Functional Design

PRINCIPLES, PATTERNS, AND PRACTICES

Robert C. Martin

✦✦ Addison-Wesley

Hoboken, New Jersey

For information about buying this title in bulk quantities, or for special sales opportunities (which may include electronic versions; custom cover designs; and content particular to your business, training goals, marketing focus, or branding interests), please contact our corporate sales department at corpsales@pearsoned.com or (800) 382-3419.

For government sales inquiries, please contact governmentsales@pearsoned.com.

For questions about sales outside the U.S., please contact intlcs@pearson.com.

Visit us on the Web: informit.com/aw

Library of Congress Control Number: 2023940397

ISBN-13: 978-0-13-817639-6
ISBN-10: 0-13-817639-6

$PrintCode

DEDICATION

To my family, my love for them explains everything I do.

First, to my wife of 50 years, the gorgeous 16-year-old with glistening brown eyes and long, flowing black hair who captured my heart and has held it for more than half a century. She remains as gorgeous as the day I met her. Those glistening brown eyes and flowing locks enrapture me every day. The mother of my children. The anchor of my life. My one and only love.

To Angela, my beautiful firstborn and ever-faithful daughter whose devastatingly contagious smile will melt your heart and convince you that all is right with the world. I once asked her what she wanted to be. Her answer was "Fun!" She went on to achieve, and far exceed, that goal. Her boundless enthusiasm for life infects everyone she encounters. She married Matt, a wonderful, hardworking, and honest (and fun) man. Together the two of them have turned the fun they share into a mountain-biking frenzy of gainful employment. They live on a wooded hilltop and have raised three beautiful, intelligent, and talented daughters for me to spoil.

To Micah, my second-born and passionately dedicated son. He inherited his mother's glistening brown eyes. I once asked him what he wanted to be. He said, "Rich!" I'm happy to report that he has done quite well. He spent the better part of a decade working with me and then founded his own software business, which he sold some years later. Then he spent a year building an airplane in his garage. Now he's running yet another software business. Much of his success is due to Angelique, the beautiful, hardworking, and deeply intelligent woman he married. They have raised two spectacular young men.

To Gina, my third-born and endlessly surprising daughter. If it is possible for a woman to be more beautiful than my wife, Gina is that woman. She became an accomplished chemical engineer, working with such pleasant substances as uranium, fluorine, and concentrated sodium hydroxide. She donned hard hats, climbed reaction vessels, and managed teams of chemical plant operators. She married Keith, a wonderful, hardworking, and honest mechanical engineer. The two of them swap stories about their adventures at big and complex chemical plants. They have produced three (2.9 as of this writing) of my grandsons. More than three years ago, struggling with the competing pressures of motherhood, work, and the pandemic, she asked me if I thought a career change to software engineer might be possible. Oh yeah, it was possible, all right. She's crushing it! And, by the way, her industrial experience is a big factor in just why she is crushing it.

To Justin, my last-born and confidently competent son. Justin is a deeply analytical soul for whom no problem is insoluble, no challenge is unmeetable, and no wrong is un-rightable. If that sounds a tad quixotic, be assured that he is also a pragmatist of the highest order. He chooses his battles well. He also has this annoying tendency to be . . . right. He called his mother and me in January of 2020 and told us a very serious pandemic was coming. He recommended getting into cryptocurrencies and made quite a nice nest egg with his speculations. He is a software engineer *par excellence* and currently runs a software team for a company in Austin. He married Ela, a fiery, gorgeous young redhead whose intelligence and integrity are exceeded only by her courage. They have produced two beautiful children—a boy and a girl—the first of my children's families to enjoy that particular privilege.

Happy is the man who has his quiverful of children and grandchildren.

Contents

FOREWORD

Uncle Bob needs little introduction. A prominent figure in the software development industry, Bob has authored several books on software design and delivery. Some of his works are taught in computer science classrooms around the world.

I was a student in university when I started functional programming. I didn't attend an elite computer science program teaching Scheme and C, but I was hungry for all things computing. Nobody was talking about functional programming then. I saw a wave of programming coming in the future; a future where developers spent more time thinking about the problem they were solving, rather than how to manage it. After reading *Functional Design*, I wish I had this book then and now, at every stage in my career, from student to professional.

Functional Design exudes "classic-on-arrival." It feels like a book written exactly for the professional software developer. Bob touches on the foundations of software engineering and expands upon them, putting into succinct words the things I've experienced for years. He elegantly pulls back the curtain to reveal how functional programming elements make software design simple yet pragmatic. He does so without alienating experienced object-oriented programmers coming from languages like C#, C++, or Java.

By introducing a comparative analysis to Java, *Functional Design* introduces functional systems design with Clojure, a Lisp dialect. Clojure isn't so pure like Haskell where one must use pure functional programming concepts. Instead, Clojure strongly encourages it, making it a great first functional programming language. *Functional Design* carefully points out the few pitfalls Clojure developers find themselves in from time to time. As a Clojure consultant myself, I can attest to this. This book teaches how to keep a language (and developer) out of the way, rather than seeking something that gets out of the way.

Clojure's critics will say that Clojure is unsuitable for any sufficiently large codebase. As you'll learn in the coming chapters, the design principles and patterns apply to Clojure just as they do to Java, C#, or C++. The design principles of SOLID will help you build better software with functional programming. Design patterns have long since been scoffed at by functional programmers, but *Functional Design* deconstructs such criticism and shows exactly why developers need them, and how developers can implement them on their own.

I've written extensively online about classic design patterns in Clojure, so I was delighted to find that this book approaches design pattern usage with thoughtful diagrams before showing the reader code. By the time you reach those chapters, you'll already be able to picture the Clojure code just from the diagrams. Then, the code follows. Finally, *Functional Design* ties it all together by walking you through an "enterprise" application in Clojure using the design principles and patterns.

—Janet A. Carr, Independent Clojure Consultant

PREFACE

This is a book for programmers in the trenches who want to learn how to use functional programming languages to get real things done. As such, I will not spend any appreciable time on the more theoretical aspects of functional programming such as Monads, Monoids, Functors, Categories, and so on. Not that these ideas aren't valid, valuable, or relevant; rather, they do not often impact the day-to-day world of the programmer. This is because they have already been "baked into the cake" of the common languages, libraries, and frameworks. If you are interested in functional theory, I recommend the writings of Mark Seemann.

This book is about how—and why—to use functional programming in our day-to-day effort to build real systems for real customers. In the pages that follow, we will be comparing and contrasting the coding structures that are common in object-oriented languages like Java to those that are common in functional languages like Clojure.

I have chosen these two languages in particular because Java is very widely known and used, and Clojure is extraordinarily simple to learn.

A Brief History of Functional and Procedural Programming

In 1936, two mathematicians, Alan Turing and Alonzo Church, independently resolved one of David Hilbert's famous challenges: *The Decidability Problem*. It is beyond the scope of this introduction to describe this problem in any detail, except to say it had to do with finding a general solution to formulae of integers.[1] This is relevant to us because every program in a digital computer is an integer formula.

The two men independently proved that no such general solution exists by demonstrating that there were integers that could never be calculated by an integer formula smaller than the integer itself.

Another way to say this is that there are numbers that no computer program can compute. And indeed, that was the approach that Alan Turing took. In his famous 1936 paper,[2] Turing invented a digital computer, and then showed that there were numbers that could not be computed—even given infinite time and space.[3]

Church, on the other hand, came to the same conclusion through his invention of lambda calculus, a mathematical formalism for manipulating functions. Using manipulations in the logic of his formalism, he was able to prove that there were logical problems that could not be solved.

Turing's invention was the forebear of all modern digital computers. Every digital computer is, for all intents and purposes, a (finite) Turing machine. Every program that has ever executed on a digital computer is, for all intents and purposes, a Turing Machine program.

---

1. Diophantine equations.

2. A. M. Turing, "On Computable Numbers, with an Application to the Entscheidungsproblem" (May 1936).

3. Given infinite time and space, a computer could calculate π or ϵ or any other irrational or transcendental number for which a formula exists. What Turing and Church proved is that there were numbers for which no such formula can exist. Such numbers are "uncomputable."

Church and Turing later collaborated to show that Turing's and Church's approaches were equivalent. That every program in a Turing machine can be represented in lambda calculus, and vice versa.

Functional programming is, for all intents and purposes, programming in lambda calculus.

So these two styles of programming are equivalent in a mathematical sense. Any program can be written using either the procedural (Turing) style or the functional (Church) style. What we are going to examine in this book is not that equivalence, but rather, the ways that using the functional approach affects the structure and design of our programs. We will seek to determine whether those different structures and designs are in any sense superior, or inferior, to those that arise from using the Turing approach.

On Clojure

I chose Clojure for this book because learning a new language and a new paradigm is a doubly difficult task. Therefore, I sought to simplify that task by choosing a language that is simple enough to not get in the way of learning functional programming and functional design.

Clojure is semantically rich but syntactically trivial. What that means is that the language itself has a very simple syntax that requires very little effort to learn. The learning curve in Clojure is all on the semantic side. The libraries and idioms require a significant effort to internalize; but the language itself requires almost no effort at all. My hope is that this book will give you a way to learn and appreciate functional programming while not being distracted by the syntax of a new language.

Having said all that, this book is not a Clojure tutorial.[4] I will explain some of the basics in the early chapters and use some explanatory footnotes throughout the text, but I will also rely upon you, gentle reader, to do your

---

4. By the end, you will think me a liar.

homework and look things up. There are several Web sites that will help. One of my favorites is https://clojure.org/api/cheatsheet.

The test framework I used in this book is speclj.[5] As the chapters progress, you'll see more and more of it. It is very similar to other popular testing frameworks, so as the pages turn, you should not find it difficult to become familiar with its various facilities.

ON ARCHITECTURE AND DESIGN

A primary focus of this book is to describe the principles of design and architecture for systems built in a functional style. Toward that end, I will employ unified modeling language (UML) diagrams and make reference to the SOLID[6] principles of software design, *Design Patterns*,[7] and the concepts of *Clean Architecture*. Fear not, I will be explaining things as we go along and will cite many external references should you need to look things up.

ON OBJECT ORIENTATION

Many have expressed the opinion that object-oriented programming and functional programming are incompatible. These pages should prove otherwise. The programs, designs, and architectures that you see here will be an admixture of both functional and object-oriented concepts. It is my experience, and my strongly held opinion, that the two styles are entirely compatible and that good programmers can, and should, apply them together.

ON "FUNCTIONAL"

In this text, I will make use of the term *functional*. I will define it and expound upon it. As the chapters roll by, I will also take some license

---

5. https://github.com/slagyr/speclj

6. Robert C. Martin, *Clean Architecture* (Pearson 2017), p. 57.

7. Erich Gamma, Richard Helm, Ralph Johnson, and John Vlissides, *Design Patterns: Elements of Reusable Object-Oriented Software* (Addison-Wesley, 1994).

with it. There will be examples that, while written in a functional language and in a functional style, will not be *purely* functional. In most such cases, I will put quotation marks around the word *functional* and use footnotes to point out the license I am taking.

Why take that license? Because this is a book about pragmatics, not theory. I am more interested in extracting the benefits from the functional *style* than in strict adherence to an ideal. For example, as we'll see in the first chapter, "functions" that take input from the user are not purely functional. I will, however, make use of such "functions" as appropriate.

The source code for all the examples in all the chapters is in a single GitHub repository named https://github.com/unclebob/FunctionalDesign.

Register your copy of *Functional Design: Principles, Patterns, and Practices* on the InformIT site for convenient access to updates and/or corrections as they become available. To start the registration process, go to informit.com/ functionaldesign and log in or create an account. The product ISBN (9780138176396) will already be populated. Look on the Registered Products tab for an Access Bonus Content link next to this product, and follow that link to access any available bonus materials. If you would like to be notified of exclusive offers on new editions and updates, please check the box to receive email from us.

Acknowledgments

Thank you to the diligent and professional folks at Pearson for helping to guide this book to completion: Julie Phifer, my ever-helpful, ever-supportive publisher of long-standing; and her compatriots, Menka Mehta, Julie Nahil, Audrey Doyle, Maureen Forys, Mark Taber, and a host of others. It has always been a joy to work with you, and I look forward to many future such endeavors.

Thank you to Jennifer Kohnke, who has produced the vast majority of the gorgeous illustrations in my books over the last three decades. Back in 1995, up against a production deadline, Jennifer, Jim Newkirk, and I pulled an all-nighter to get the illustrations for my very first book formatted and organized just the way I wanted.

Thank you to Michael Feathers, who suggested 20 years ago that I investigate functional programming. He was learning Haskell at the time and was enthusiastic about the possibilities. I found his enthusiasm contagious.

Thank you to Mark Seemann (@ploeh) for his consistently insightful works, his keen and devastatingly rational reviews of my works, and also for his moral courage.

Thanks to Stuart Halloway, who wrote the first book I read about Clojure. It was more than a decade and a half ago that I started that adventure, and I have never looked back. Stuart was kind enough to coach me through my very first experiments with functional programming. Also to Stuart, an apology for once, long ago, speaking out of turn.

Thanks to Rich Hickey who debated with me in the early '90s regarding C++ and object-oriented design and then went on to create and masterfully guide the development of Clojure. Rich's insights into software continue to amaze me.

Though I have never met them, I owe a debt of gratitude to Harold Abelson, Gerald Jay Sussman, and Julie Sussman for the book that truly inspired me to pursue functional programming. That book, *The Structure and Interpretation of Computer Programs (SICP)*, may be the most consequential of all the books on software that I have read. It is available for free online. Just search for "SICP."

Thank you to Janet Carr for her Foreword. I stumbled onto Janet's work while perusing Twitter one day and found that she had come to many of the same conclusions regarding functional programming and Clojure that I had.

And for writing the Afterword, thank you to Gina Martiny, my lovely daughter and an accomplished chemical and software engineer. More about her in my dedication.

About the Author

Robert C. Martin (Uncle Bob) has been a programmer since 1970. He is founder of Uncle Bob Consulting, LLC, and cofounder with his son Micah Martin of The Clean Coders, LLC. Martin has published dozens of articles in various trade journals and is a regular speaker at international conferences and trade shows. He has authored and edited many books, including *Designing Object-Oriented C++ Applications Using the Booch Method*, *Pattern Languages of Program Design 3*, *More C++ Gems*, *Extreme Programming in Practice*, *Agile Software Development: Principles, Patterns, and Practices*, *UML for Java Programmers*, *Clean Code*, *The Clean Coder*, *Clean Architecture*, *Clean Craftsmanship*, and *Clean Agile*. A leader in the industry of software development, Martin served for three years as editor-in-chief of the *C++ Report*, and he served as the first chairman of the Agile Alliance.

FUNCTIONAL BASICS

IMMUTABILITY 1

WHAT IS FUNCTIONAL PROGRAMMING?

If you were to ask the average programmer what functional programming is, you might get any of the following answers.

- Programming with functions.
- Functions are "first class" elements.
- Programming with referential transparency.
- A programming style based upon lambda calculus.

While these assertions might be true, they are not particularly helpful. I think a better answer is: *Programming without assignment statements.*

Perhaps you don't think that definition is much better. Perhaps it even frightens you. After all, what do assignment statements have to do with functions; and how can you possibly program without them?

Good questions. Those are the questions that I intend to answer in this chapter.

Consider the following simple C program:

```
int main(int ac, char** av) {
    while(!done())
        doSomething();
}
```

This program is the core loop of virtually every program ever written. It quite literally says: "Do something until you are done." What's more, this program has no visible assignment statements. Is it functional? And if so, does that mean every program ever written is functional?

Let's actually make this function do something. Let's have it compute the sum of the squares of the first ten integers [1..10]:

```
int n=1;
int sum=0;
```

```
int done() {
  return n>10;
}

void doSomething() {
  sum+=n*n;
  ++n;
}

void sumFirstTenSquares() {
    while(!done())
        doSomething();
}
```

This program is not functional because it uses two assignment statements in the doSomething function. It's also just plain ugly with those two global variables. Let's improve it:

```
int sumFirstTenSquares() {
  int sum=0;
  int i=1;
loop:
  if (i>10)
    return sum;
  sum+=i*i;
  i++;
  goto loop;
}
```

This is better; the two globals have become local variables. But it's still not functional. Perhaps you are worried about that goto. It is there for a good reason. Bear with me as you consider this small modification that uses a worker function to convert the local variables into function arguments:

```
int sumFirstTenSquaresHelper(int sum, int i) {
loop:
  if (i>10)
    return sum;
```

```
    sum+=i*i;
    i++;
    goto loop;
}


int sumFirstTenSquares() {
    return sumFirstTenSquaresHelper(0, 1);
}
```

This program is still not functional; but it's an important *milestone* that we'll refer to in a moment. But now, with one last change, something magical happens:

```
int sumFirstTenSquaresHelper(int sum, int i) {
    if (i>10)
        return sum;
    return sumFirstTenSquaresHelper(sum+i*i, i+1);
}


int sumFirstTenSquares() {
    return sumFirstTenSquaresHelper(0, 1);
}
```

All the assignment statements are gone, and this program is functional. It's also recursive. That's no accident. If you want to get rid of assignment statements, you *have* to use recursion. Recursion allows you to replace the assignment of local variables with the *initialization* of function arguments.

It also burns up a lot of space on the stack. However, there is a little trick we can use to fix that problem.

Notice that the last call to sumFirstTenSquaresHelper is also the last use of sum and i in that function. Holding those two variables on the stack after initializing the two arguments of the recursive call is pointless; they'll never be used. What if, instead of creating a new stack frame for the recursive call, we simply reused the current stack frame by jumping back to the top of the function with a goto, as we did in the *milestone* program?

This cute little trick is called *tail call optimization (TCO)* and all functional languages make use of it.[1]

Notice TCO effectively turns that last program into the *milestone* program. The last three lines of sumFirstTenSquaresHelper in the *milestone* program are, in effect, the recursive function call. Does that mean the *milestone* program is functional too? No, it just behaves identically. At the source code level, that program is not functional because it has assignment statements. But if we take one step back and ignore the fact that the local variables changed as opposed to being reinstantiated in a new stack frame, then the program *behaves* as a functional program.

As we will discover in the next section, that is not a distinction without a difference. In the meantime, just remember when you use recursion to eliminate assignment statements, you are not necessarily wasting lots of space on the stack. The language you are using is almost certainly using TCO.

THE PROBLEM WITH ASSIGNMENT

First let's define what we mean by *assignment*. Assigning a value to a variable *changes* the original value of the variable to the newly assigned value. It is the change that makes it assignment.

In C we initialize a variable this way:

```
int x=0;
```

But we assign a variable this way:

```
x=1;
```

---

1. In one way or another. The *Java virtual machine (JVM)* complicates TCO a bit. C, of course, does not do TCO and so all my recursive examples in C will grow the stack.

In the first case, the variable x comes into existence with the value 0; prior to the initialization, there was no variable x. In the second case, the value of x is changed to 1. This may not seem significant, but the implications are profound.

In the first case, we do not know if x is actually a variable. It could be a constant. In the second case, there is no doubt. We are varying x by assigning it a new value. Thus, we can say that functional programming is programming *without variables*. The values in functional programs *do not vary*.

Why is this desirable? Consider the following:

```
.

//Block A

.

x=1;

.

//Block B

.
```

The *state of the system* during the execution of Block A is different from the state of the system in Block B. This means that Block A must execute *before* Block B. If the position of the two blocks were swapped, the system would likely not execute correctly.

This is called a *sequential or temporal coupling*—a coupling in time; and it is something you are probably quite familiar with. Open must be called before close. New must be called before delete. Malloc must be called before free. The list of pairs[2] like this is endless. And in many ways, they are a bane of our existence.

How many times have you forgotten to close a file, or release a block of memory, or close a graphics context, or release a semaphore? How many

---

2. They are like the Sith; always two there are.

times have you debugged a pernicious problem only to find that you can fix it by swapping the position of two function calls?

And then there's garbage collection.

Garbage collection is a horrible[3] hack that we have accepted into our languages because we are just so bad at managing temporal couplings. If we were adept at keeping track of allocated memory, we would not depend on some nasty background process to clean up after us. But the sad fact is we are so truly terrible at managing temporal couplings that we celebrate the crutches we build to protect ourselves from them.

And that doesn't take into account multiple threads. When two or more threads are competing for the processor, keeping the temporal couplings in the correct order becomes a much more significant challenge. Those threads may get the order correct 99.99 percent of the time; but every once in a great while they may execute in the wrong order and cause all manner of mayhem. We call those situations *race conditions*.

Temporal couplings and race conditions are the natural consequence of programming with variables—of using assignment. Without assignment, there are no temporal couplings and there are no race conditions.[4] You cannot have a concurrent update problem if you never update anything. You cannot have an ordering issue within a function if the system state never changes within that function.

But perhaps it's time for a simple example. Here's our nonfunctional algorithm again; this time without the goto:

```
1: int sumFirstTenSquaresHelper(int sum, int i) {
2:    while (i<=10) {
3:      sum+=i*i;
```

---

3. And, no, reference counting isn't any better.

4. We'll see later that this is not entirely correct. As Spock was fond of saying: "There are always possibilities."

```
4:     i++;
5:   }
6:   return sum;
7: }
```

Now let's say you'd like to log the progress of the algorithm with a statement like this:

```
log("i=%d, sum=%d", i, sum);
```

Where would you put that line? There are three possibilities. If you add the `log` statement after line 2 or 4, then the logged data will be correct, and the difference will simply be whether you are logging before or after the computation. If you insert the `log` statement after line 3, then the logged data will be incorrect. That is a temporal coupling—an ordering problem.

Now consider our functional solution, with one interesting cosmetic change:

```
int sumFirstTenSquaresHelper(int sum, int i) {
   return (i>10) ? sum : sumFirstTenSquaresHelper(sum+i*i, i+1);
}
```

There is only one place we can put our `log` statement, and it will log correct data.

So Why Is It Called Functional?

A function is a mathematical object that maps inputs to outputs. Given $y = f(x)$, there is a value of y for every value of x. Nothing else matters to f. If you give x to f, you will get y every single time. The state of the system in which f executes is irrelevant to f.

Or to say that a different way, there are no temporal couplings with f. There is no special order in which f must be invoked. If you call f with x, you will get y no matter what else may have changed.

Functional programs are true functions in this mathematical sense. If you decompose a functional program into many smaller functions, each of those will also be a true function in the same mathematical sense. This is called *referential transparency*.

A function is referentially transparent if you can always replace the function call with its value. Let's try that with our functional algorithm for calculating the sum of the squares of the first ten integers:

```
int sumFirstTenSquaresHelper(int sum, int i) {
  return (i>10) ? sum : sumFirstTenSquaresHelper(sum+i*i, i+1);
}


int sumFirstTenSquares() {
  return sumFirstTenSquaresHelper(0, 1);
}
```

When we replace the first call to sumFirstTenSquaresHelper with its implementation, it becomes:

```
int sumFirstTenSquares() {
  return (1>10) ? 0 : sumFirstTenSquaresHelper(0+1*1, 1+1);
}
```

When we replace the next function call, it becomes:

```
int sumFirstTenSquares() {
  return
    (1>10) ? 0 :
      (2>10) ? 0+1*1
              : sumFirstTenSquaresHelper((0+1*1)+2*2,
                                         (1+1)+1);
}
```

I think you can see where this is going. Each call to sumFirstTenSquares Helper simply gets replaced with its implementation with the arguments properly replaced.

Notice that you cannot do this simple replacement with the nonfunctional version of the program. Oh, you can unwind the loop if you like; but that's not the same as simply replacing each function call with its implementation.

So, functional programs are composed of true mathematical, referentially transparent functions. And that's why this is called functional programming.

No Change of State?

If there are no variables in functional programs, then functional programs cannot change state. How can we expect a program to be useful if it cannot change state?

The answer is that functional programs compute a new state from an old state, *without changing the old state*. If this sounds confusing, then the following example should clear it up:

```
State system(State s) {
   return isFinal(s) ? s : system(s);
}
```

You can start the system in some initial state, and it will successively move the system from state to state until the final state is reached. The system does not change a state variable. Instead, at each iteration, a new state is created from the old state.

If we turn TCO off and allow the stack to grow with each recursive call, then the stack will contain all the previous states, unchanged. Moreover, the system functions as a true function in the mathematical sense. If you call system with state1, it will return state2 every single time.

If you look closely at our functional version of sumFirstTenSquares, you will see that it uses precisely this approach to the changing of state. There are no variables, and no internal state. Rather, the algorithm moves from the initial state to the final state, one state change at a time.

Of course, our system function does not appear to be able to respond
to any inputs. It simply starts at some initial state and then runs to
completion. But with a simple modification we can create a "functional"
program that responds quite nicely to input events:

```
State system(State state, Event event) {
  return done(state) ? state : system(state, getEvent());
}
```

Now, the computed next state of the system is a function of the current
state and an incoming event. And voila! We have created a very traditional
finite state machine that can react to events in real time.

Notice the quotes I put around the word *functional* above. That is
because getEvent is not referentially transparent. Every time you call it
you will get a different result. Thus, you cannot replace the call with its
return value. Does this mean that our program is not actually functional?

Strictly speaking, any program that takes input in this manner cannot be
purely functional. But this is not a book about purely functional programs.
This is a book about functional *programming*. The style of the program
above is "functional," even if the input is not pure; and it is that style we
are interested in here.

So here, for your entertainment, is a simple little real-time finite state
machine that is written in C and is "functional." It is the time-honored
subway turnstile example. Have fun with it.

```
#include <stdio.h>

typedef enum {locked, unlocked, done} State;
typedef enum {coin, pass, quit} Event;

void lock() {
  printf("Locking.\n");
}
```

```
void unlock() {
  printf("Unlocking.\n");
}

void thankyou() {
  printf("Thanking.\n");
}

void alarm() {
  printf("Alarming.\n");
}

Event getEvent() {
  while (1) {
    int c = getchar();
    switch (c) {
      case 'c': return coin;
      case 'p': return pass;
      case 'q': return quit;
    }
  }
}

State turnstileFSM(State s, Event e) {
  switch (s) {
    case locked:
    switch (e) {
      case coin:
      unlock();
      return unlocked;

      case pass:
      alarm();
      return locked;

      case quit:
      return done;
    }
```

```
    case unlocked:
    switch (e) {
      case coin:
      thankyou();
      return unlocked;

      case pass:
      lock();
      return locked;

      case quit:
      return done;
    }
    case done:
    return done;
  }
}

State turnstileSystem(State s) {
  return (s==done)? 0
                : turnstileSystem(
                      turnstileFSM(s, getEvent()));
}

int main(int ac, char** av) {
  turnstileSystem(locked);
  return 0;
}
```

Keep in mind that C does not use TCO, and so the stack will grow until it is exhausted—though that may require quite a few operations in this case.

IMMUTABILITY

What all this means is that functional programs contain no variables. Nothing in a functional program changes state. State changes are passed from one invocation of a recursive function to the next, without altering any of the previous states. If those previous states aren't needed, TCO can optimize them away; but in spirit they all still exist, unchanged, somewhere in a past stack frame.

If there are no variables in a functional program, then the values we name are all *constants*. Once initialized, those constants never go away and never change. In spirit, the entire history of every one of those constants remains intact, unchanged, and immutable.

2 PERSISTENT DATA

So far this has seemed relatively simple. Programs written in the "functional" style are simply programs that have no variables. Rather than reassign values to variables, we use recursion to initialize new function arguments with new values. Simple.

But data elements are seldom as simple as we have so far imagined them to be. So let's take a look at a slightly more complicated problem, *The Sieve of Eratosthenes*:

```java
package sieve;

import java.util.ArrayList;
import java.util.Arrays;
import java.util.List;

public class Sieve {
  boolean[] isComposite;

  static List<Integer> primesUpTo(int upTo) {
    return (new Sieve(upTo).getPrimes());
  }

  private Sieve(int upTo) {
    if (upTo<1)
      upTo=1;
    isComposite = new boolean[upTo+1];
    Arrays.fill(isComposite, false);
    isComposite[0]=isComposite[1] = true;
    for (int i=0; i<isComposite.length; i++)
      if (!isComposite[i])
        for (int c=i+i; c<isComposite.length; c+=i)
          isComposite[c] = true;
  }

  public List<Integer> getPrimes() {
    ArrayList<Integer> primes = new ArrayList<>();
    for (int i=0; i<isComposite.length; i++)
      if (!isComposite[i])
```

```
        primes.add(i);
    return primes;
    }
}
```

This cute little Java program computes the prime numbers up to a limit. Notice all the assignment statements. There are variables everywhere, so this program must not be functional.

But then again, look at the static function at the top. Sieve.primesUpTo is a true mathematical function. Every time you call it with n, it will return the prime numbers up to n. So we can cheat and say that despite the fact that the underlying algorithm uses variables, the result of that algorithm is functional.

On Cheating

Our computers are, in some sense, finite *Turing machines*; they are not based upon lambda calculus. The Church–Turing thesis tells us that Turing machines and lambda calculus are equivalent forms; but that doesn't mean you can easily translate from one to the other. A functional program is a program that *looks like* lambda calculus but is implemented in a finite Turing machine. And that implementation requires that we cheat.

The first cheat we saw was TCO. We waved it away with an argument about pragmatics. After all, since we were never going to need all those historical stack frames, why should we keep them? But that's still a cheat. Under the hood, our implementation was changing the values of existing variables. From the Turing machine's point of view, all our supposed constants were actually variables.

We could continue to push that cheat upward. This lovely little Sieve algorithm runs entirely in the constructor, so it's all initialization! And as we learned, initialization is not assignment. So the fact that this program has variables under the hood is no different from TCO. In the end, the result is still functional.

This is fun! We can keep pushing that cheat upward. We can push it up until it is outside our finite Turing machine of a computer. And then we could say to ourselves: "Every program that runs in this computer is functional because it will always produce the same outputs when given the same inputs. Never mind that the inputs and outputs include every single bit in the computer's memory. Never mind that. Yeah. That's the ticket."

Of course, if we take that view, then there's not much point in studying functional programming, is there? So let's back down from that highest-level cheat and keep pushing the cheats back down until we simply cannot practically escape them.

There is no reasonable escape from TCO. We don't have an infinite stack. We don't want our functional programs uselessly consuming gigabytes of stack space until they crash. So TCO is a practically unavoidable cheat.

MAKING COPIES

So, what about that `Sieve` algorithm: Can we push the cheating down lower than that? Can we write that algorithm so it does not use any assignment statements?

The problem, of course, is all those `for` loops. We need to turn those into recursive functions in order to get rid of the assignment statements. We also need to do something about the two arrays. We can't be changing elements in existing arrays, can we? That would make those arrays variables. So we'll have to make copies of them whenever we need to change an element:

```
package sieve;

import java.util.ArrayList;
import java.util.Arrays;
import java.util.List;
```

```java
public class Sieve {
  static List<Integer> primesUpTo(int upTo) {
    return getPrimes(
      computeSieve(
        makeSieve(Math.max(upTo, 1)),
        0),
      new ArrayList<>(), 0);
  }

  private static boolean[] makeSieve(int upTo) {
    boolean[] sieve = new boolean[upTo+1];
    Arrays.fill(sieve, false);
    sieve[0] = sieve[1] = true;
    return sieve;
  }

  private static boolean[] computeSieve(boolean[] sieve, int n) {
    if (n>=sieve.length)
      return sieve;
    else if (!sieve[n])
      return computeSieve(markMultiples(sieve, n, 2), n+1);
    else return computeSieve(sieve, n+1);
  }

  private static boolean[] markMultiples(boolean[] sieve,
                                         int prime,
                                         int m) {
    int multiple = prime * m;
    if (multiple>=sieve.length)
      return sieve;
    else {
      var markedSieve = Arrays.copyOf(sieve, sieve.length);
      markedSieve[multiple] = true;
      return markMultiples(markedSieve, prime, m+1);
    }
  }
}
```

```
  public static List<Integer> getPrimes(boolean[] sieve,
                                         List<Integer> primes,
                                         int n) {
    if (n>=sieve.length)
      return primes;
    else if (!sieve[n]) {
      var newPrimes = new ArrayList<>(primes);
      newPrimes.add(n);
      return getPrimes(sieve, newPrimes, n+1);
    } else {
      return getPrimes(sieve, primes, n+1);
    }
  }
}
```

That's not very pretty, is it? It is, however, pretty functional. You might complain about the assignments in makeSieve, and I agree that's a bit of a cheat, but it looks close enough to an initialization to satisfy me.

So, yes, all the significant assignment operations have been eliminated. All the named entities are constants, and the stack (if not deleted by TCO) contains the history of each invocation of each recursive function.

But at what cost? Every time either of the two arrays is modified, a new array is created in order to prevent the previous one from being changed. The amount of memory used by this algorithm could be enormous. Imagine finding all the primes up to 100,000. How many sieve arrays would be created? How many primes arrays?

And what about execution time? Copying all those arrays over and over again must eat up a terrifying number of cycles.

Is that, then, the cost of functional programming? Must we live with such a huge extravagance of memory and time?

STRUCTURAL SHARING

Fortunately, no. It turns out that there are data structures that behave very much like arrays but that also efficiently maintain the history of their past states. These data structures are *n*-ary trees. The bigger the *n*, the more efficient they are. But for the sake of simplicity, I will choose an *n* of 2—binary trees—for the following examples.

Let us say that we wish to represent a simple array of integers from 1 to 8. The binary tree that achieves this is shown in Figure 2.1.

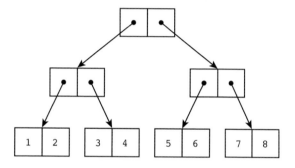

Figure 2.1. A binary tree representing an array of integers [1..8]

If you look at the leaves and ignore the branches, you will see that the leaves form an array. The branches simply provide a way to traverse to each leaf in some ordered way. That order is the index of the array!

To get to the element at index 0 of the array, simply take the leftmost branch of each node. To get to the element at index 1, go left at each node but right at the last node.

I won't belabor this point. I'm sure you all understand binary trees.

Now, let's say we want to append a 42 on the end of this array while preserving the existence of the previous array. The binary tree that achieves this is shown in Figure 2.2.

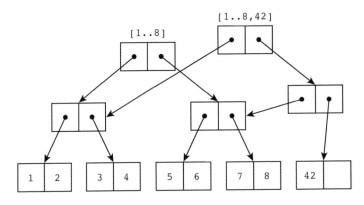

Figure 2.2. A binary tree that represents [1..8, 42] but also preserves the original [1..8] array

Now the tree has *two roots*. The root at the top left still represents the array from 1..8. The root at the top right represents the new array with a 42 appended after the 8.

Stop now and think carefully about this. It should be clear that representing linear arrays as trees, in the manner shown, will allow us to represent additions, insertions, and deletions while preserving all previous arrangements, without massive copying of the array.

Oh, there is some copying going on. We may have to copy a leaf node, or some of the branch nodes, depending on what operation we are performing. But the amount of memory and the number of cycles are drastically less than simply maintaining copies of all the past versions of the array.

In the end, every past version of the array will be represented by a new root node connected to a small number of additional branch nodes, allowing the majority of the elements of the array to be shared among all the versions.

Now consider what happens if we use 32-ary trees instead of binary trees. For arrays of a million elements, the tree depth is on the order of four or five branches. Copying five nodes of 32 elements each is *a lot* faster and requires *a lot* less memory than copying a million elements. Indeed, the cost, while not zero, is so small as to be inconsequential for most applications.

So we have a way to represent an indexable linear array that can be versioned over time while preserving all past versions. We call this *persistence*.[1] A persistent data structure has the ability to undergo change while remembering all past versions of itself.

But what about higher-level data structures like hash maps, sets, stacks, and queues? How do we make all of them as persistent as our linear indexed array? Of course, all those data structures can be implemented using indexed arrays. Indeed, since the memory of the computer is nothing more than one big indexed linear array, every data structure that you can represent within a computer can also be represented in a persistent array.

And so the problem we confronted at the start of this chapter, the problem of copying, can be set aside. The cost of functional programming, in memory and cycles, need not dissuade us from further study and pursuit of the benefits of functional programming.

And with that problem solved, all future examples will be written in Clojure, a language that intrinsically supports persistent data structures.

---

1. Not to be confused with the overloaded term used to describe data in offline storage.

RECURSION AND ITERATION 3

KOHNKE

In Chapter 1, Immutability, I stated that functional programming makes use of recursion in order to eliminate assignment. In this chapter, we will look at the two different varieties of recursion; one we will call iteration and the other will retain the original name: recursion.

Iteration

TCO is the remedy for the infinite stack depth implied by infinite recursive loops. However, TCO is only applicable if the recursive call is the very last thing to be executed within the function. Such functions are often called *tail call functions*.

Here is a very traditional implementation of a function to create a list of Fibonacci numbers:

```
(defn fibs-work [n i fs]
  (if (= i n)
    fs
    (fibs-work n (inc i) (conj fs (apply + (take-last 2 fs))))))

(defn fibs [n]
  (cond
    (< n 1) []
    (= n 1) [1]
    :else (fibs-work n 2 [1 1])))
```

This program is written in Clojure, which is a variant of Lisp. You call this function like this:

```
(fibs 15)
```

And it returns an array of the first 15 Fibonacci numbers:

```
[1 1 2 3 5 8 13 21 34 55 89 144 233 377 610]
```

Many programmers experience eyestrain headaches the first few times they look at Lisp, mostly because the parentheses don't seem to make any sense. So let me give you a very brief tutorial about those parentheses.

Very Brief Clojure Tutorial

1. This is a typical function call in C, C++, C#, and Java: `f(x);`.
2. Here is the same function in Lisp: `(f x)`.
3. Now you know Lisp. Here ends the tutorial.

That's not much of an exaggeration. The syntax of Lisp is really that simple.

The syntax of Clojure is just a bit more complicated. So let's take the above program apart, one statement at a time.

First there's `defn`, which looks like it is being called as a function. Let's go with that for now. The truth is mostly compatible with that view. So the `defn` "function" defines a new function from its arguments. The functions being defined are named `fibs-work` and `fibs`. The square brackets after the function name enclose the names of the arguments of the function.[1] So the `fibs` function takes a single argument named n, while the `fibs-work` function takes three arguments named n, i, and fs.

Following the argument list is the body of the function. So the body of the `fibs` function is a call to the `cond` function. Think of `cond` like a switch statement that returns a value. The `fibs` function returns the value returned by `cond`.

The arguments to `cond` are a set of pairs. The first element in each pair is a predicate, and the second is the value that `cond` will return if that predicate is `true`. The `cond` function walks down the list of pairs until it sees a true predicate, and then it returns the corresponding value.

---

1. Actually, the square brackets are Clojure syntax for a "vector" (an array). In this case, that vector contains the symbols that represent the arguments.

The predicates are just function calls. The (< n 1) predicate simply calls the < function with n and 1. It returns true if n is less than 1. The (= n 1) predicate calls the = function, which returns true if its arguments are equal. The :else predicate is considered true.

The value returned by cond for the (< n 1) predicate is [], an empty vector. If (= n 1), then cond returns a vector containing 1. Otherwise, cond returns the value produced by the fibs-work function.

So, the fibs function returns [] if n is less than 1, [1] if n is equal to 1, and (fibs-work n 2 [1 1]) in every other case.

Got it? Make sure you do. Go back over it until you do.

The))) at the end of the fibs function are just the closing parentheses of the defn, cond, and fibs-work function calls. I could have written fibs like this:

```
(defn fibs [n]
  (cond
    (< n 1) []
    (= n 1) [1]
    :else (fibs-work n 2 [1 1])
  )
)
```

Perhaps that makes you feel better. Perhaps that relieves the eyestrain headache you felt coming on. And indeed, many new Lisp programmers use this technique to reduce their parentheses anxiety. That's certainly what I did a decade and a half ago when I first started learning Clojure.

After a few years, however, it becomes obvious that there is no reason to put trailing parentheses on their own lines, and the technique simply becomes an annoyance. Trust me. You'll see.

Anyway, that brings us to the heart of the matter, the fibs-work function. If you have gotten comfortable with the fibs function, you have probably already worked out most of the details of the fibs-work function. But let's go through it step by step just to be sure.

First, the arguments: [n i fs]. The n argument tells us how many Fibonacci numbers to return. The i argument is the index of the next Fibonacci number to compute. The fs argument is the current list of Fibonacci numbers.

The if function is a lot like the cond function. Think of (if p a b) as (cond p a :else b). The if function takes three arguments. It evaluates the first as a predicate. If the predicate is true, it returns the second argument; otherwise, it returns the third.

So, if (= i n), then we return fs. Otherwise... Well, let's walk through that one carefully.

```
(fibs-work n (inc i) (conj fs (apply + (take-last 2 fs))))
```

This is a recursive call to fibs-work, passing in n unchanged, i incremented by one, and fs with a new Fibonacci number appended.

It is the conj function that does the appending. It takes two arguments: a vector and the value to append to that vector. Vectors are a kind of list. We'll talk about them later.

The take-last function takes two arguments: a number n and a list. It returns a list containing the last n elements of the list argument.

The apply function takes two arguments: a function and a list. It calls the function with the list as its arguments. So, (apply + [3 4]) is equivalent to (+ 3 4).

OK, so now you should have a good working grasp of Clojure. There's more to the language that we'll encounter as we go along. But for now, let's get back to the topic of iteration and recursion.

ITERATION

Notice the recursive call to `fibs-work` is a tail call. The very last thing done by the `fibs-work` function is to call itself. Therefore, the language can employ TCO to eliminate previous stack frames and turn the recursive call into a `goto`, effectively converting the recursion to pure iteration.

So, then, functions that employ tail calls are, for all intents and purposes, iterative.

TCO, CLOJURE, AND THE JVM

The *Java virtual machine (JVM)* does not make it easy for languages to employ TCO. Indeed, the code I just showed you does not use TCO and therefore grows the stack throughout the iteration. Thus, in Clojure, we *explicitly* invoke TCO by using the `recur` function as follows:

```
(defn fibs-work [n i fs]
  (if (= i n)
    fs
    (recur n (inc i) (conj fs (apply + (take-last 2 fs)))))))
```

The `recur` function can only be called from a tail position, and it effectively reinvokes the enclosing function without growing the stack.

RECURSION

There is a much more natural and elegant way to write the Fibonacci algorithm using true recursion:

```
(defn fib [n]
  (cond
    (< n 1) nil
```

```
    (<= n 2) 1
    :else (+ (fib (dec n)) (fib (- n 2)))))))

(defn fibs [n]
  (map fib (range 1 (inc n))))
```

The fib function should be self-explanatory by now. After all, *fib(n)* is just *fib(n–1)* + *fib(n–2)*. Notice, however, the calls to fib are not on the tail of the function. The last thing executed by the :else clause is the + function. This means we cannot use the recur function and that TCO is not possible. This also means that the stack will grow as the algorithm proceeds.

The range function takes two arguments, *a* and *b*, and returns a list of all the integers from *a* to *b–1*. The map function takes two arguments, *f* and *l*. The *f* argument must be a function and the *l* argument must be a list. It calls *f* with each member of *l* and returns a list containing the results.

This version of fib is extraordinarily inefficient. Consider this execution profile:

```
fib 20 = 6765
"Elapsed time: 1.459277 msecs"
fib 25 = 75025
"Elapsed time: 11.735279 msecs"
fib 30 = 832040
"Elapsed time: 106.490355 msecs"
fib 34 = 5702887
"Elapsed time: 735.689834 msecs"
```

I didn't bother to analyze the algorithm. But a quick curve fit suggests that the algorithm is $O(n^3)$. So, as elegant as the implementation appears, it will never do.

We can vastly improve the performance by using iteration as follows:

```
(defn ifib
  ([n a b]
```

```
    (if (= 0 n)
      b
      (recur (dec n) b (+ a b))))

  ([n]
   (cond
     (< n 1) nil
     (<= n 2) 1
     :else (ifib (- n 2) 1 1)))
  )
```

The ifib function has two overloads: [n a b] and [n]. Since it is iterative, it does not grow the stack, and it is also much faster than the previous recursive version. Indeed, I believe most of that time was spent in printing rather than true computation.

```
ifib 20 = 6765
"Elapsed time: 0.185508 msecs"
ifib 25 = 75025
"Elapsed time: 0.177111 msecs"
ifib 30 = 832040
"Elapsed time: 0.14596 msecs"
ifib 34 = 5702887
"Elapsed time: 0.148221 msecs"
```

Of course, we've lost a lot of the expressive power of the recursive algorithm. We can reclaim that by remembering *referential transparency*: In a functional language, functions always return the same values given the same inputs. Thus, it is never necessary to reevaluate a function. Once we have computed the value of (fib 20), we can remember it instead of recomputing it.

We do this by using the memoize function as follows:

```
(declare fib)

(defn fib-w [n]
  (cond
    (< n 1) nil
```

```
    (<= n 2) 1
    :else (+ (fib (dec n)) (fib (- n 2))))))

(def fib (memoize fib-w))
```

The declare function creates an unbound symbol, which can be used by other functions so long as it is bound before its use. I used declare in this case because the definition of fib comes after fib-w, and Clojure wants all names declared or defined before they are used.

The memoize function takes an argument *f*, which must be a function, and returns a new function *g*. Calls to *g* with argument *x* will call *f* with *x* if, and only if, *g* has never been called with *x* before. It then remembers those arguments and the return value. Any subsequent call to *g* with *x* will return the remembered value.

This version of the algorithm is just as fast as the iterative version because we have short-circuited the vast majority of the recursion without sacrificing the elegance of the algorithm. We pay for that with a little extra memory, but that seems a small price to pay.

```
fib 20 = 6765
"Elapsed time: 0.168678 msecs"
fib 25 = 75025
"Elapsed time: 0.16232 msecs"
fib 30 = 832040
"Elapsed time: 0.151619 msecs"
fib 34 = 5702887
"Elapsed time: 0.15134 msecs"
```

What we have learned here is that iteration and recursion are very different approaches. Iterative functions must use tail calls to drive the iteration and should use TCO to prevent the growth of the stack. Recursive functions do not use tail calls and therefore will grow the stack. Truly recursive functions can be quite elegant, and memoization can be used to prevent that elegance from significantly affecting performance.

Although Clojure was used as the language in this chapter, the concepts are the same in virtually every other functional language, and could even be implemented in nonfunctional languages, though with a substantial loss of elegance. ;-)

4 Laziness

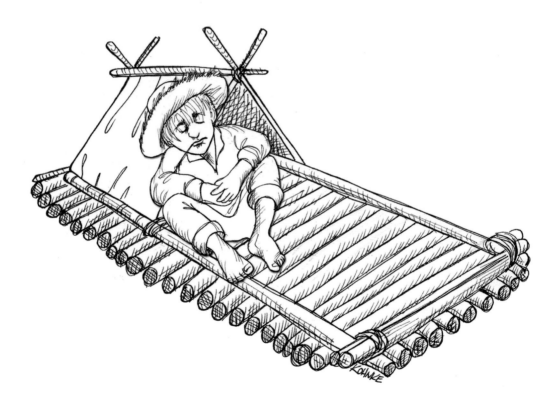

Consider the following boldfaced change to our program that calculates a list of Fibonacci numbers:

```
(declare fib)

(defn fib-w [n]
  (cond
    (< n 1) nil
    (<= n 2) 1
    :else (+ (fib (dec n)) (fib (- n 2)))))

(def fib (memoize fib-w))


(defn lazy-fibs []
  (map fib (rest (range)))
  )
```

The `lazy-fibs` function may look a little strange to you. Let's walk through it. You already understand the `map` function. The `rest` function takes a list and returns that list without the first element. And that brings us to the range function.

The range function, as called here, returns a list of integers starting at zero. How many integers, you ask? As many as you need. The range function is *lazy*. Or, rather, the range function returns a *lazy* list.

What is a lazy list? A lazy list is an object that knows how to compute its next value. In Java, C++, and C#, we called such objects *iterators*. A lazy list is an iterator masquerading as a list.

Clojure is friends with lazy lists. Most of the library functions return lazy lists if possible. So, in the above program, `rest` and `map` both return a lazy list. And that means `lazy-fibs` also returns a lazy list.

How would you use `lazy-fibs`? Like so:

```
(take 10 (lazy-fibs))
returns: (1 1 2 3 5 8 13 21 34 55)
```

The `take` function takes two arguments: a number n and a list. It returns a list that contains the first n elements of the argument list. Actually, that's not quite right, but I'll get to that in a minute.

So, now let's walk through `lazy-fibs` again. The `range` function returns a lazy list of integers starting at zero. The `rest` function takes that list, drops the first element, and then returns a lazy list of the remaining integers, which in this instance, are the integers starting at one. The `map` function applies each of those integers to the `fib` function returning a lazy list of the Fibonacci numbers starting at (`fib 1`).

You can have as many Fibonacci numbers as you like, so long as there are no overflows or other machine limitations. So, for example:

```
(nth (lazy-fibs) 50)
returns: 20365011074
```

The `nth` function takes a list and an integer n and returns the nth element of the list. So this returns the 50th Fibonacci number.

Now consider this:

```
(def list-of-fibs (lazy-fibs))
```

The `def` function (it's not really a function, but pretend that it is) creates a new symbol and associates it with a value. So the symbol `list-of-fibs` refers to a lazy list of Fibonacci numbers, as you can see from the following:

```
(take 5 list-of-fibs)
returns: (1 1 2 3 5)
```

Now note: When we executed the `def` that created `list-of-fibs`, no Fibonacci numbers were calculated, and no memory was allocated for Fibonacci numbers. The calculations only take place, and the memory is only allocated, as the elements of the list are accessed. Remember, behind the scenes, the lazy lists are really just iterators that know how to calculate their next element. Once that calculation takes place, the memory is allocated and the value is placed into a real list.[1]

It is tempting to think of lazy lists as being infinite. Of course they are not. They are simply unbounded. You can walk through as many items as you like, but that number will always be finite.

LAZY ACCUMULATION

It should be clear that if you continue to pass lazy lists through functions like map, rest, and take (yes, take actually returns a lazy list), you will accumulate a long chain of iterators behind the scenes. Each of those iterators must hold on to the function that calculates its next value. It must also hold on to all the data required for that calculation.

I have written applications that have lists with thousands of elements, each of which holds on to other lists with thousands of other elements; and all these lists are lazy. Now remember, we are *deferring* calculations. None of the calculations take place until the final results are accessed. So a huge backlog of deferred iterators can get chained through all those lists.

This works fine until you run out of the memory allocated for holding all those deferred iterators. So, from time to time, it might be a good idea to convert your lazy lists into real lists. In Clojure, we do that with the doall function:

```
(def real-list-of-fibs (doall (take 50 (lazy-fibs))))
```

The doall function makes real-list-of-fibs a real list that occupies memory and contains no deferred iterators. All calculations have been done.

---

1. That's a convenient way to think of it for now. Actually, as we'll see shortly, the memory is only allocated and the list only grows, if the program needs to hold those values.

OK, BUT WHY?

Good question! Laziness is not free. It requires memory and cycles to defer calculations. Then there's the problem of accumulation that can lead to memory exhaustion.

Yet despite these costs, laziness is a common—if not universal—feature in functional languages. Some languages, like Haskell, are intrinsically lazy. Clojure is not intrinsically lazy, but so many of the library functions are lazy that you cannot easily avoid the laziness. F# and Scala allow laziness, but you must be explicit about it.

Why? Why do all these languages accept the costs of laziness?

Because laziness decouples *what* you need to do from *how much* you need to do. You can write a program that creates a lazy sequence without knowing how big a sequence your users are going to want. Your users can determine how much of your sequence they need.

So, for example:

```
(nth (lazy-fibs) 500)
```

returns 225591516161936330872512695036072072046011324913758190588638
➡88664184746277386868834050159870527969684986 26N

Since `lazy-fibs` puts no limit on the number of Fibonacci numbers it creates, you can ask for as many as you like.

Or, consider this example. I could create a list of 51 integers like this:

```
(range 51)
```

Or like this:

```
(take 51 (range))
```

Notice in the first example, the 51 is far more coupled than in the second. In the first, I have to get that 51 into the range function somehow. I might be able to pass it as an argument, but that's a pretty strong coupling. In the second example, the range function doesn't care at all. That 51 could be way out in some other part of the code, far removed from the call to range.

By the way, you might be interested to know that in the lazy-fibs example above, (fib 1) through (fib 499) have likely been garbage-collected. Since I'm not holding on to the list itself, the runtime system is free to dispose of the previously calculated elements. Thus, it would be possible to create and traverse a lazy list with trillions of elements and yet never hold more than one[2] of them in memory at a time.

CODA

There is much more to learn about laziness. My purpose here has been to make you aware of it because it is so common in functional languages. We will be seeing much more of it in the pages to come, but it will almost always be in the background.

---

2. Or at least some n, where n is small and is the "chunk" size of the lazy engine.

STATEFULNESS 5

In the end, every program ever written is just a form of $y = f(x)$, where x is all the input you give to the program and y is all the output it delivers in response.

This definition is sufficient for all batch jobs. For example, in a payroll system, the input x is all the employee records and timecards and the output y is all the paychecks and reports.

But perhaps this batch definition is too simplistic. After all, in interactive applications, the input you give to the program is often based on the output it just gave you. So perhaps we should think of interactive software systems as:

```
void p(Input x) {
  while (x != DONE)
    x = (getInput(f(x))
}
```

In other words, our program is a loop that computes $y = f(x)$ and then hands y to some source of input that is passed back into f until f finally returns DONE.

In some very real sense, the state of this program during each iteration is x. If you were debugging some malfunction, you would want to know the value of x and would likely call x the state of the system.

And indeed, in the program above, there is a variable named x that holds the state of the system and is updated upon each iteration.

However, we can eliminate that variable by writing the program "functionally" as follows:

```
void p(Input x) {
  if (x!=DONE)
    p(getInput(f(x)));
}
```

Now this program has no variable that is updated to hold the state of the system. Instead, that state is passed as an argument from one invocation of p to the next.

A few years ago I wrote a functional program in Clojure that looked very much like this. It was a version of the old computer game *Spacewar!*. You can see (and play) this program at https://github.com/unclebob/spacewar. The game is visual and interactive, and it is written in the "functional" style.

The internal state of the spacewar program is enormously complex. It consists of the *Enterprise*, dozens of Klingons, hundreds of stars, many dozens of torpedoes, phaser blasts, kinetic projectiles, bases, transports, and a plethora of other entities and attributes. All that complexity is maintained within a single object that I called world. And the flow of spacewar is, for all intents and purposes:

```
(defn spacewar [world]
  (when (:done? world)
    (System/exit 0))
  (recur (update-world world (get-input world))))
```

In other words, the spacewar program is a loop that exits if the :done?[1] attribute of the world is true, and otherwise presents the world to the user and gets input that it uses to update the world.

Here is the actual update-world function as it currently exists within spacewar:

```
(defn update-world [ms world]
  ;{:pre [(valid-world? world)]
  ;  :post [(valid-world? %)]}
  (->> world
       (game-won ms)
```

---

1. Keywords in Clojure are prefixed with colons. So :done? is a keyword, which is just a constant that can be used as an identifier. Often, they are used as keys into hash maps. When used as a function, a keyword behaves like an accessor into a hash map. Thus, (:done? world) simply returns the :done? element of the world hash map.

```
(game-over ms)
(ship/update-ship ms)
(shots/update-shots ms)
(explosions/update-explosions ms)
(clouds/update-clouds ms)
(klingons/update-klingons ms)
(bases/update-bases ms)
(romulans/update-romulans ms)
(view-frame/update-messages ms)
(add-messages)
))
```

The threading macro (->>) simply passes the argument world into game-won, the output of which gets passed to game-over, the output of which gets passed to ship/update-ship, and so on. Each of those functions returns an updated version of the world.

Note the ms argument. It contains the number of milliseconds since the last update and is the primary input to the game as a whole. As an object moves across the screen, its position is updated based upon its velocity vector and the number of milliseconds that have transpired since its position was last updated.

I'm showing this to you to give you a glimpse of the complexity being managed by this program. Keep in mind that the world is not a mutable variable. Each of those threaded functions into which the world is being passed is returning a new version of the world and passing it to the next. It is not being held in a variable and being mutated.

Let me give you one more glimpse of the complexity:

```
(s/def ::ship (s/keys :req-un
                [::x ::y ::warp ::warp-charge
                 ::impulse ::heading ::velocity
                 ::selected-view ::selected-weapon
                 ::selected-engine ::target-bearing
                 ::engine-power-setting
                 ::weapon-number-setting
```

```
::weapon-spread-setting
::heading-setting
::antimatter ::core-temp
::dilithium ::shields
::kinetics ::torpedos

::life-support-damage ::hull-damage
::sensor-damage ::impulse-damage
::warp-damage ::weapons-damage
::strat-scale
::destroyed
::corbomite-device-installed]))
```

What you are looking at is a small portion of the type specification of the *Enterprise*, the player's ship. Clojure provides a mechanism called `clojure .spec` that give us the ability to very specifically design our data structures with even more precision and control than most statically typed languages.

All this complexity of state is managed within the `spacewar` program by passing the `world` from function to function to function, and then recursively passing it back to `spacewar`. The `world` is never held in a variable.

And, the game operates on a large screen at 30 frames per second.

The bottom line here is that there is no level of complexity that demands that we abandon immutability and deviate from the functional style. On the other hand, there are other factors that do, from time to time, make that demand.

WHEN WE MUST MUTATE

The spacewar program uses a graphical user interface (GUI) framework called *Quil*.[2] This framework allows the programs that use it to be written in a "functional" style. It may not actually be functional in its internals, but from the outside looking in, there need not be any visible mutable state.

---

2. See www.quil.info. Quil uses *Processing* behind the scenes. *Processing* is a Java framework that is certainly not functional. Quil pretends to be functional by hiding the mutable variables, or at least by not forcing you to mutate those variables.

On the other hand, I am currently writing an application in Clojure named more-speech[3] that uses Java's Swing framework. Swing *is not functional.* Mutable state drips from every appendage of the framework. It is a definitionally mutable object framework.

This makes it a challenge to use with Clojure and maintain a "functional" style. To make matters worse, Swing uses a model-view approach, and the models are defined and controlled by Swing. So building an immutable model is virtually impossible.

Swing is not the only framework that forces you into the mutable world. There are many others. So, even if you are determined to use the "functional" style, you must be able to deal with the fact that a large panoply of existing software frameworks will force you out of that style.

Worse, many such frameworks also force you into the multithreaded world. Swing, for example, runs in its own special thread. Programmers should not use that thread for regular processing but must specifically enter that thread when mutating Swing data structures.

This puts the users of such frameworks into the double jeopardy of mutating state from within multiple threads. The dreaded result of that, of course, is race conditions and concurrent update anomalies.

Fortunately, there are functional languages that provide facilities that reduce the problems of mutation and allow the functional style to interface tolerably well with the multithreaded, nonfunctional style.

SOFTWARE TRANSACTIONAL MEMORY (STM)

STM is a set of mechanisms that treat internal memory as though it were a transactional commit/rollback database. The transactions are functions that are protected from concurrent update by a *compare-and-swap* protocol.

---

3. https://github.com/unclebob/more-speech

If that was too much of a word salad, perhaps an example would be clarifying.

Let us say that we have an object o and a function f that mutates o. So $o_f = f(o)$ where o_f is the original o mutated by f.

The problem is that f takes time to do its work, and there is a chance that some other thread will interrupt f and apply its own operation g on o: $o_g = g(o)$. When f finally completes, what is the state of o? Is it o_f? Or is it o_g? Or have both mutations been applied, giving us o_{fg}?

The typical concurrent update problem would most often yield o_f, causing the operation of g to be lost. Programmers often resolve this kind of problem by *locking* o so that g cannot interrupt f, and vice versa. The lock forces the interrupting thread to wait until o is unlocked. The problem, however, is that this can lead to the dreaded *deadly embrace*.[4]

Imagine that we have two objects o and p and two functions $f(o, p)$ and $g(p, o)$. These functions lock their arguments before operating on them. Suppose f and g are executing in different threads and g interrupts f just after f locks o. Now g locks p but cannot lock o because o is locked by f, so g waits. Now f wakes up and tries to lock p but cannot because p is locked by g—and nothing can proceed. The functions f and g are in a deadly embrace.

The problem of deadly embrace can be avoided by locking everything in the same order every time. If f and g agree to lock o first and p second, then the embrace cannot happen. However, these agreements are hard to enforce, and as systems get more and more complicated, a correct locking order can be very difficult to divine.

STM solves this problem by *not* locking, and instead using a commit/rollback technique. Let's call this technique *swap*. We can enact it with *swap(o, f)*, which will hold the current value of o in o_h, compute

---

4. Sometimes known as *deadlock*.

$o_f = f(o)$, and then, in an *atomic*[5] operation, compare the current value of o with o_b and, if they are the same, swap o with o_f. If the compare fails, then the operation is repeated from the beginning and will continue repeating until the compare succeeds.

There are several ways to use STM in Clojure, but the simplest is the atom. An atom is an *atomic* value that can be altered using the swap! function. Here's an example:

```
(def counter (atom 0))

(defn add-one [x]
  (let [y (inc x)]
    (print (str "(" x ")"))
    y))

(defn increment [n id]
  (dotimes [_ n]
    (print id)
    (swap! counter add-one)))

(defn -main []
  (let [ta (future (increment 10 "a"))
        tx (future (increment 10 "x"))
        _ @ta
        _ @tx]
    (println "\nCounter is: " @counter)))
```

The first line creates the atom named counter. The -main program starts two threads, using future, both of which call the increment function. The @ta and @tx expressions wait for the respective threads to complete.

---

5. Atomic operations cannot be interrupted.

The add-one function adds one to its argument, but that print function can allow another thread to jump in; and that's exactly what happens. Here's an example of the output:

```
a(0)a(1)a(2)a(3)a(4)xa(5)x(5)(6)(6)x(7)(7)a(8)(8)
x(9)(9)a(10)(10)x(11)a(11)(12)(12)a(13)x(13)(14)(14)
x(15)(15)(16)x(17)x(18)x(19)
Counter is:  20
```

At first, thread a runs without interruption for a while. But at the fifth increment, the x thread jumps in, and the two fight each other. Notice the repeated values as the swap! detects the collisions and repeats. Finally, thread a finishes and thread x experiences no further interruptions. The end count of 20 is correct.

LIFE IS HARD, SOFTWARE IS HARDER

It would be nice to live, full time, in a functional world. Multiple threads in a functional world generally do not have race conditions.[6] After all, if you never update, you can't have concurrent update problems. But all too often we are forced back into the multithreaded, nonfunctional world by frameworks, or legacy code. And when that happens, the mechanisms of STM can help us avoid the worst of an otherwise horrific situation.

---

6. See Chapter 15, Concurrency, for when they do.

II COMPARATIVE ANALYSIS

What follows is a comparative analysis of a series of exercises written in traditional *object-oriented (OO)* style and in "functional" style. The first two exercises may appear familiar to you; the OO portions come from examples that I published in *Clean Craftsmanship*.[1]

Both versions of each of the examples were created using the discipline of *test-driven development (TDD)*. The tests are shown with the code in an incremental fashion. You'll see how the first test was passed, then the second, then the third, and so on.

The point of this part of the book is to explore and examine the differences between OO implementations and functional implementations.

The exercises increase in complexity from one to the next. Prime Factors is pretty simple. Bowling Game is a bit more complicated and Gossiping Bus Drivers is more complicated still. The last exercise, Payroll, is the most complex of the examples. I explored it in great detail in Section 3 of *Agile Software Development: Principles, Patterns, and Practices*.[2] So to save space I've only included the functional version.

---

1. Robert C. Martin, *Clean Craftsmanship* (Addison-Wesley, 2021).

2. Robert C. Martin, *Agile Software Development: Principles, Patterns, and Practices* (Pearson, 2002).

As the complexity increases, the differences between the approaches become more apparent. You should find this educational. But you should also be prepared for a few surprises; this may not end the way you think it should.

P**RIME** F**ACTORS**

Is functional programming better than programming with mutable variables? Let's do a comparative analysis of some familiar exercises. Here, for example, is the traditional Java derivation of the Prime Factors kata using TDD, roughly as it was presented in Chapter 2 of *Clean Craftsmanship*.[3] A related video, *Prime Factors*, is also available. You can access the video by registering at https://informit.com/functionaldesign.

JAVA VERSION

We begin with a simple test:

```
public class PrimeFactorsTest {
  @Test
  public void factors() throws Exception {
    assertThat(factorsOf(1), is(empty()));
  }
}
```

And we make it pass in this simple way:

```
private List<Integer> factorsOf(int n) {
  return new ArrayList<>();
}
```

Of course, this passes. So the next most degenerate test is 2:

```
assertThat(factorsOf(2), contains(2));
```

We make this pass with some trivial and obvious code:

```
private List<Integer> factorsOf(int n) {
  ArrayList<Integer> factors = new ArrayList<>();
  if (n>1)
```

---

3. Martin, *Clean Craftsmanship*, p. 52.

```
    factors.add(2);
  return factors;
}
```

Next comes 3,

```
assertThat(factorsOf(3), contains(3));
```

which we make pass by being a bit clever and replacing the 2 with n:

```
private List<Integer> factorsOf(int n) {
  ArrayList<Integer> factors = new ArrayList<>();
  if (n>1)
    factors.add(n);
  return factors;
}
```

Next comes 4, which is the first time our list will have more than one factor in it:

```
assertThat(factorsOf(4), contains(2, 2));
```

And we make it pass with what appears to be a pretty awful hack:

```
private List<Integer> factorsOf(int n) {
  ArrayList<Integer> factors = new ArrayList<>();
  if (n>1) {
    if (n % 2 == 0) {
      factors.add(2);
      n /= 2;
    }
  }
  if (n>1)
    factors.add(n);
  return factors;
}
```

The next three tests pass without any changes:

```
assertThat(factorsOf(5), contains(5));
assertThat(factorsOf(6), contains(2,3));
assertThat(factorsOf(7), contains(7));
```

The 8 case is the first time we've seen more than two elements in the list of factors:

```
assertThat(factorsOf(8), contains(2, 2, 2));
```

And we pass this with the elegant transformation of one of the `if` statements into a `while`:

```
private List<Integer> factorsOf(int n) {
  ArrayList<Integer> factors = new ArrayList<>();
  if (n>1) {
    while (n % 2 == 0) {
      factors.add(2);
      n /= 2;
    }
  }
  if (n>1)
    factors.add(n);
  return factors;
}
```

The next test, 9, must also fail because nothing in our solution factors out 3:

```
assertThat(factorsOf(9), contains(3, 3));
```

To solve it, we need to factor out 3's. We could do that as follows:

```
private List<Integer> factorsOf(int n) {
  ArrayList<Integer> factors = new ArrayList<>();
  if (n>1) {
    while (n % 2 == 0) {
```

```
      factors.add(2);
      n /= 2;
    }
    while (n % 3 == 0) {
      factors.add(3);
      n /= 3;
    }
  }
  if (n>1)
    factors.add(n);
  return factors;
}
```

But this is horrific because it implies endless duplication. We can solve that by changing another if to a while:

```
private List<Integer> factorsOf(int n) {
  ArrayList<Integer> factors = new ArrayList<>();
  int divisor = 2;
  while (n>1) {
    while (n % divisor == 0) {
      factors.add(divisor);
      n /= divisor;
    }
    divisor++;
  }
  if (n>1)
    factors.add(n);
  return factors;
}
```

Just a little bit of refactoring and we get this:

```
private List<Integer> factorsOf(int n) {
  ArrayList<Integer> factors = new ArrayList<>();

  for (int divisor = 2; n > 1; divisor++)
    for (; n % divisor == 0; n /= divisor)
      factors.add(divisor);
```

```
    return factors;
  }
```

And that algorithm is sufficient to compute the prime factors of any[4] integer.

CLOJURE VERSION

OK, so what does this look like in Clojure?

As before, we begin with a simple degenerate test:[5]

```
(should= [] (prime-factors-of 1))
```

And we make that pass as one might expect, by returning an empty list:

```
(defn prime-factors-of [n] [])
```

The next test follows the Java version pretty closely:

```
(should= [2] (prime-factors-of 2))
```

So does the solution:

```
(defn prime-factors-of [n]
  (if (> n 1) [2] []))
```

And the solution to the third test employs the same clever replacement of 2 by n:

```
(should= [3] (prime-factors-of 3))
```

```
(defn prime-factors-of [n]
  (if (> n 1) [n] []))
```

---

4. Given enough time and space.

5. Using the speclj testing framework.

But with the test for 4, the Clojure and Java solutions begin to diverge:

```
(should= [2 2] (prime-factors-of 4))

(defn prime-factors-of [n]
  (if (> n 1)
    (if (zero? (rem n 2))
      (cons 2 (prime-factors-of (quot n 2)))
      [n])
    []))
```

The solution is recursive. The cons function prepends a 2 onto the beginning of the list returned by prime-factors-of. Convince yourself that you understand why! The rem and quot functions are just the integer remainder and quotient operations, respectively.

At this point in the Java program, there was no iteration. The two if(n>1) segments were a tantalizing hint of the iteration that was to come, but the solution was still just straight linear logic.

In the functional version, however, we see full-blown recursion. It's not even tail-called.

The next four tests pass outright, even the test for 8:

```
(should= [5] (prime-factors-of 5))
(should= [2 3] (prime-factors-of 6))
(should= [7] (prime-factors-of 7))
(should= [2 2 2] (prime-factors-of 8))
```

In some ways, this is a shame since it was the test for 8 that caused us to transform an if to a while in the Java solution. No such elegant transformation takes place in the Clojure solution; though I have to say that the recursion is the better solution—so far.

Next comes the test for 9. And here the Java and Clojure versions face the similar dilemma of duplicated code:

```
(should= [3 3] (prime-factors-of 9))

(defn prime-factors-of [n]
  (if (> n 1)
    (if (zero? (rem n 2))
      (cons 2 (prime-factors-of (quot n 2)))
      (if (zero? (rem n 3))
        (cons 3 (prime-factors-of (quot n 3)))
        [n]))
    []))
```

This solution is not sustainable. It would force us to add the 5, 7, 11, 13... cases all the way up to the maximum prime that our language could hold. But this solution does imply an interesting iterative/recursive solution:

```
(defn prime-factors-of [n]
  (loop [n n
         divisor 2
         factors []]
    (if (> n 1)
      (if (zero? (rem n divisor))
        (recur (quot n divisor) divisor (conj factors divisor))
        (recur n (inc divisor) factors))
      factors)))
```

The `loop` function creates a new anonymous function in situ. The `recur` function, when nested inside a `loop` expression, causes the in situ function to be reinvoked with TCO. The arguments to the in situ function are n, divisor, and factors. Each is followed by its initializer. So the n within the loop is initialized to the value of n outside the loop (the two n identifiers are distinct), divisor is initialized to 2, and factors is initialized to [].

The recursion in this solution is iterative because the recursive calls are at the tail. Note that the cons has been changed to a conj because the ordering of the list construction has changed. The conj function appends[6] to factors. Convince yourself that you understand why the ordering has changed!

CONCLUSION

There are several things to note about this example. First, the sequence of tests is the same between the Java and Clojure versions. This is significant because it implies that the change to functional programming has little to no impact on the way we express our tests. Tests are somehow more basic, more abstract, or more essential than the programming style.

Second, the solution strategy between the two deviated even before any iteration was required. In Java, the test for 4 did not require iteration; but in Clojure, it caused us to use recursion. This implies that recursion is somehow more semantically essential than standard looping with while statements.

Third, the derivation in Java was relatively straightforward; there were few, if any, surprises from one test to the next. But the Clojure derivation took a U-turn once we got to the test for 9. This was because we chose to use non-tail recursion instead of the iterative loop construct to solve the test for 4. This implies that, when we have a choice, we should prefer tail-recursive constructs to non-tail recursion.

The end result is an algorithm that is similar to the Java solution but has at least one surprising difference: It is not a doubly nested loop. The Java solution has one loop that increments the divisor and another that repeatedly adds the current divisor as a factor. The Clojure solution replaces that doubly nested loop with two independent recursions.

Which solution is better? The Java solution is a lot faster because Java is a lot faster than Clojure. But otherwise, I see no particular benefit to either. To those who know both languages well, neither is easier than the

---

6. In this case because factors is a vector.

other to read or understand. Neither is riskier or better structured than the other. From my point of view, it's a wash. Other than the intrinsic speed of Java, there is no advantage to either style that overrides the other.

However, this is the last example for which the results will be ambiguous. As we proceed from example to example, the differences will become more and more significant.

7
BOWLING GAME

Now let's look at another traditional TDD exercise: the Bowling Game kata. What follows is a much-abbreviated version of that kata that appeared in *Clean Craftsmanship*.[1] A related video, *Bowling Game*, is also available. You can access the video by registering at https://informit.com/functionaldesign.

JAVA VERSION

We begin, as always, with a test that does nothing, just to prove we can compile and execute:

```
public class BowlingTest {
  @Test
  public void nothing() throws Exception {
  }
}
```

Next, we assert that we can create an instance of the Game class:

```
@Test
public void canCreateGame() throws Exception {
  Game g = new Game();
}
```

And then we make that compile and pass by directing the integrated development environment (IDE) to create the missing class:

```
public class Game {
}
```

Next, we see if we can roll one ball:

```
@Test
public void canRoll() throws Exception {
  Game g = new Game();
```

---

1. Robert C. Martin, *Clean Craftsmanship* (Addison-Wesley, 2021).

```
    g.roll(0);
}
```

And then we make that compile and pass by directing the IDE to create the roll function, and we give the argument a reasonable name:

```
public class Game {
  public void roll(int pins) {
  }
}
```

There's a bit of duplication in the tests already. We should get rid of it. So we factor out the creation of the game into the setup function:

```
public class BowlingTest {
  private Game g;

  @Before
  public void setUp() throws Exception {
    g = new Game();
  }
}
```

This makes the first test completely empty. So we delete it. The second test is also pretty useless since it doesn't assert anything, so we delete it as well.

Next, we want to assert that we can score a game. But to do that we need to roll a complete game:

```
@Test
public void gutterGame() throws Exception {
  for (int i=0; i<20; i++)
    g.roll(0);
  assertEquals(0, g.score());
}

public int score() {
  return 0;
}
```

Next come all ones:

```
@Test
public void allOnes() throws Exception {
  for (int i=0; i<20; i++)
    g.roll(1);
  assertEquals(20, g.score());
}

public class Game {
  private int score;

  public void roll(int pins) {
    score += pins;
  }

  public int score() {
    return score;
  }
}
```

The duplication in the tests can be eliminated by extracting a function called rollMany:

```
public class BowlingTest {
  private Game g;

  @Before
  public void setUp() throws Exception {
    g = new Game();
  }

  private void rollMany(int n, int pins) {
    for (int i=0; i<n; i++) {
      g.roll(pins);
    }
  }
```

```java
@Test
public void gutterGame() throws Exception {
  rollMany(20, 0);
  assertEquals(0, g.score());
}

@Test
public void allOnes() throws Exception {
  rollMany(20, 1);
  assertEquals(20, g.score());
}
}
```

OK, next test. One spare, with one extra bonus ball, and all the rest gutter balls:

```java
@Test
public void oneSpare() throws Exception {
  rollMany(2, 5);
  g.roll(7);
  rollMany(17, 0);
  assertEquals(24, g.score());
}
```

This test fails, of course. We have to refactor the algorithm in order to get this to pass. We move the computation of the score out of the roll method and into the score method, and we walk through the rolls array two balls (one frame) at a time:

```java
public int score() {
  int score = 0;
  int frameIndex = 0;
  for (int frame = 0; frame < 10; frame++) {
    if (isSpare(frameIndex)) {
      score += 10 + rolls[frameIndex + 2];
      frameIndex += 2;
    } else {
      score += rolls[frameIndex] + rolls[frameIndex + 1];
```

```
      frameIndex += 2;
    }
  }
  return score;
}

private boolean isSpare(int frameIndex) {
  return rolls[frameIndex] + rolls[frameIndex + 1] == 10;
}
```

One strike is next:

```
@Test
public void oneStrike() throws Exception {
  g.roll(10);
  g.roll(2);
  g.roll(3);
  rollMany(16, 0);
  assertEquals(20, g.score());
}
```

Passing it is just a matter of adding the strike condition, and then we refactor a bit:

```
public int score() {
  int score = 0;
  int frameIndex = 0;
  for (int frame = 0; frame < 10; frame++) {
    if (isStrike(frameIndex)) {
      score += 10 + strikeBonus(frameIndex);
      frameIndex++;
    } else if (isSpare(frameIndex)) {
      score += 10 + spareBonus(frameIndex);
      frameIndex += 2;
    } else {
      score += twoBallsInFrame(frameIndex);
      frameIndex += 2;
    }
```

```
  }
  return score;
}
```

Lastly, we test for a perfect game:

```
@Test
public void perfectGame() throws Exception {
  rollMany(12, 10);
  assertEquals(300, g.score());
}
```

And this passes without change.

CLOJURE VERSION

Things start out quite differently in Clojure. We have no classes to create, and there is no need for a roll method. So our first test is the gutter game:

```
(should= 0 (score (repeat[2] 20 0)))

(defn score [rolls] 0)
```

Followed quickly by all ones:

```
(should= 20 (score (repeat 20 1)))

(defn score [rolls]
  (reduce + rolls))
```

---

2. The repeat function returns a sequence of repeating values. In this case, it is a sequence of 20 zeros.

No surprises here. The reduce[3] function simply applies the + function across the entire list. So our next test is one spare:

```
(should= 24 (score (concat [5 5 7] (repeat 17 0)))))
```

To make this pass, we go through several steps. The first is to break the rolls array up into frames and sum up the frames. At first, we assume that frames have just two rolls:

```
(defn to-frames [rolls]
  (partition[4] 2 rolls))

(defn add-frame [score frame]
  (+ score (reduce + frame)))

(defn score [rolls]
  (reduce add-frame 0 (to-frames rolls)))
```

Now the reduce function has come into its own. It cycles through the pairs of rolls, accumulating them into a score.

This change keeps all the previous tests passing, but it still fails the spare test. To pass that we have to add special processing to the to-frames and add-frame functions. Our goal is to put all the rolls needed to calculate a frame into the frame data.

```
(defn to-frames [rolls]
  (let [frames (partition 2 rolls)
```

---

3. You will want to look this function up. It does much more than this paragraph suggests. But you'll see that soon enough.

4. The partition function breaks the rolls list into a list of pairs. So [1 2 3 4 5 6] becomes [[1 2][3 4][5 6]].

```
      possible-bonuses (map #(take 1 %)⁵ (rest frames))
      possible-bonuses⁶ (concat⁷ possible-bonuses [[0]])]
  (map concat frames possible-bonuses)))


(defn add-frame [score frame-and-bonus]
  (let [frame (take 2 frame-and-bonus)]
    (if (= 10 (reduce + frame))
      (+ score (reduce + frame-and-bonus))
      (+ score (reduce + frame)))))


(defn score [rolls]
  (reduce add-frame 0 (to-frames rolls)))
```

Look closely at this code. There are lots of little tricks and workarounds in it. Why? Because Clojure is full of lots of lovely, tempting little tools that you can use to get data into *almost* the form you want, and then use little tricks to maneuver the data into *exactly* the form you want. If you aren't careful, those little tricks can start to dominate the code.

So, for example, see if you can figure out why I am passing [[0]] into the concat function in to-frames.[8] As another example, ask yourself why I used #(take 1 %) instead of just first.[9]

Because of the trickiness in this code, don't be too concerned if you are struggling to understand it. I struggled too when looking back over it. And so...

---

5. The #(…) form creates an anonymous function. The % symbol is the argument to that function. You can also use %n, where n is an integer representing the *n*th argument. So #(take 1 %) is a function that returns a list containing the first element of its argument.

6. This is not a reassignment, or even a reinitialization. The second possible-bonuses value is distinct from the first. Think of it like a local variable in Java hiding a function argument or a member variable of the same name.

7. The concat function concatenates lists together. So (concat [1 2] [3 4]) returns [1 2 3 4].

8. Since bonuses are based on the next frame, possible-bonuses had one too few elements. That would have terminated the final call to map one element too early.

9. (take 1 x) returns a list containing the first element in x. first returns the first element.

When these little tricks proliferate it's time to rethink the solution. So I refactored the solution into a simple loop:

```
(defn to-frames [rolls]
  (loop [remaining-rolls rolls
         frames []]
    (cond
      (empty? remaining-rolls)
      frames

      (= 10 (reduce + (take 2 remaining-rolls)))
      (recur (drop 2 remaining-rolls)
             (conj frames (take 3 remaining-rolls)))
      :else
      (recur (drop 2 remaining-rolls)
             (conj frames (take 2 remaining-rolls))))))

(defn add-frames [score frame]
  (+ score (reduce + frame)))

(defn score [rolls]
  (reduce add-frames 0 (to-frames rolls)))
```

This is looking a lot better. Moreover, it's starting to look a bit like the Java solution. The next test is one strike:

```
(should= 20 (score (concat [10 2 3] (repeat 16 0)))))
```

And we make that pass by adding one more case to the cond:

```
(defn to-frames [rolls]
  (loop [remaining-rolls rolls
         frames []]
    (cond
      (empty? remaining-rolls)
      frames

      (= 10 (first remaining-rolls))
```

```
            (recur (rest remaining-rolls)
                   (conj frames (take 3 remaining-rolls)))

            (= 10 (reduce + (take 2 remaining-rolls)))
            (recur (drop 2 remaining-rolls)
                   (conj frames (take 3 remaining-rolls)))
            :else
            (recur (drop 2 remaining-rolls)
                   (conj frames (take 2 remaining-rolls))))))))

(defn add-frames [score frame]
  (+ score (reduce + frame)))

(defn score [rolls]
  (reduce add-frames 0 (to-frames rolls)))
```

Trivial, right? So all that's left is the perfect game. And if this goes like the Java version, this test should just pass without modification:

```
(should= 300 (score (repeat 12 10)))))
```

But it doesn't! Can you see why? Perhaps the fix will elucidate that for you:

```
(defn score [rolls]
  (reduce add-frames 0 (take 10 (to-frames rolls)))))
```

The to-frames function happily creates more than ten frames. It just runs to the end of the rolls list making as many frames as it can. But a game of bowling is only ten frames.

Conclusion

There are quite a few interesting differences between the Java and Clojure versions of this problem. First, the Clojure version has no Game class. So all the machinations we used to create that class in the Java version simply don't occur in the Clojure version.

You might think that the loss of the Game class is a weakness of the Clojure version. After all, it's convenient to be able to just create a Game, toss it a bunch of rolls, and then get the score. However, the Clojure version has decoupled the accumulation of the rolls from the computation of the score. Those concepts are not bound together in the Clojure version. And that makes me think that the Java version has a subtle violation of the Single Responsibility Principle.[10]

Second, as we tried to solve the one spare case, we saw how the Clojure version got polluted with all those nasty little tricks. This is a real problem with Clojure programs (or perhaps Clojure programmers). It's just too easy to add one more nasty little trick to get things to work.

Third, the Clojure solution is significantly different from the Java solution. Oh, there are some points of similarity, to be sure. That cond structure in the Clojure version is very reminiscent of the if/else structure in the Java version. However, those two similar structures produced radically different results. The Java version produced the score. The Clojure version produced a frame that included the bonus balls for spares and strikes.

This is an interesting separation of concerns. It is a fact that computing the score forces both versions to identify all the rolls that impact each frame. However, the Java version does this in situ, whereas the Clojure version nicely separates those two concerns.

Which of these versions is better? The Java version ended up a bit simpler than the Clojure version; but it was also a bit more coupled. The separation of concerns in the Clojure version convinces me that between the two, it would be more flexible and useful.

But, of course, we are only talking about a dozen lines of code.

---

10. See Robert C. Martin, *Clean Architecture* (Pearson, 2017).

GOSSIPING BUS DRIVERS

So far in this comparative analysis we haven't found a strong reason to prefer functional programming over OO programming. So let's examine a slightly more interesting problem.

Object orientation was born in 1966 when Ole-Johan Dahl and Kristen Nygaard added some modifications to the ALGOL-60 language in order to make the language more amenable to discrete event simulation.[1] The new language was called SIMULA-67 and is considered to be the first true OO programming language.

So let's do a comparative analysis of a simple discrete event simulator. That should keep the problem squarely in the OO wheelhouse. A nice problem to choose is the Gossiping Bus Drivers kata.[2]

Given n drivers, each with their own circular route of stops, determine how many steps are required until all gossip known to each bus driver is known by all. Drivers only gossip if they arrive together at the same stop.

So, let's say that Bob knows rumor X and drives route [p,q,r]. Jim knows rumor Y and drives route [s,t,u,p]. When will Bob and Jim be able to share their gossip? If they start at time 0, then at time 3 they will both be at stop p; remember, the routes are circular.

The process is limited to 480 steps.

This problem gets more interesting when there are more than two drivers and more complex routes.

JAVA SOLUTION

I wrote a solution to this problem in Java. I started out with a very traditional kind of OO analysis and design (see Figure 8.1).

---

1. Legend has it that they were simulating Norwegian ocean shipping.

2. https://kata-log.rocks/gossiping-bus-drivers-kata

The Simulator holds many Drivers. Each Driver has a Route, and each Route contains many Stops. Each Stop has many Drivers, and each Driver has many Rumors.

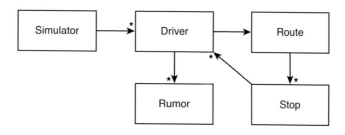

Figure 8.1. Simple object model for the Java version

This is a fairly simple object model. There's not even any inheritance or polymorphism implied. So it should be a pretty straightforward implementation.

I wrote the Java code using TDD, of course. Here are the tests. As you can see, they are fairly wordy; but at least they all fit into a single test class:[3]

```
package gossipingBusDrivers;

import org.junit.Before;
import org.junit.Test;

import static org.hamcrest.MatcherAssert.assertThat;
import static org.hamcrest.collection.IsEmptyCollection.empty;

import static org.hamcrest.collection.
  IsIterableContainingInAnyOrder.containsInAnyOrder;
import static org.junit.Assert.assertEquals;

public class GossipTest {
```

---

3. If you read my book *Clean Craftsmanship* (Addison-Wesley, 2021), you'll understand why this is a good thing.

```
    private Stop stop1;
    private Stop stop2;
    private Stop stop3;
    private Route route1;
    private Route route2;
    private Rumor rumor1;
    private Rumor rumor2;
    private Rumor rumor3;
    private Driver driver1;
    private Driver driver2;

    @Before
    public void setUp() {
      stop1 = new Stop("stop1");
      stop2 = new Stop("stop2");
      stop3 = new Stop("stop3");
      route1 = new Route(stop1, stop2);
      route2 = new Route(stop1, stop2, stop3);
      rumor1 = new Rumor("Rumor1");
      rumor2 = new Rumor("Rumor2");
      rumor3 = new Rumor("Rumor3");
      driver1 = new Driver("Driver1", route1, rumor1);
      driver2 = new Driver("Driver2", route2, rumor2, rumor3);
    }

    @Test
    public void driverStartsAtFirstStopInRoute() throws Exception {
      assertEquals(stop1, driver1.getStop());
    }

    @Test
    public void driverDrivesToNextStop() throws Exception {
      driver1.drive();
      assertEquals(stop2, driver1.getStop());
    }

    @Test
    public void driverReturnsToStartAfterLastStop()
    throws Exception {
```

```
    driver1.drive();
    driver1.drive();
    assertEquals(stop1, driver1.getStop());
}

@Test
public void firstStopHasDriversAtStart() throws Exception {
  assertThat(stop1.getDrivers(), containsInAnyOrder(driver1,
                                                    driver2));
  assertThat(stop2.getDrivers(), empty());
}

@Test
public void multipleDriversEnterAndLeaveStops()
throws Exception {
  assertThat(stop1.getDrivers(), containsInAnyOrder(driver1,
                                                    driver2));
  assertThat(stop2.getDrivers(), empty());
  assertThat(stop3.getDrivers(), empty());
  driver1.drive();
  driver2.drive();
  assertThat(stop1.getDrivers(), empty());
  assertThat(stop2.getDrivers(), containsInAnyOrder(driver1,
                                                    driver2));
  assertThat(stop3.getDrivers(), empty());
  driver1.drive();
  driver2.drive();
  assertThat(stop1.getDrivers(), containsInAnyOrder(driver1));
  assertThat(stop2.getDrivers(), empty());
  assertThat(stop3.getDrivers(), containsInAnyOrder(driver2));
  driver1.drive();
  driver2.drive();
  assertThat(stop1.getDrivers(), containsInAnyOrder(driver2));
  assertThat(stop2.getDrivers(), containsInAnyOrder(driver1));
  assertThat(stop3.getDrivers(), empty());
}

@Test
public void driversHaveRumorsAtStart() throws Exception {
```

```
    assertThat(driver1.getRumors(), containsInAnyOrder(rumor1));
    assertThat(driver2.getRumors(), containsInAnyOrder(rumor2,
                                                       rumor3));
  }


  @Test
  public void noDriversGossipAtEmptyStop() throws Exception {
    stop2.gossip();
    assertThat(driver1.getRumors(), containsInAnyOrder(rumor1));
    assertThat(driver2.getRumors(), containsInAnyOrder(rumor2,
                                                       rumor3));
  }


  @Test
  public void driversGossipAtStop() throws Exception {
    stop1.gossip();
    assertThat(driver1.getRumors(), containsInAnyOrder(rumor1,
                                                       rumor2,
                                                       rumor3));

    assertThat(driver2.getRumors(), containsInAnyOrder(rumor1,
                                                       rumor2,
                                                       rumor3));
  }


  @Test
  public void gossipIsNotDuplicated() throws Exception {
    stop1.gossip();
    stop1.gossip();
    assertThat(driver1.getRumors(), containsInAnyOrder(rumor1,
                                                       rumor2,
                                                       rumor3));

    assertThat(driver2.getRumors(), containsInAnyOrder(rumor1,
                                                       rumor2,
                                                       rumor3));
  }
```

```
@Test
public void driveTillEqualTest() throws Exception {
  assertEquals(1, Simulation.driveTillEqual(driver1,
                                             driver2));
}

@Test
public void acceptanceTest1() throws Exception {
  Stop s1 = new Stop("s1");
  Stop s2 = new Stop("s2");
  Stop s3 = new Stop("s3");
  Stop s4 = new Stop("s4");
  Stop s5 = new Stop("s5");
  Route r1 = new Route(s3, s1, s2, s3);
  Route r2 = new Route(s3, s2, s3, s1);
  Route r3 = new Route(s4, s2, s3, s4, s5);
  Driver d1 = new Driver("d1", r1, new Rumor("1"));
  Driver d2 = new Driver("d2", r2, new Rumor("2"));
  Driver d3 = new Driver("d3", r3, new Rumor("3"));
  assertEquals(6, Simulation.driveTillEqual(d1, d2, d3));
}

@Test
public void acceptanceTest2() throws Exception {
  Stop s1 = new Stop("s1");
  Stop s2 = new Stop("s2");
  Stop s5 = new Stop("s5");
  Stop s8 = new Stop("s8");
  Route r1 = new Route(s2, s1, s2);
  Route r2 = new Route(s5, s2, s8);
  Driver d1 = new Driver("d1", r1, new Rumor("1"));
  Driver d2 = new Driver("d2", r2, new Rumor("2"));
  assertEquals(480, Simulation.driveTillEqual(d1, d2));
}
}
```

The solution code is broken up into several small files.

DRIVER

```java
package gossipingBusDrivers;

import java.util.Arrays;
import java.util.HashSet;
import java.util.Set;

public class Driver {
  private String name;
  private Route route;
  private int stopNumber = 0;
  private Set<Rumor> rumors;

  public Driver(String name, Route theRoute,
                Rumor... theRumors) {
    this.name = name;
    route = theRoute;
    rumors = new HashSet<>(Arrays.asList(theRumors));
    route.stopAt(this, stopNumber);
  }

  public Stop getStop() {
    return route.get(stopNumber);
  }

  public void drive() {
    route.leave(this, stopNumber);
    stopNumber = route.getNextStop(stopNumber);
    route.stopAt(this, stopNumber);
  }

  public Set<Rumor> getRumors() {
    return rumors;
  }

  public void addRumors(Set<Rumor> newRumors) {
    rumors.addAll(newRumors);
  }
}
```

ROUTE

```java
package gossipingBusDrivers;

public class Route {
  private Stop[] stops;

  public Route(Stop... stops) {
    this.stops = stops;
  }

  public Stop get(int stopNumber) {
    return stops[stopNumber];
  }

  public int getNextStop(int stopNumber) {
    return (stopNumber + 1) % stops.length;
  }

  public void stopAt(Driver driver, int stopNumber) {
    stops[stopNumber].addDriver(driver);
  }

  public void leave(Driver driver, int stopNumber) {
    stops[stopNumber].removeDriver(driver);
  }
}
```

STOP

```java
package gossipingBusDrivers;

import java.util.ArrayList;
import java.util.HashSet;
import java.util.List;
import java.util.Set;

public class Stop {
  private String name;
```

```java
    private List<Driver> drivers = new ArrayList<>();

    public Stop(String name) {
        this.name = name;
    }

    public String toString() {
        return name;
    }

    public List<Driver> getDrivers() {
        return drivers;
    }

    public void addDriver(Driver driver) {
        drivers.add(driver);
    }

    public void removeDriver(Driver driver) {
        drivers.remove(driver);
    }

    public void gossip() {
        Set<Rumor> rumorsAtStop = new HashSet<>();
        for (Driver d : drivers)
            rumorsAtStop.addAll(d.getRumors());
        for (Driver d : drivers)
            d.addRumors(rumorsAtStop);
    }
}
```

RUMOR

```java
package gossipingBusDrivers;

public class Rumor {
    private String name;
```

```
  public Rumor(String name) {
    this.name = name;
  }

  public String toString() {
    return name;
  }
}
```

SIMULATION

```
package gossipingBusDrivers;

import java.util.HashSet;
import java.util.Set;

public class Simulation {
  public static int driveTillEqual(Driver... drivers) {
    int time;
    for (time = 0; notAllRumors(drivers) && time < 480; time++)
      driveAndGossip(drivers);
    return time;
  }

  private static void driveAndGossip(Driver[] drivers) {
    Set<Stop> stops = new HashSet<>();
    for (Driver d : drivers) {
      d.drive();
      stops.add(d.getStop());
    }
    for (Stop stop : stops)
      stop.gossip();
  }

  private static boolean notAllRumors(Driver[] drivers) {
    Set<Rumor> rumors = new HashSet<>();
    for (Driver d : drivers)
      rumors.addAll(d.getRumors());
```

```
    for (Driver d : drivers) {
      if (!d.getRumors().equals(rumors))
        return true;
    }
    return false;
  }
}
```

A quick perusal of this code will convince you that it is written in a very
traditional OO style and that the objects encapsulate their own state
relatively well.

CLOJURE

When writing the Clojure version I did not start out with a design sketch.
Rather, I depended upon my TDD tests to help me with the design. The
tests are as follows:

```clojure
(ns gossiping-bus-drivers-clojure.core-spec
  (:require [speclj.core :refer :all]
            [gossiping-bus-drivers-clojure.core :refer :all]))


(describe "gossiping bus drivers"
  (it "drives one bus at one stop"
    (let [driver (make-driver "d1" [:s1] #{:r1}⁴)
          world [driver]
          new-world (drive world)]
      (should= 1 (count new-world))
      (should= :s1 (-> new-world first :route first))))

  (it "drives one bus at two stops"
    (let [driver (make-driver "d1" [:s1 :s2] #{:r1})
          world [driver]
          new-world (drive world)]
      (should= 1 (count new-world))
      (should= :s2 (-> new-world first :route first))))
```

---

4. #{. . .} represents a set in Clojure. A *set* is a list of items that has no duplicates.

```
(it "drives two buses at some stops"
  (let [d1 (make-driver "d1" [:s1 :s2] #{:r1})
        d2 (make-driver "d2" [:s1 :s3 :s2] #{:r2})
        world [d1 d2]
        new-1 (drive world)
        new-2 (drive new-1)]
    (should= 2 (count new-1))
    (should= :s2 (-> new-1 first :route first))
    (should= :s3 (-> new-1 second :route first))
    (should= 2 (count new-2))
    (should= :s1 (-> new-2 first :route first))
    (should= :s2 (-> new-2 second :route first))))

(it "gets stops"
  (let [drivers #{{:name "d1" :route [:s1]}
                  {:name "d2" :route [:s1]}
                  {:name "d3" :route [:s2]}}]
    (should= {:s1 [{:name "d1" :route [:s1]}
                   {:name "d2" :route [:s1]}]
              :s2 [{:name "d3", :route [:s2]}]}
             (get-stops drivers)))
  )

(it "merges rumors"
  (should= [{:name "d1" :rumors #{:r2 :r1}}
            {:name "d2" :rumors #{:r2 :r1}}]
           (merge-rumors [{:name "d1" :rumors #{:r1}}
                          {:name "d2" :rumors #{:r2}}])))

(it "shares gossip when drivers are at same stop"
  (let [d1 (make-driver "d1" [:s1 :s2] #{:r1})
        d2 (make-driver "d2" [:s1 :s2] #{:r2})
        world [d1 d2]
        new-world (drive world)]
    (should= 2 (count new-world))
    (should= #{:r1 :r2} (-> new-world first :rumors))
    (should= #{:r1 :r2} (-> new-world second :rumors))))
```

```
(it "passes acceptance test 1"
  (let [world [(make-driver "d1" [3 1 2 3] #{1})
               (make-driver "d2" [3 2 3 1] #{2})
               (make-driver "d3" [4 2 3 4 5] #{3})]]
    (should= 6 (drive-till-all-rumors-spread world))))

(it "passes acceptance test 2"
  (let [world [(make-driver "d1" [2 1 2] #{1})
               (make-driver "d2" [5 2 8] #{2})]]
    (should= :never (drive-till-all-rumors-spread world))))
)
```

There are some interesting similarities between the Java tests and the Clojure tests. They are both quite wordy; although the Clojure tests contain half as many lines. The Java version has 12 tests whereas the Clojure version has only 8. This difference has a lot to do with the way the two different solutions were partitioned. The Clojure tests also play pretty fast and loose with the data.

Consider, for example, the "merges rumors" test. The merge-rumors function expects a list of drivers; however, the test does not create completely formed drivers. Rather, it creates abbreviated structures that look like drivers as far as the merge-rumors function is concerned.

The solution is all contained in a single, very short file:

```
(ns gossiping-bus-drivers-clojure.core
  (:require [clojure.set :as set]))

(defn make-driver [name route rumors]
  (assoc⁵ {} :name name :route (cycle⁶ route) :rumors rumors))

(defn move-driver [driver]
```

---

5. assoc adds elements to a map. (assoc {} :a 1) returns {:a 1}.

6. cycle returns a lazy (and "infinite") list that simply repeats the input list endlessly. Thus, (cycle [1 2 3]) returns [1 2 3 1 2 3 1 2 3 …].

```
    (update⁷ driver :route rest))

(defn move-drivers [world]
  (map move-driver world))

(defn get-stops [world]
  (loop [world world
         stops {}]
    (if (empty? world)
      stops
      (let [driver (first world)
            stop (first (:route driver))
            stops (update stops stop conj driver)]
        (recur (rest world) stops)))))

(defn merge-rumors [drivers]
  (let [rumors (map :rumors drivers)
        all-rumors (apply set/union⁸ rumors)]
    (map #(assoc % :rumors all-rumors) drivers)))

(defn spread-rumors [world]
  (let [stops-with-drivers (get-stops world)
        drivers-by-stop (vals⁹ stops-with-drivers)]
    (flatten¹⁰ (map merge-rumors drivers-by-stop))))

(defn drive [world]
  (-> world move-drivers spread-rumors))

(defn drive-till-all-rumors-spread [world]
  (loop [world (drive world)
```

---

7. The update function returns a new map with one element changed. (update m k f a) changes the k element of m by applying the function (f e a), where e is the old value of element k. Thus, (update {:x 1} :x inc) returns {:x 2}.

8. The union function is from the set namespace. Notice the ns at the top aliases the clojure.set namespace to just set.

9. vals returns a list of all the values in a map. keys returns a list of all the keys in a map.

10. The flatten function turns a list of lists into a list of all the elements. So (flatten [[1 2][3 4]]) returns [1 2 3 4].

```
        time 1]
  (cond
    (> time 480) :never
    (apply = (map :rumors world)) time
    :else (recur (drive world) (inc time)))))))
```

This solution is 42 lines, whereas the Java solution is 145 lines spread among five files.

Both solutions have the concept of a Driver, but I made no attempt to encapsulate the concepts of Route, Stop, and Rumor into independent objects. They all just happily live within the Driver.

Worse, the Driver "object" is not an object in the traditional OO sense. It has no methods. There is one method in the system, move-driver, that operates on a single Driver, but it's just a little helper function for the more interesting move-drivers function.

Six out of the eight functions take only the world as an argument. Thus, we might say that the only true object in this system is the world, and it has five methods. But even that is a stretch.

Even if we decide that the Driver is a kind of object, it is not mutable. The simulated world is nothing more than a list of immutable Drivers. The drive function accepts the world and produces a new world in which all the Drivers have been moved one step, and Rumors have been spread at any stop where more than one Driver has arrived.

That drive function is an example of an important concept. Notice how the world passes through a pipeline of functions. In this case there are only two, move-drivers and spread-rumors, but in larger systems the pipeline can be quite long. At each stage along that pipeline the world is modified into a slightly new form.

This tells us that the partitioning of this system is not about objects, but about functions. The relatively unpartitioned data passes from one independent function to the next.

You might argue that the Java code is relatively straightforward, whereas the Clojure code is too dense and obscure. Believe me when I say that it does not take very long to get comfortable with that density and that the perceived obscuration is an illusion based on unfamiliarity.

Is the lack of partitioning in the Clojure version a problem? Not at its current size; but if this program were to grow the way most systems grow, that problem would assert itself with a vengeance. Partitioning OO programs is a bit more natural than partitioning functional programs because the dividing lines are much more obvious and pronounced.

On the other hand, the dividing lines we chose for the Java version are not guaranteed to lead to an *effective* partitioning. The warning is in the drive function of the Clojure program. It seems likely that a better partitioning of this system might lie along the different operations that manipulate the world, rather than things like Routes, Stops, and Rumors.

CONCLUSION

We saw some differences in the Prime Factors and Bowling Game katas; but the differences were relatively minor. The differences in the Gossiping Bus Drivers kata were much more pronounced. This is likely because that last kata was a bit larger than the first two (I'd say twice the size), and also because it was a true finite state machine.

A *finite state machine* moves from state to state, taking actions that depend upon the incoming events and the current state. When such systems are written in an OO style, the state tends to be stored in mutable objects that have dedicated methods. But in a functional style, the state remains externalized in immutable data structures that are passed through pipelines of functions.

We can perhaps conclude from this that programs that do simple calculations, like Prime Factors, are little affected by the OO or functional style. They are, after all, simple functions without any change of state. Programs in which state change is restricted to minor issues, such as array indexing, are only slightly affected by the difference in style. But those programs that are driven by changes of state from one moment to the next, like the Gossiping Bus Drivers program, will see profound differences between the two styles.

The OO style leads to a partitioning that is strongly related to data cohesion, whereas the functional style leads to a partitioning that is strongly related to behavioral cohesion. Which of these two is better is a question that I will leave for subsequent chapters.

OBJECT-ORIENTED PROGRAMMING

In the preceding chapter, we saw that the OO style of programming is strongly related to data types and the cohesion of data. But that's not all there is to object orientation. Indeed, data cohesion may be secondary to another attribute of object orientation: polymorphism.

In *Clean Architecture*,[1] I made the point that the OO style has three attributes: encapsulation, inheritance, and polymorphism. I then led you through the reasoning that, of the three, polymorphism is the most beneficial. The other two are, at best, ancillary.

The examples in the previous chapters did not lend themselves to any polymorphism. Let's correct that by examining how we might solve the Payroll problem from Section 3 of *Agile Software Development: Principles, Patterns, and Practices*.[2]

The requirements are as follows.

- There is a database of employee records.
- The payroll program runs daily, generating payments for those employees who should be paid on that day.
- Salaried employees are paid on the last business day of the month. Their monthly salary is a field in their employee record.
- Commissioned employees are paid every other Friday. They are paid a base salary plus commission. The base salary and the commission rate are fields in their employee record. Commission is calculated by multiplying the commission rate by the total of the sales receipts for that employee.
- Hourly employees are paid every Friday. Their hourly rate is a field in their employee record. Their pay is calculated by multiplying their hourly rate by the sum of the hours on their timecards for the week. If

---

1. Robert C. Martin, *Clean Architecture* (Pearson, 2017).

2. Robert C Martin, *Agile Software Development: Principles, Patterns, and Practices* (Pearson, 2002).

that sum is greater than 40, the remaining hours are paid at 1.5 times their hourly rate.

- Employees are given the option to have their paychecks mailed to their home address, held at their paymaster's office, or directly deposited into their bank account. The address, paymaster, and bank information are fields in their employee record.

The typical OO solution to this problem is shown in the unified modeling language (UML) diagram in Figure 9.1.

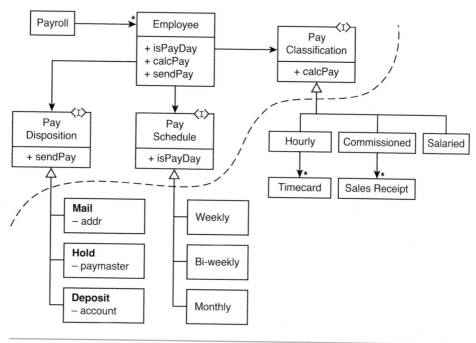

Figure 9.1. Object model for the Payroll problem

Perhaps the best place to begin is with the Payroll class. In Java, it has a run method that looks like this:

```
void run() {
  for (Employee e : db.getEmployees()) {
```

```
    if (e.isPayDay()) {
      Pay pay = e.calcPay();
      e.sendPay(pay);
    }
  }
}
```

I have made the point many times, and in many places, including the aforementioned books, that this little snippet of code is the *pure truth*. For each employee, if today is the day they should be paid, then calculate their pay and send it to them.

From that little snippet of code, the rest of the implementation ought to be pretty clear. There are three uses of the *Strategy*[3] pattern: one to implement calcPay, another to implement isPayDay, and the last to implement sendPay.

It should also be clear that this structure of objects must be built up by the getEmployees function, which reads the employees from the database and arranges them properly. It is unlikely that the data in the database looks like the object structure seen here.

There is also a very clear architectural boundary (dashed line) that cuts across all those inheritance relationships, dividing the high-level abstractions from the low-level details.

FUNCTIONAL PAYROLL

Figure 9.2 shows what this might look like as a functional program.

---

3. Erich Gamma, Richard Helm, Ralph Johnson, and John Vlissides, *Design Patterns: Elements of Reusable Object-Oriented Software* (Addison-Wesley, 1995), 315.

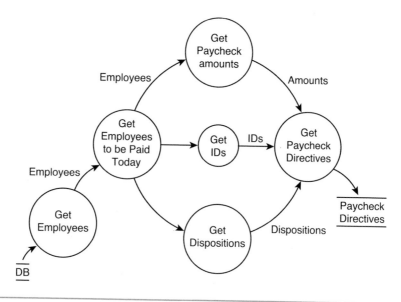

Figure 9.2. Data flow diagram of the Payroll problem

Isn't it interesting that I chose a data flow diagram (DFD) to represent the functional solution? DFDs are very helpful in depicting the relationships between processes and data elements, but they are not nearly as helpful as UML class diagrams when it comes to depicting architectural decisions.

Still, the DFD helps us propose the functional version of the *pure truth*:

```
(defn payroll [today db]
  (let [employees (get-employees db)
        employees-to-pay (get-employees-to-be-paid-today
                           today employees)
        amounts (get-paycheck-amounts employees-to-pay)
        ids (get-ids employees-to-pay)
        dispositions (get-dispositions employees-to-pay)]
    (send-paychecks ids amounts dispositions)))
```

Notice that this differs from the Java version in that it is not an iterative approach. Rather, the list of employees flows through the program, getting modified at each stage according to the data flow diagram. This is typical of the way functional programs are conceived and written. Functional programs tend to be more like *plumbing* than step-by-step procedures. They regulate and modify the flow of data, rather than iterating step by step through the data.

So, what about the architecture? There was that nice architectural boundary in the UML diagram of the OO version. Where is the architectural boundary in the functional version?

Let's look a bit deeper. The tests may give us some hints:

```
(it "pays one salaried employee at end of month by mail"
  (let [employees [{:id "emp1"
                    :schedule :monthly
                    :pay-class [:salaried 5000]
                    :disposition [:mail "name" "home"]}]
        db {:employees employees}
        today (parse-date "Nov 30 2021")]
    (should= [{:type :mail
               :id "emp1"
               :name "name"
               :address "home"
               :amount 5000}]
             (payroll today db))))
```

In this test, the database contains a list of employees, and each employee is a hash map with specific fields. That's not so different from an object, is it? The payroll function returns a list of paycheck directives, each of which is also a hash map—another object. Interesting.

```
(it "pays one hourly employee on Friday by Direct Deposit"
  (let [employees [{:id "empid"
```

```
                 :schedule :weekly
                 :pay-class [:hourly 15]
                 :disposition [:deposit "routing" "account"]}]
        time-cards {"empid" [["Nov 12 2022" 80/10⁴]]}
        db {:employees employees :time-cards time-cards}
        friday (parse-date "Nov 18 2022")]
   (should= [{:type :deposit
              :id "empid"
              :routing "routing"
              :account "account"
              :amount 120}]
            (payroll friday db))))
```

This test shows how the employee and paycheck-directive objects vary based upon the :schedule, :pay-class, and :disposition. It also shows that the database contains time-cards associated with employee ids. From this, the third test ought to be predictable:

```
(it "pays one commissioned employee on an even Friday by Paymaster"
  (let [employees [{:id "empid"
                    :schedule :biweekly
                    :pay-class [:commissioned 100 5/100]
                    :disposition [:paymaster "paymaster"]}]
        sales-receipts {"empid" [["Nov 12 2022" 15000]]}
        db {:employees employees :sales-receipts sales-receipts}
        friday (parse-date "Nov 18 2022")]
   (should= [{:type :paymaster
              :id "empid"
              :paymaster "paymaster"
              :amount 850}]
            (payroll friday db))))
```

Notice that the payments are being properly calculated, the dispositions are being correctly interpreted, and—as far as we can tell—the schedules are being followed. So how is this all being accomplished?

---

4. This is not 80 divided by 10. Rather, it is the rational number 80/10. This ensures that subsequent mathematics will not treat the value as an integer.

Here's the key to it all:

```
(defn get-pay-class [employee]
  (first (:pay-class employee)))

(defn get-disposition [paycheck-directive]
  (first (:disposition paycheck-directive)))

(defmulti is-today-payday :schedule)
(defmulti calc-pay get-pay-class)
(defmulti dispose get-disposition)

(defn get-employees-to-be-paid-today [today employees]
  (filter⁵ #(is-today-payday % today) employees))

(defn- build-employee [db employee]
  (assoc employee :db db))

(defn get-employees [db]
  (map (partial⁶ build-employee db) (:employees db)))

(defn create-paycheck-directives [ids payments dispositions]
  (map #(assoc {} :id %1 :amount %2 :disposition %3)
       ids payments dispositions))

(defn send-paychecks [ids payments dispositions]
  (for⁷ [paycheck-directive
         (create-paycheck-directives ids payments dispositions)]
    (dispose paycheck-directive)))

(defn get-paycheck-amounts [employees]
```

---

5. (filter predicate list) calls predicate for every member of list and returns a sequence of all the members for which predicate was not *falsey*.

6. The partial function takes a function and some arguments, and returns a new function in which all those arguments have already been initialized. Thus, ((partial f 1) 2) is equivalent to (f 1 2).

7. In this case, the for function calls dispose for each paycheck-directive in the list returned by create-paycheck-directives.

```
  (map calc-pay employees))

(defn get-dispositions [employees]
  (map :disposition employees))

(defn get-ids [employees]
  (map :id employees))
```

Do you see those `defmulti` statements (in bold)? They are analogous, though not identical, to a Java interface. Each `defmulti` defines a polymorphic function. However, that function does not dispatch based upon an intrinsic type, the way Java or C# or even Ruby and Python do. Rather, they dispatch upon the result of the function specified right after the name.

So, the `get-pay-class` function returns the value that the `calc-pay` function will polymorphically dispatch on. What does `get-pay-class` return? It returns the first element of the `pay-class` field of the `employee`. According to our tests, those values are `:salaried`, `:hourly`, and `:commissioned`.

So where are the implementations of the `calc-pay` functions? They are *further down* in the program:

```
(defn-[8] get-salary [employee]
  (second (:pay-class employee)))

(defmethod calc-pay :salaried [employee]
  (get-salary employee))

(defmethod calc-pay :hourly [employee]
  (let [db (:db employee)
        time-cards (:time-cards db)
        my-time-cards (get[9] time-cards (:id employee))
```

---

8. The trailing - makes this a private function, so only functions in this file can access it.

9. (get m k) returns the value of k in the map m.

```
      [_ hourly-rate]¹⁰ (:pay-class employee)
      hours (map second my-time-cards)
      total-hours (reduce + hours)]
  (* total-hours hourly-rate)))

(defmethod calc-pay :commissioned [employee]
  (let [db (:db employee)
        sales-receipts (:sales-receipts db)
        my-sales-receipts (get sales-receipts (:id employee))
        [_ base-pay commission-rate] (:pay-class employee)
        sales (map second my-sales-receipts)
        total-sales (reduce + sales)]
    (+ (* total-sales commission-rate) base-pay)))
```

I italicized the words *further down* because that is significant in a Clojure program. Clojure programs cannot call functions that are declared below the point of call. But these functions *are* declared below the point of call. That means there is a source code dependency inversion. The calc-pay implementations are called by the payroll function; but the payroll function is above the calc-pay implementations.

Indeed, I could move all the implementations of the defmulti function to a different source file that the payroll source file does not require.

If we draw the relationships between those source files, we get the diagram in Figure 9.3.

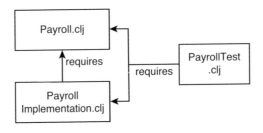

Figure 9.3. Dependency inversion

---

10. *Destructures* the pay-class of the employee and ignores the first element.

The arrows depict the `requires` relationships between the source files. The source code of those `requires` in the `payroll-implementation.clj` file looks like this:

```
(ns payroll-implementation
  (:require [payroll :refer [is-today-payday calc-pay dispose]]))
```

The source code dependency inversion should be obvious. The `payroll` function in `payroll.clj` calls the `is-today-payday`, `calc-pay`, and `dispose` implementations in the `payroll-implementation.clj` file, but the `payroll.clj` file does not depend upon the `payroll-implementation.clj` file. The dependency points the other way around.

What does all this inversion mean? It means that the low-level details in `payroll-implementation.clj` depend upon the high-level policy in `payroll.clj`. And whenever low-level details depend upon high-level policy, we have the potential for an architectural boundary. We could even draw it as shown in Figure 9.4.

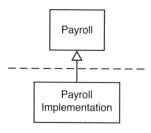

Figure 9.4. Architectural boundary

Notice that I used a UML implements arrow. It's almost as if `Payroll` and `PayrollImplementation` were classes in a Java program.

But we can do even better than this. We can move all the `defmulti` statements, along with their supporting functions, into their own `payroll-interface` namespace and source file, like this:

```
(ns payroll-interface)

(defn- get-pay-class [employee]
  (first (:pay-class employee)))

(defn- get-disposition [paycheck-directive]
  (first (:disposition paycheck-directive)))

(defmulti is-today-payday :schedule)
(defmulti calc-pay get-pay-class)
(defmulti dispose get-disposition)
```

And now we can draw the architecture diagram as shown in Figure 9.5.

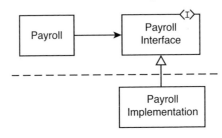

Figure 9.5. Architecture with interface

This is starting to look more and more like the UML diagram of a Java or C# program. It looks like we got a `Payroll` class, a `PayrollInterface` class, and a `PayrollImplementation` class. And indeed, from an architectural point of view, that's a pretty accurate statement.

But there are some interesting differences. Where, for example, are the `PaySchedule`, `PayClassification`, and `PayDisposition` classes that we saw in the UML of the OO Java program?

We could easily pull them out of the Clojure program by splitting the `PayrollImplementation.clj` file into three namespaces and files, as shown in Figure 9.6.

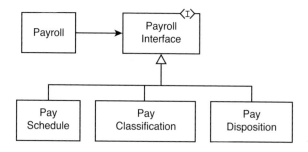

Figure 9.6. Split architecture

This is not the kind of thing you can do in Java or C# since there is no way, in those languages, to implement each function of an interface in a different module. However, it's perfectly possible in Clojure. The important thing to remember is that this is an *architectural* diagram, not a class diagram. PaySchedule, PayClassification, and PayDisposition are namespaces and source files, not classes. We do not make instances of them. They don't represent objects in an OO sense.

Not that there aren't objects in our Clojure solution. There certainly are. The employee, the paycheck-directive, and even the pay-class and disposition are objects. They do not have methods as strongly associated with them as they would if they were written in an OO language; but there are functions through which those objects flow.

NAMESPACES AND SOURCE FILES

In Clojure especially, namespaces and source files are deeply connected. Each namespace must be contained in its own source file, and the name of that file must correspond[11] to the name of the namespace. This is very similar to the way Java forces public classes into their own source file named for the class. It is also very similar to the file/class convention used by C++ and C# programmers. This could lead you to consider that each Clojure namespace is something like a class.

---

11. Through a simple translation algorithm.

The correspondence is not perfect, of course. The contents of a Clojure namespace need not be class-like at all. But, in general, the concept is not a bad one.

One of the great temptations in functional languages like Clojure is to group functions into namespaces in a kind of ad hoc, by-feel way. Without the OO structure to force us to divide functions into classes that exist in their own source files, we often wind up with source file structures that are ricketier and more fragile than they ought to be.

So, when writing functional programs, it is not a bad idea to consider the partitioning disciplines of OO and continue to apply them. We'll see more of this later as we investigate principles, patterns, and architecture.

Conclusion

First of all, functional programs and OO programs are different. Functional programs tend to be constructions of plumbing that regulate data flow transformations, while mutable OO programs tend to iterate step by step over objects. However, from an architectural point of view, the two styles are quite compatible. It turns out that we can partition the functions of a functional program into the same kinds of architecturally significant elements as an OO program. From an architectural point of view, there's very little difference.

Functional programs may not be composed of syntactically enforced classes that enclose methods and define objects. Yet, objects still exist in functional programs. Those objects are less tightly bound to the functions that operate upon them than they would be in an OO language. Whether that is an advantage or a disadvantage is something we will continue to probe in the chapters that follow.

We shall see as these pages turn more and more toward design and architecture, the differences between functional programs and the object orientation of immutable objects start to become less and less relevant.

10 TYPES

KOHNKE

The preceding chapter may have left you somewhat distressed. Those things that I called objects were just hash maps and were completely untyped. Anybody could stick anything into them without any constraint. The salary in the :pay-class could hold a string instead of a number. The :schedule field could hold an integer instead of the appropriate keyword.

In short, these objects are not statically typed. The compiler does not check them. And therefore, *all hell could break loose*!

Many functional languages, as well as many OO languages, are statically typed in order to prevent that hell. Other languages, like Clojure, Python, and Ruby, depend upon other mechanisms to prevent that hell.

Those of us who practice TDD are not usually very concerned about that hell. Our tests generally ensure that the objects that we pass around are properly constructed. Still, in complex systems, where the totality of all the objects can end up being quite complex, there is a need for a more formal and complete way to ensure the integrity of our types than a dynamically typed language (and even most statically typed languages) can give us.

In Clojure, I use the clojure.spec library to achieve the goal of type integrity. The type specification for our payroll example looks like this:

```
(s/def ::id string?)
(s/def ::schedule #{:monthly :weekly :biweekly})
(s/def ::salaried-pay-class (s/tuple #(= % :salaried) pos[1]?))
(s/def ::hourly-pay-class (s/tuple #(= % :hourly) pos?))
(s/def ::commissioned-pay-class (s/tuple #(= % :commissioned)
                                         pos? pos?))
(s/def ::pay-class (s/or :salaried ::salaried-pay-class
                         :Hourly ::hourly-pay-class
                         :Commissioned ::commissioned-pay-class))

(s/def ::mail-disposition (s/tuple #(= % :mail) string? string?))
(s/def ::deposit-disposition (s/tuple #(= % :deposit)
```

---

1. (pos? x) returns true if x is a number greater than zero.

```
                                           string? string?))
(s/def ::paymaster-disposition (s/tuple #(= % :paymaster)
                                        string?))
(s/def ::disposition (s/or :mail ::mail-disposition
                           :deposit ::deposit-disposition
                           :paymaster ::paymaster-disposition))


(s/def ::employee (s/keys :req-un [::id ::schedule
                                   ::pay-class ::disposition]))
(s/def ::employees (s/coll-of ::employee))


(s/def ::date string?)
(s/def ::time-card (s/tuple ::date pos?))
(s/def ::time-cards (s/map-of ::id (s/coll-of ::time-card)))


(s/def ::sales-receipt (s/tuple ::date pos?))
(s/def ::sales-receipts (s/map-of
                          ::id (s/coll-of ::sales-receipt)))


(s/def ::db (s/keys :req-un [::employees]
                    :opt-un [::time-cards ::sales-receipts]))


(s/def ::amount pos?)
(s/def ::name string?)
(s/def ::address string?)
(s/def ::mail-directive (s/and #(= (:type %) :mail)
                              (s/keys :req-un [::id
                                              ::name
                                              ::address
                                              ::amount])))


(s/def ::routing string?)
(s/def ::account string?)
(s/def ::deposit-directive (s/and #(= (:type %) :deposit)
                                 (s/keys :req-un [::id
                                                 ::routing
                                                 ::account
                                                 ::amount])))
```

```
(s/def ::paymaster string?)
(s/def ::paymaster-directive (s/and #(= (:type %) :paymaster)
                                    (s/keys :req-un [::id
                                                    ::paymaster
                                                    ::amount]))))


(s/def ::paycheck-directive (s/or
                                :mail ::mail-directive
                                :deposit ::deposit-directive
                                :paymaster ::paymaster-directive))

(s/def ::paycheck-directives (s/coll-of ::paycheck-directive))
```

If this looks scary, it should. There's a lot of detail in there. Keep in mind, however, that this is the level of detail that you would have to specify within the modules of a statically typed language in order to capture all the type constraints.

Understanding this type specification is not actually difficult. Look down toward the middle and find the definition of ::db. This just says that the database is a hash map with a required :employees field and two optional fields for :time-cards and :sales-receipts.

If you look a bit higher in the specification, you'll see that ::employees is just a collection of ::employee, ::sales-receipts is a collection of ::sales-receipt, and ::time-cards is a collection of ::time-card. Don't let the double colons bother you; they are a namespace convention. You can read the Clojure docs later if you want to understand them. For now, just look at the keywords and ignore how many colons there are.

As we continue to work our way up, we see that an ::employee is a hash map that is required to have the keys :id, :schedule, :pay-class, and :disposition. Keep exploring and you'll find that the :id must be a string; the :schedule must be one of :monthly, :weekly, or :biweekly; and a :salaried-pay-class is a tuple containing :salaried, followed by a positive number.

The s/or statements might bother you a bit. The arguments come in pairs, and the first in each pair is just the name of that alternative. So, in the ::disposition definition, :mail is just the name of the ::mail-disposition alternative. Don't worry anymore about this. It will become clear if you decide one day to read the clojure.spec docs.

So, given this elaborate type specification, how do we use it? I sometimes use it in my tests as follows:

```
(it "pays one salaried employee at end of month by mail"
  (let [employees [{:id "emp1"
                    :schedule :monthly
                    :pay-class [:salaried 5000]
                    :disposition [:mail "name" "home"]}]
        db {:employees employees}
        today (parse-date "Nov 30 2021")]
    (should (s/valid? ::db db))
    (let [paycheck-directives (payroll today db)]
      (should (s/valid? ::paycheck-directives
                        paycheck-directives))
      (should= [{:type :mail
                 :id "emp1"
                 :name "name"
                 :address "home"
                 :amount 5000}]
               paycheck-directives))))
```

Look for the calls to s/valid?, which is a function that returns true if the data matches the spec. Look carefully and you'll see that I'm checking the ::db spec on the way in and the ::paycheck-directives spec on the way out. This is pretty secure. If my tests have high coverage, and they all check the specs for the inputs and outputs of the functions they call, then violations of type ought to be extremely rare.

I have, upon occasion, also used Clojure's :pre and :post features to run the specs on critical data before and after the main processing functions of my applications.

Here, for example, is the main processing step of the spacewar[2] game I wrote some years ago:

```
(defn update-world [ms world]
  ;{:pre [(valid-world? world)]
  ; :post [(valid-world? %)]}
  (->> world
       (game-won ms)
       (game-over ms)
       (ship/update-ship ms)
       (shots/update-shots ms)
       (explosions/update-explosions ms)
       (clouds/update-clouds ms)
       (klingons/update-klingons ms)
       (bases/update-bases ms)
       (romulans/update-romulans ms)
       (view-frame/update-messages ms)
       (add-messages)))
```

The :pre and :post statements are commented out,[3] but they are ready to be reasserted should I suspect some kind of terrible type corruption.

CONCLUSION

There is a lot of wailing and gnashing of teeth over the static versus dynamic typing issue. Each side yells at the other without listening to what either side has to say. I think both sides have valid points. Dynamic typing makes code easier to write. Static typing makes code a lot safer, easier to understand, and much more internally consistent. It seems to me that a library like clojure.spec strikes a great balance. It gives you the ability to have as much or as little type checking as you need. It allows you to specify when types *are* checked and when they are *not*. What's more, it allows you to specify dynamic constraints that no static type system *can* check. So, for my money, libraries like this give you better than the best of both worlds.

---

2. https://github.com/unclebob/spacewar

3. I don't much care for commented-out code. I'd remove these lines as the project matured.

III

FUNCTIONAL DESIGN

11 Data Flow

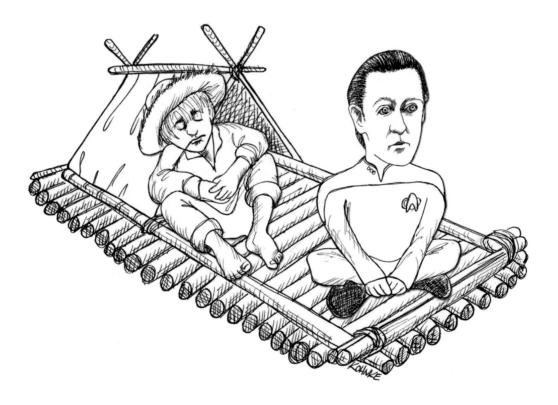

In Chapter 9, Object-Oriented Programming, I suggested that the design of a functional program is more like plumbing than procedure. There is a definite data flow bias to it. This is because we tend to use map, filter, and reduce to transform the contents of lists into other lists, rather than iterating through the problem one element at a time to produce results.

We can see this bias in many of our previous examples, including the Bowling Game, Gossiping Bus Drivers, and Payroll applications in Part II, Comparative Analysis.

As another example, consider this interesting problem from day ten of Advent of Code 2022.[1] The goal was to render pixels on a 6-by-40 screen. The pixels were drawn from left to right, one at a time, based on a clock circuit. Clock cycles were counted starting at 0. If a certain register x matched the clock cycle number, then the pixel at the appropriate screen position was turned on; otherwise, it was turned off.

This is actually quite typical of the way old CRT[2] displays used to work. You had to energize the electron beam at just the right moment as it rastered over the screen. So you matched the bits in the bitmap to the clock that drove that beam. If, according to the clock, the beam was at position 934, and if the 934th bit in the bitmap was set, then you energized the beam for an instant to display that pixel.

The Advent of Code problem was a bit more interesting. It asked us to simulate a simple processor that had two instructions. The first instruction was noop, which took one clock cycle but had no other effect. The other instruction was addx, which took an integer argument n that it added to the x register of the processor. This instruction consumed two clock cycles and only changed the x register after both cycles had completed. Pixels on

---

1. https://adventofcode.com/2022/day/10

2. Cathode ray tube. A *cathode ray* is an electron. CRTs have electron guns that create narrow beams of electrons that are rastered across the screen using regularly changing magnetic fields. The beam strikes phosphors on the screen and makes them glow, thus creating a raster image.

the screen would be visible for a clock cycle if, and only if, at the beginning of that cycle the x register matched the clock cycle number.

So if according to the clock, the beam was over screen position 23, and if the x register was 23 at the start of cycle 23, then the beam would be energized for that clock cycle.

To complicate matters just a little more, the matching of the x register to the clock cycle was widened so that 22, 23, and 24 would match clock cycle 23. In other words, the x register specified a window that was three pixels wide. So long as the clock cycle fell within that window, the beam would be energized.

Since the screen is 40 pixels wide and 6 pixels tall, the matching of the clock cycle to x is modulus 40.

The task was to execute a set of instructions and produce a list of six strings that were 40 characters each, with "#" indicating a pixel that was visible and "." indicating one that was not visible.

If you were to write this program in Java, C, Go, C++, C#, or any other procedural/OO language, you might create a loop that iterated one cycle at a time while accumulating the appropriate pixels for each cycle. The loop would consume instructions and modify the x register as directed.

Here's a typical example in Java:

```
package crt;

public class Crt {
  private int x;
  private String pixels = "";
  private int extraCycles = 0;
  private int cycle = 0;
  private int ic;
  private String[] instructions;
```

```
public Crt(int x) {
  this.x = x;
}

public void doCycles(int n, String instructionsLines) {
  instructions = instructionsLines.split("\n");
  ic = 0;
  for (cycle = 0; cycle < n; cycle++) {
    setPixel();
    execute();
  }
}

private void execute() {
  if (instructions[ic].equals("noop"))
    ic++;
  else if (instructions[ic].startsWith("addx ")
          && extraCycles == 0) {
    extraCycles = 1;
  }
  else if (instructions[ic].startsWith("addx ")
          && extraCycles == 1) {
    extraCycles = 0;
    x += Integer.parseInt(instructions[ic].substring(5));
    ic++;
  } else
    System.out.println("TILT");
}

private void setPixel() {
  int pos = cycle % 40;
  int offset = pos - x;
  if (offset >= -1 && 1 >= offset)
    pixels += "#";
  else
    pixels += ".";
}
```

```
  public String getPixels() {
    return pixels;
  }

  public int getX() {
    return x;
  }
}
```

Notice all the mutated state. Notice how it iterates, cycle by cycle, to populate the pixels. Notice also the funny business of extraCycles to account for the fact that addx takes two cycles to execute.

Finally, notice that although the program is nicely partitioned into a few smallish functions, those functions are all coupled together by the mutable state variables. That is, of course, the usual situation for methods of a mutable class.

I solved this problem in Clojure today. And the solution I came up with was very different from the Java code above. Remember as you read this to start at the bottom. Clojure programs are always written from the bottom up.

```
(ns day10-cathode-ray-tube.core
  (:require [clojure.string :as string]))

(defn noop [state]
  (update state :cycles conj (:x state)))

(defn addx [n state]
  (let [{:keys [x cycles]} state]
    (assoc state :x (+ x n)
                 :cycles (vec (concat cycles [x x])))))

(defn execute [state lines]
  (if (empty? lines)
    state
    (let [line (first lines)
          state (if (re-matches #"noop" line)
```

```
                    (noop state)
                    (if-let [[_ n] (re-matches
                                    #"addx (-?\d+)" line)]
                      (addx (Integer/parseInt n) state)
                      "TILT"))]³
        (recur state (rest lines)))))

(defn execute-file [file-name]
  (let [lines (string/split-lines (slurp file-name))
        starting-state {:x 1 :cycles []}
        ending-state (execute starting-state lines)]
    (:cycles ending-state)))

(defn render-cycles [cycles]
  (loop [cycles cycles
         screen ""
         t 0]
    (if (empty? cycles)
      (map #(apply str %) (partition 40 40 "" screen))
      (let [x (first cycles)
            offset (- t x)
            pixel? (<= -1 offset 1)
            screen (str screen (if pixel? "#" "."))
            t (mod (inc t) 40)]
        (recur (rest cycles) screen t)))))

(defn print-screen [lines]
  (doseq [line lines]
    (println line))
  true)

(defn -main []
  (-> "input"
      execute-file
      render-cycles
      print-screen))
```

---

3. TILT is my favorite error message. Long ago, pinball machines would put up this message and cancel your game if you physically tilted the machine in order to manipulate the ball.

The execute-file function transforms the list of instructions in the named file into a list of resulting x values. The render-cycles function then transforms the list of x values into a list of pixels, which it finally partitions into strings of 40 characters.

Notice that there are, of course, no mutable variables. Instead, the state value flows through each of the functions as though through a pipeline.

The state value begins in execute-file and then flows to execute, then repeatedly to noop or addx, and then back to execute, and finally back to execute-file. At each stage in that flow, a new value of state is created from the old without changing the old.

If this seems eerily familiar to you, it should. This is very much like the pipes and filters we have gotten used to in our command-line shells. Data flows into a command from a pipe, is transformed by that command, and then flows out to the next command through a pipe.

Here's a recent command I've been using at the shell:

```
ls -lh private/messages | cut -c 32-37,57-64
```

It lists the private/messages directory and then cuts out certain fields. The data flows out of the ls command, through the pipe, and then into the cut command. This has the same kind of feel as the state value flowing through the execute, addx, and noop functions.

As a result of this pipelining, you should notice that my cathode-ray-tube program is partitioned into a set of smallish functions that are not coupled to one another by mutable state. Whatever coupling exists is merely the coupling of the data formats that flow from function to function through the pipes.

Finally, notice that there is none of the funny business we saw in the Java program surrounding the two cycles of the addx instruction. Instead, the two cycles are neatly accounted for by simply adding two x values to the `:cycles` element of the `state`.

Of course, I didn't have to use the data flow style. I could have created a Clojure algorithm that was much closer to the Java algorithm. But that's not the way I think about things when I'm writing in a functional language. Instead, I am biased toward data flow solutions.

Some of the newer features in Java and C# lend themselves to the data flow style. But they are wordy and appear to me to be bolted onto the languages in awkward ways. Your mileage may vary; but I find that when I use procedural/OO languages I tend to iterate much more than I tend to plumb.

Or, to say this differently:

In mutable languages, behaviors flow through objects. In functional languages, objects flow through behaviors.

12

SOLID

I wrote about the SOLID principles over two decades ago in the context of OO design. Because of that context, many have come to associate those principles with OO and regard them as anathema to functional programming. This is unfortunate because the SOLID principles are general principles of software design that are not specific to any particular programming style. In this chapter, I will endeavor to explain how the SOLID principles apply to functional programming.

The following chapters are summaries, not complete descriptions, of the principles. For those of you who are interested in more detail, I recommend the following sources.

- *Agile Software Development: Principles, Patterns, and Practices.*[1]
- *Clean Architecture.*[2]
- Cleancoder.com. Check out the blog posts and articles. There are lots and lots of things to learn on this Web site about principles and more.
- Cleancoders.com. This Web site has videos that explain each principle in great detail and with compelling examples.

THE SINGLE RESPONSIBILITY PRINCIPLE (SRP)

The *SRP* is a simple statement about focusing our modules on the sources that cause them to change. Those sources are, of course, *people*. It is

1. Robert C. Martin (Pearson, 2002).

2. Robert C. Martin (Pearson, 2017).

people who request changes to software, and therefore it is people to whom our modules are responsible.

These people can be separated into groups called *roles* or *actors*. An actor is a person, or a group of people, who require the same things from the system. The kinds of changes they request will be consistent with each other. On the other hand, different actors have different needs. The changes one actor requests will affect the system in very different ways from the changes requested by other actors. Those disparate changes may even be at cross purposes to each other.

When a module is responsible to more than one actor, the changes requested by those competing actors can interfere with each other. This interference often leads to the design smell of *fragility*; causing the system to break in unexpected ways when simple changes are made.

Nothing can be quite so terrifying to managers and customers than systems that suddenly misbehave in startling ways after simple feature changes are made. If this repeats too often, the only conclusion they can come to is that the developers have lost control of the system and don't know what they are doing.

A violation of the SRP can be as simple as mixing GUI formatting and business rule code together in the same module. Or it can be as complex as using stored procedures in the database to implement business rules.

Here's a simple example of a nasty SRP violation written in Clojure. First, let's look at the tests because they tell the story:

```
(describe "Order Entry System"
  (context "Parsing Customers"
    (it "parses a valid customer"
      (should=
        {:id "1234567"
         :name "customer name"
         :address "customer address"
```

```
      :credit-limit 50000}
   (parse-customer
     ["Customer-id: 1234567"
      "Name: customer name"
      "Address: customer address"
      "Credit Limit: 50000"])))

(it "parses invalid customer"
  (should= :invalid
           (parse-customer
             ["Customer-id: X"
              "Name: customer name"
              "Address: customer address"
              "Credit Limit: 50000"]))
  (should= :invalid
           (parse-customer
             ["Customer-id: 1234567"
              "Name: "
              "Address: customer address"
              "Credit Limit: 50000"]))
  (should= :invalid
           (parse-customer
             ["Customer-id: 1234567"
              "Name: customer name"
              "Address: "
              "Credit Limit: 50000"]))
  (should= :invalid
           (parse-customer
             ["Customer-id: 1234567"
              "Name: customer name"
              "Address: customer address"
              "Credit Limit: invalid"])))
(it "makes sure credit limit is <= 50000"
  (should= :invalid
           (parse-customer
             ["Customer-id: 1234567"
              "Name: customer name"
              "Address: customer address"
              "Credit Limit: 50001"])))))
```

The first test tells us that we are parsing some text input into a customer record. That record has four fields: id, name, address, and credit-limit. The next four tests tell us about syntax errors such as missing or malformed input.

The last test is the interesting one. It tests a business rule. Testing a business rule as part of parsing the input is a clear SRP violation. The parsing code can safely validate syntax errors, but it should avoid all *semantic* checks because those checks are in the domain of a different actor. The actor who specifies the input format is not the same as the actor who specifies the largest allowable credit limit.[3]

The code that passes these tests exacerbates the problem:

```
(defn validate-customer
  [{:keys [id name address credit-limit] :as customer}]
  (if (or (nil? id)
          (nil? name)
          (nil? address)
          (nil? credit-limit))
    :invalid
    (let [credit-limit (Integer/parseInt credit-limit)]
      (if (> credit-limit 50000)
        :invalid
        (assoc customer :credit-limit credit-limit)))))

(defn parse-customer [lines]

  (let [[_ id] (re-matches #"^Customer-id: (\d{7})$"
                           (nth lines 0))
        [_ name] (re-matches #"^Name: (.+)$" (nth lines 1))
        [_ address] (re-matches #"^Address: (.+)$" (nth lines 2))
        [_ credit-limit] (re-matches #"^Credit Limit: (\d+)$"
                                     (nth lines 3))]
```

---

3. This is true even when the two actors are the same person. In that case, that person is playing two different roles.

```
(validate-customer
  {:id id
   :name name
   :address address
   :credit-limit credit-limit}))) 
```

Look at how the validate-customer function mixes the syntax checks with the semantic business rule that limits the credit limit to 50,000. That semantic check belongs in an entirely different module, not tangled in with all those syntax checks.

Worse, consider a programmer who conscientiously uses clojure/spec to dynamically define the type of customer:

```
(s/def ::id (s/and
              string?
              #(re-matches #"\d+" %)))
(s/def ::name string?)
(s/def ::address string?)
(s/def ::credit-limit (s/and int? #(<= % 50000)))
(s/def ::customer (s/keys :req-un [::id ::name
                                   ::address ::credit-limit]))
```

This specification properly constrains the customer data structure to be syntactically correct; but it also imposes the semantic business rule constraint that the credit limit must not be greater than 50,000.

Why am I concerned about mixing the credit limit constraint with the syntax of the data structure? It is because I expect the syntax of the data structure and the credit limit constraint to be specified by different actors. And I expect those different actors will request changes at different times and for different reasons. I don't want a change to the syntax to inadvertently break a business rule.

Of course, this begs the question: Where do semantic validations belong? The answer to that is semantic validations belong in the modules responsible to the actors who are likely to change them. If, for example, there is a business rule that says that credit limits must not exceed 50,000, then the enforcement code should go in the module that handles all the other credit limit processing.

> *Gather together the things that change for the*
> *same reasons, and at the same times.*
> *Separate those things that change for different*
> *reasons or at different times.*

THE OPEN-CLOSED PRINCIPLE (OCP)

The *OCP* was first stated by Bertrand Meyer in his classic 1988 book, *Object-Oriented Software Construction*.[4] To paraphrase, it says that software modules should be open for extension but closed for modification. This means that you want to design your modules such that extending or changing their behavior does not require you to modify their code.

This may sound oxymoronic, but it's actually something that we do all the time. Consider, for example, the copy program in C:

```c
void copy() {
  int c;
  while ((c = getchar()) != EOF)
    putchar(c);
}
```

---

4. Pearson, 1988.

This program copies characters from stdin to stdout. I can add new devices to the operating system anytime I like. For example, I could add an optical character recognition (OCR) and a text-to-speech synthesizer to the system. This program would still operate without complaint and would happily copy characters from the OCR to the voice synthesizer without needing to be modified or even recompiled.

This is a very powerful idea that allows us to separate high-level policy from low-level detail and keep the high-level policy immune from changes to the low-level detail. However, it requires that the high-level policy access the low-level detail through an abstraction layer.

In OO programs, we typically create that abstraction layer through polymorphic interfaces. In statically typed languages like Java, C#, and C++, those interfaces are classes[5] with abstract methods. High-level policies are given access through those interfaces to the low-level details that implement, or inherit from, those interfaces.

In dynamically typed OO languages like Python and Ruby, these interfaces are duck types. *Duck types* have no particular syntax within the language. They are simply sets of function signatures called by the high-level policies and implemented by the low-level details. The dynamic type system determines the polymorphic dispatch at runtime by matching those signatures.

Some functional languages, like F# and Scala, sit on top of an OO foundation and thus can take advantage of the polymorphic interfaces of that foundation. But functional languages have long had another mechanism by which the abstraction layer for the OCP can be created: functions.

---

5. The keyword interface in Java and C# defines classes where every method is abstract.

FUNCTIONS

Consider this simple Clojure program:

```
(defn copy [read write]
  (let [c (read)]
    (if (= c :eof)
      nil
      (recur read (write c)))))
```

This is essentially the same program as the copy program written in C, except that the functions to read and write have been passed in as arguments.[6] Nevertheless, the abstraction layer for the OCP is intact.

By the way, I tested this program using the following tests. I think you'll find this interesting.

```
(def str-in (atom nil))
(def str-out (atom nil))

(defn str-read []
  (let [c (first @str-in)]
    (if (nil? c)
      :eof
      (do
        (swap! str-in rest)
        c))))

(defn str-write [c]
  (swap! str-out str c)
  str-write)

(describe "copy"
  (it "can read and write using str-read and str-write"
```

---

6. Functions that are passed as arguments, or returned as values from functions, are sometimes called *higher-order functions.*

```
(reset! str-in "abcedf")
(reset! str-out "")
(copy str-read str-write)
(should= "abcdef" @str-out)))
```

I used the atoms because I/O is a side effect and is therefore not purely functional. After all, when you read from an input or write to an output, you are mutating their states. Thus, the low-level I/O functions are not purely functional and use Software Transactional Memory to manage the mutation of state.

OBJECTS WITH VTABLES

For those of you who are pining for OO, you can pass an "object" into copy using the following technique:

```
(defn copy [device]
  (let [c ((:getchar device))]
    (if (= c :eof)
      nil
      (do
        ((:putchar device) c)
        (recur device)))))
```

The test simply loads the device map with the functions:

```
(it "can read and write using str-read and str-write"
    (reset! str-in "abcedf")
    (reset! str-out "")
    (copy {:getchar str-read :putchar str-write})
    (should= "abcdef" @str-out))
```

C++ programmers will recognize that the device argument is just a vtable—which is the polymorphism mechanism in C++. In any case, it should be obvious that you can define many different devices for the copy program to use. You can extend the behavior of copy without having to modify it.

MULTI-METHODS

Still another variation on this theme is the use of multi-methods. Many languages, functional or otherwise, support multi-methods in one way or another. *Multi-methods* are another form of duck typing, because they create a loose grouping of methods that are dynamically dispatched based on their function signature and the "type"[7] of the arguments.

In Clojure, we use the time-honored approach of a *dispatching function* to specify that "type":

```
(defmulti getchar (fn [device] (:device-type device)))
(defmulti putchar (fn [device c] (:device-type device)))
```

Here we see `getchar` and `putchar` declared as multi-methods. Each has a dispatching function that takes the same arguments that `getchar` and `putchar` will be called with. We can change the copy program to call those multi-methods:

```
(defn copy [device]
  (let [c (getchar device)]
    (if (= c :eof)
      nil
      (do
        (putchar device c)
        (recur device)))))
```

The test for this new copy function is below. Notice that the test `device` is no longer a vtable containing pointers to functions. Instead, it now contains the input and output atoms, and also a :device-type. It is that :device-type that the multi-methods will be dispatching on.

```
(it "can read and write using multi-method"
  (let [device {:device-type :test-device
```

---

7. I used quotes here because the "type" of the arguments is not necessarily associated with their specific data types. Indeed, that "type" can be a completely different concept.

```
          :input (atom "abcdef")
          :output (atom nil)}]
    (copy device)
    (should= "abcdef" @(:output device)))))
```

All that remains are the implementations of the multi-methods. They should not be too surprising.

```
(defmethod getchar :test-device [device]
  (let [input (:input device)
        c (first @input)]
    (if (nil? c)
      :eof
      (do
        (swap! input rest)
        c))))

(defmethod putchar :test-device [device c]
  (let [output (:output device)]
    (swap! output str c)))
```

These are the implementations that will be dispatched when the :device-type is :test-device. It should be clear that many other such implementation methods could be created for various different devices. Those new devices will extend the copy program without forcing any modification.

INDEPENDENT DEPLOYABILITY

One of the benefits we expect to get from the OCP is the ability to compile high-level policies and low-level details in separate modules and to deploy them independently. In Java and C#, this would mean compiling them down into separate jar or dll files that can be dynamically loaded. In C++, we would compile the modules and place the binaries into dynamically loadable shared libraries.

The Clojure solutions shown above do not achieve that goal. The high-level policy and the low-level detail cannot be dynamically loaded from two separate jar files.

This is much less of an issue than it would be in Java or C# because "loading" a Clojure program almost always[8] involves compiling it. Thus, while the high-level policies and low-level details may not be dynamically loaded from jar files, they are dynamically compiled and loaded from *source* files. Therefore, most of the benefits of independently deployable jar files are preserved.

However, if you absolutely must have total and complete independent deployability, there is another option. You can use Clojure's protocols and records:

```
(defprotocol device
  (getchar [_])
  (putchar [_ c]))
```

The protocol will become a Java `interface` that can be independently compiled into a jar file for dynamic loading. The implementation of the protocol (shown below) can likewise be independently compiled and loaded:

```
(defrecord str-device [in-atom out-atom]
  device
  (getchar [_]
    (let [c (first @in-atom)]
      (if (nil? c)
        :eof
        (do
          (swap! in-atom rest)
          c))))

  (putchar [_ c]
    (swap! out-atom str c)))

(describe "copy"
  (it "can read and write using str-read and str-write"
    (let [device (->str-device (atom "abcdef") (atom nil))]
```

---

8. Clojure allows for precompilation in some cases.

```
(copy device)
(should= "abcdef" @(:out-atom device)))))
```

Notice the ->str-device function in the test. That's essentially the Java constructor of the str-device class that implements the device protocol. Notice also that I loaded the atoms into the device as in the previous example.

Indeed, I did not change the copy program to get this example to work. The copy program is exactly as it was in the multi-method example. Now that's the OCP at work!

If the protocol/record mechanism of Clojure feels like OO, that's because it is OO. The JVM is an OO foundation, and Clojure fits very nicely upon that foundation.

THE LISKOV SUBSTITUTION PRINCIPLE (LSP)

Any language that supports the OCP must also support the LSP. The two principles are linked because every violation of the LSP is a latent violation of the OCP.

The *LSP* was first described by Barbara Liskov in 1988,[9] providing a more or less formal definition of a subtype. In essence, she said that a subtype must be substitutable for its base type in any program that uses the base type.

To clarify that, let us say that we have some program pay that uses a type employee:

```
(defn pay [employee pay-date]
  (let [is-payday? (:is-payday employee)
        calc-pay (:calc-pay employee)
        send-paycheck (:send-paycheck employee)]
    (when (is-payday? pay-date)
      (let [paycheck (calc-pay)]
        (send-paycheck paycheck)))))
```

Notice that I'm using the vtable approach to create the type. Notice also that the data within the type is completely hidden from the pay function. All the pay function can see is the methods within the employee type. How much more OO can you get?

Here's the test code that uses this type. Notice that the make-test-employee function makes an object that uses *duck typing* to conform to the employee type:

```
(defn test-is-payday [employee-data pay-date]
  true)

(defn test-calc-pay [employee-data]
  (:pay employee-data))

(defn test-send-paycheck [employee-data paycheck]
  (format "Send %d to: %s at: %s"
          paycheck
          (:name employee-data)
          (:address employee-data)))
```

---

9. Coincidentally, that's the same year that Bertrand Meyer published the OCP.

```
(defn make-test-employee [name address pay]
  (let [employee-data {:name name
                       :address address
                       :pay pay}

        employee {:employee-data employee-data
                  :is-payday (partial test-is-payday
                                      employee-data)
                  :calc-pay (partial test-calc-pay employee-data)
                  :send-paycheck (partial test-send-paycheck
                                          employee-data)}]

    employee))

(describe "Payroll"
  (it "pays a salaried employee"
    (should= "Send 100 to: name at: address"
             (pay (make-test-employee "name" "address" 100)
                  :now))))
```

Notice the make-test-employee function uses the pointer to implementation (PIMPL)[10] pattern to hide the data in the :employee-data field and expose only the methods. Finally, notice that all the polymorphic methods are given the employee-data as their first arguments. Oh, just so OO! And yet entirely functional.

It should be clear that I could create many different kinds of employee objects and pass them to the pay function without modifying the pay function at all. This is the OCP.

However, to achieve that I must be very careful to make sure that every employee object I create conforms to the expectations of the pay function. If one of those methods does something that pay doesn't expect, then pay will malfunction.

---

10. Holding all the data behind a single field to help keep it private. See https://cpppatterns.com /patterns/pimpl.html.

For example, this test fails:

```
(it "does not pay an employee whose payday is not today"
  (should-be-nil
    (pay (make-later-employee "name" "address" 100)
         :now)))
```

It fails because `make-later-employee` does not conform to the pay function's expectations for the :is-payday method. As you can see below, it returns :tomorrow instead of `false`:

```
(defn make-later-employee [name address pay]
  (let [employee (make-test-employee name address pay)
        is-payday? (partial (fn [_ _] :tomorrow)
                            (:employee-data employee))]
    (assoc employee :is-payday is-payday?)))
```

This is an LSP violation.

Now imagine you were the author of the pay function, and you were tasked with debugging why certain employees were getting paychecks at the wrong times. You find that many employee objects are using the :tomorrow convention instead of returning a boolean as they should. What do you do?[11]

You *could* fix all those employees. Or you could add an extra condition to the pay function:

```
(defn pay [employee pay-date]
  (let [is-payday? (:is-payday employee)
        calc-pay (:calc-pay employee)
        send-paycheck (:send-paycheck employee)]
```

---

11. Of course, a statically typed language would solve that particular issue. So would a well-timed call to s/valid?, given appropriate specs. But that's not the case we are investigating at the moment.

```
(when (= true (is-payday? pay-date))
  (let [paycheck (calc-pay)]
    (send-paycheck paycheck)))))
```

Yeah, that's pretty ugly.[12] It's also an OCP violation because we've modified high-level policy due to the misbehavior of a low-level detail.

THE ISA RULE

The OO literature often uses the term *ISA* (pronounced, and meaning, "is a") to describe subtypes. To describe the above situation in those terms we would say that the test-employee ISA employee, and the later-employee ISA employee. This usage can be confusing.

First, the later-employee is not an employee because it does not conform to the expectations of the pay function; and it is the pay function, and all the other functions that operate on employees, that define what the employee type is.

But second, and perhaps more important, the term *ISA* can be deeply misleading. The ancient and venerable square/rectangle conundrum is often used to make this point.

Let us say that we have an object that describes a rectangle. In Clojure, it might look like this:

```
(defn make-rect [h w]
  {:h h :w w})
```

A simple test of this rectangle object might look like this:

```
(it "calculates proper area after change in size"
  (should= 12 (-> (make-rect 1 1) (set-h 3) (set-w 4) area)))
```

---

12. Think long and hard about why that is ugly and why many programmers would be tempted to delete the = true, thus re-exposing the bug.

To make this work we'll need the set-h, set-w, and area functions as follows:

```
(defn set-h [rect h]
  (assoc rect :h h))

(defn set-w [rect w]
  (assoc rect :w w))

(defn area [rect]
  (* (:h rect) (:w rect)))
```

Nothing here should be surprising. The rectangle object is not mutable. The set-h and set-w functions simply create new rectangles with the changed parameters.

So let's flesh this out a bit and create a small system that uses our rectangle. Here are the tests:

```
(describe "Rectangle"
  (it "calculates proper area and perimeter"
    (should= 25 (area (make-rect 5 5)))
    (should= 18 (perimeter (make-rect 4 5)))
    (should= 12 (-> (make-rect 1 1) (set-h 3) (set-w 4) area)))

  (it "minimally increases area"
    (should= 15 (-> (make-rect 3 4) minimally-increase-area area))
    (should= 24 (-> (make-rect 5 4) minimally-increase-area area))
    (should= 20 (-> (make-rect 4 4) minimally-increase-area area))))
```

And here are the functions that pass those tests:

```
(defn perimeter [rect]
  (let [{:keys [h w]}13 rect]
    (* 2 (+ h w))))
```

---

13. This *destructures* the map into the named components. In this case, it is equivalent to (let [h (:h rect) w (:w rect)]...

```
(defn minimally-increase-area [rect]
  (let [{:keys [h w]} rect]
    (cond
      (>= h w) (make-rect (inc h) w)
      (> w h) (make-rect h (inc w))
      :else :tilt)))
```

Again, there's nothing very surprising about this. Perhaps you are confused by the `minimally-increase-area` function. This function simply increases the area of the rectangle by the smallest integral amount possible.[14]

So now let's imagine that this system has been in operation for years and has been very successful. But lately the customers of this system have been asking for squares. How do we add squares to our system?

If we apply the ISA rule, we might decide that a square is a rectangle, and therefore, we should make the functions that accept rectangles also accept squares. In Java, we might accomplish this by deriving the class `Square` from the class `Rectangle`. In Clojure, we can do this by simply creating rectangles with equal sides:

```
(defn make-square [side]
  (make-rect side side))
```

This should bother us slightly because the size of the `square` object is the same as the size of the `rectangle` object. Objects of type `square` ought to be smaller since they don't need both the height and the width. But memory is cheap, and we want to keep things simple, right?

The question is, will all our tests still pass? They should, of course, because our squares are really just rectangles (ah, that's just the ISA rule!).

---

14. Presuming all the lengths and widths are integers.

These tests pass just fine:

```
(should= 36 (area (make-square 6)))
(should= 20 (perimeter (make-square 5)))
```

So does this one, but it's bothersome because somewhere in there, "squareness" got lost:

```
(should= 12 (-> (make-square 1) (set-h 3) (set-w 4) area))
```

The functions set-h and set-w do not return a square when passed a square. That's a bit strange; but in some bizarre way it actually makes sense. I mean, if you set the height of a square without changing the width, it's not going to be a square anymore, right?

If you feel a little itching at the back of your brain right now, you should probably pay attention to it.

Anyway, what about our minimally-increase-area test? Does it pass?

```
(should= 30 (-> (make-square 5) minimally-increase-area area))
```

Yes, that passes too. And of course, it should since the function simply increases the height or width as necessary.

So it looks like we're done, and this worked just great!

NOPE!

Our customer calls us up a few days later, and he's not very happy. He's been trying to minimally increase the area of his squares, and it's just not working.

"When I increase the area of a 5-by-5 square," he bleats, "I get a rectangle back with an area of 30. I need to get a *square* back with an area of 36!"

Uh-oh. Looks like we guessed wrong. This is an LSP violation. We created a subtype that does not conform to the expectations of the functions that use the base type. The expectation of `minimally-increase-area` is that height and width can be modified independently. According to our customer, that's not true for a `square`.

So, what should we do?

We could add a `:type` field to the objects and have the constructors put either `:square` or `:rectangle` into the field, respectively. And of course, then we'd have to put an `if` statement into the `minimally-increase-area` function. We'd also have to change `set-h` and `set-w` to change the type to `:rectangle`. And those changes violate the OCP, because every violation of the LSP is a latent violation of the OCP.

I'll leave other solutions as an exercise. You might try using multi-methods. You might try using protocols and records. You might try using vtables. Or you might just keep the two types absolutely separate and never pass a `square` into a function that takes a `rectangle`.

THE REPRESENTATIVE RULE

I prefer this last option. That's because I don't much care for the ISA rule. You see, while it is *geometrically* true that a square is a rectangle, none of the objects in my code were actual rectangles or squares. My code had objects that *represented* squares and rectangles, but they were *neither* squares *nor* rectangles. And here's the thing about representatives:

> *The representatives of things do not share the relationships of the things they represent.*

Just because a square is a rectangle in geometry, it does not mean that a square object in code is a `rectangle` object in code. That relationship is not shared because objects of type `square` do not behave the way objects of type `rectangle` behave.

When you see two objects in the real world that are obviously connected by the phrase "is a," you may be tempted to create a subtype relationship in your code. Be careful with that. You may just run afoul of the representative rule and violate the LSP.

THE INTERFACE SEGREGATION PRINCIPLE (ISP)

The name of this principle derives from its origins in statically typed OO languages. The example I usually use to describe the ISP works quite well for such languages as Java, C#, and C++, because those languages depend upon declared interfaces. In dynamically typed languages like Ruby, Python, JavaScript, and Clojure, those examples don't work particularly well, because in those languages, interfaces are undeclared and are already segregated by duck typing.

For example, consider the following Java interface:

```
interface AtmInteractor {
  void requestAccount();
  void requestAmount();
  void requestPin();
}
```

Here we see three methods bound together in the AtmInteractor interface. Any user of this interface therefore depends upon all three methods, even if that user only calls one of those methods. Thus, that user depends upon more than it needs. If the signature of one of those methods changes, or if another method is added to that interface, then that user will have to be recompiled and redeployed, making the design unnecessarily fragile.

We solve this weakness in statically typed OO languages by segregating the interfaces as follows:

```
interface AccountInteractor {
  void requestAccount();
}

interface AmountInteractor {
  void requestAmount();
}

interface PinInteractor {
  void requestPin();
}
```

Then each user can depend only upon the methods that it needs to call while the implementation can multiply implement those interfaces:

```
public class AtmInteractor implements AccountInteractor,
                                      AmountInteractor,
                                      PinInteractor {
```

```
    void requestAccount() {…};
    void requestAmount() {…};
    void requestPin() {…};
}
```

Perhaps the UML diagram in Figure 12.1 will make this clearer. By segregating the interfaces, the three users depend only on the methods that they need; and yet those methods can be implemented by a single class.

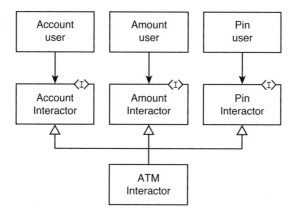

Figure 12.1. Segregated interfaces

In Clojure, we could use one of our duck typing techniques to address this problem:

```
(defmulti request-account :interactor)
(defmulti request-amount :interactor)
(defmulti request-pin :interactor)
```

Those three multi-methods are not bound together under a single declaration. Indeed, they do not even need to be kept together in the same source file. They could instead be declared in modules that are specific to their function. Thus, if the signature of one changed, or if a new multi-method were added, there would be no impact upon the users of the multi-methods that were not changed. If they were precompiled,[15] they would not require recompilation.

This means that in dynamically typed languages, like Clojure, it is easier to avoid depending on things you don't need. But that doesn't mean that the principle doesn't apply.

DON'T DEPEND ON THINGS YOU DON'T NEED

Back to the name. The word *Interface* in *Interface Segregation Principle* is not tied solely to the interface classes in Java, C#, and C++. Rather, it applies to the generic meaning of the word. The "interface" of a module is simply the list of all the access points within that module.

Java and C# (and, by strong convention, C++) are class-based languages in which there is a strong coupling between classes and source files. Java in particular demands that each source file be named after the sole public class declared within that source file. This automatically sets up the conditions that the ISP is trying to avoid. Groups of methods are coupled together into a single module that users will depend upon, even if they don't depend upon every one of those methods. Thus, unless the designer is careful, those users will depend upon things they don't need.

Dynamically typed languages like Ruby, Python, and Clojure do not have this class-to-module constraint. You can declare anything you like within any source file you like. You can write the entire application in a single source file if you like![16] Therefore, it is even easier in those languages to set up the conditions that will cause users of a module to depend upon things they don't need.

This is not a situation that is specific to functional languages. It is also not a situation from which functional languages are immune. Designers can easily pollute the interfaces of their modules with all kinds of access points that the majority of their users don't need.

---

15. Clojure allows modules to be precompiled for faster loading.

16. Not recommended. ;-)

WHY?

Why do we care about depending on modules that have more than we need? Why should it bother us if our module only uses one of the ten functions in another module?

In statically typed languages the cost can be severe because a change to one of the functions we don't use can force our module to be recompiled and redeployed. If our module is just one of many modules in a binary component (like a jar file), then that entire component will need to be redeployed. Those are couplings that every serious designer should be careful about.

In dynamically typed languages, the cost is reduced but is not zero. In Clojure, for example, there is a strict requirement[17] that the source code dependencies between modules must be acyclic. The more functions that a module contains, the more outgoing and incoming source code dependencies impinge upon that module and thus the greater the probability that it will participate in a cycle.

But possibly the best reason for caring about these dependencies is that a module structure that limits extraneous dependencies is *cogent*. It is an indication that intelligent human beings have cared enough to separate the concerns and lower the coupling. The readers of your code will thank you for that care.

CONCLUSION

The real meaning of the ISP is:

> *Gather together the things that are used together.*
> *Separate those things that are used separately.*
> *Don't depend on things you don't need.*

---

17. We'll encounter this in Chapter 17, Wa-Tor.

THE DEPENDENCY INVERSION PRINCIPLE (DIP)

Of the SOLID principles, one could say that the OCP is the moral heart, the SRP is the organizing force, while the LSP and the ISP are caution signs surrounding the potholes created by carelessness. That leaves the DIP, which is the underlying mechanism behind all the others. In almost every case when we find a principle violation, the solution involves the inversion of one or more critical dependencies.

In decades long past, software was constructed with a completely constrained and parallel dependency structure. Source code dependencies paralleled runtime dependencies. The structure looked like Figure 12.2.

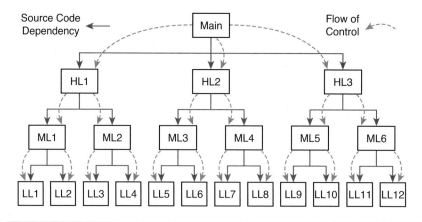

Figure 12.2. The ancient parallel dependency structure

The dashed arrows are runtime dependencies. They show that high-level modules call mid-level modules, which call low-level modules. The solid arrows are source code dependencies. They show that each source code module depends upon the modules it calls. Those source code dependencies were statements like #include, import, require, and using that mentioned the name of the downstream source file.

In those ancient days of yore, those two kinds of dependencies were always[18] parallel to each other. If module X had a runtime dependency on module Y, it also had a source code dependency on module Y.

This meant that high-level policy was inextricably dependent upon low-level detail. Think hard about the implications of that statement.

But in the late '60s, Ole-Johan Dahl and Kristen Nygaard moved a data structure[19] in the ALGOL compiler from the stack to the heap and discovered OO.[20] And with that discovery came the ability for programmers to invert dependencies easily and safely.

It took another 25 years before OO languages started to move into the mainstream. But since then, virtually all programmers have been able to effortlessly break that parallel dependence. They do it as shown in Figure 12.3.

---

18. Well, not quite always. In the late '50s and early '60s, Herculean efforts were expended by operating system engineers to invert a few, very strategic dependencies in order to create the abstraction of device independence. They had no tool other than explicit pointers to functions, so they were very, very careful.

19. The data structure was the stack frame of function calls. The language they created was Simula 67.

20. The history of the invention of Simula is fascinating. It is briefly described in the 1972 book *Structured Programming* by Edsger W. Dijkstra, Ole-Johan Dahl, and C. A. R. Hoare (Academic Press), and in much more detail in the paper "The Development of the Simula Languages" by Dahl and Nygaard (https://hannemyr.com/cache/knojd_acm78.pdf).

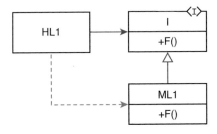

Figure 12.3. Inverting the dependency by inserting an interface

HL1 has a runtime dependency on F() within ML1; but HL1 has no source code dependency, either direct or transitive, upon ML1. Instead, they both depend upon the interface I.[21]

This ability to take any source code dependency and invert it provides us with an immense amount of power. We can easily and safely arrange the source code dependencies of our software to ensure that high-level modules *do not* depend upon low-level modules.

This allows us to create structures like that shown in Figure 12.4.

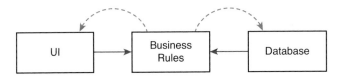

Figure 12.4. Plug-in structure

Here we see the high-level business rules have runtime dependencies upon the user interface (UI) and the database but have no source code dependencies on those modules. This application of the DIP means that the UI and database are *plug-ins* to the business rules and could easily be replaced with different implementations without affecting the business rules, thereby conforming to the OCP.

---

21. In dynamically typed languages, the interface I would not exist as a source code module. Rather, it would be a duck type that HL1 and ML1 would conform to.

Of course, what's really going on is that the UI and the database are implementing interfaces contained within the business rules. The business rules operate upon those interfaces, allowing the flow of control to go outward toward the UI and database while keeping the source code dependencies inverted inward toward the business rules (see Figure 12.5).

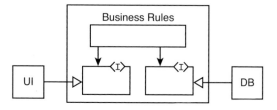

Figure 12.5. The interfaces within the business rules allow plug-ins.

Notice that all the dependencies point toward abstractions. This leads us to one way to describe the DIP:

Where possible, point all source code dependencies at abstractions.

A BLAST FROM THE PAST

But enough theory. Let's see this at work. I'm going to borrow a nostalgic example from my friend and mentor, Martin Fowler. He presented this *Video Store*[22] example in the first edition of his wonderful book, *Refactoring*.[23] Of course, I'm going to use Clojure instead of Java.

Here are the tests:

```
(describe "Video Store"
  (with customer (make-customer "Fred"))

  (it "makes statement for a single new release"
    (should= (str "Rental Record for Fred\n"
                  "\tThe Cell\t9.0\n"
```

---

22. Video killed the radio store and the Internet killed the video store. Yes, boys and girls, there was a time when we would go to the video store to rent videotapes and DVDs.

23. Addison-Wesley, 1999.

```
                            "You owed 9.0\n"
                            "You earned 2 frequent renter points\n")
                  (make-statement
                    (make-rental-order
                      @customer
                      [(make-rental
                         (make-movie "The Cell" :new-release)
                         3)]))))

  (it "makes statement for two new releases"
    (should= (str "Rental Record for Fred\n"
                  "\tThe Cell\t9.0\n"
                  "\tThe Tigger Movie\t9.0\n"
                  "You owed 18.0\n"
                  "You earned 4 frequent renter points\n")
             (make-statement
               (make-rental-order
                 @customer
                 [(make-rental
                    (make-movie "The Cell" :new-release)
                    3)
                  (make-rental
                    (make-movie "The Tigger Movie" :new-release)
                    3)]))))

  (it "makes statement for one childrens movie"
    (should= (str "Rental Record for Fred\n"
                  "\tThe Tigger Movie\t1.5\n"
                  "You owed 1.5\n"
                  "You earned 1 frequent renter points\n")
             (make-statement
               (make-rental-order
                 @customer
                 [(make-rental
                    (make-movie "The Tigger Movie" :childrens)
                    3)]))))

  (it "makes statement for several regular movies"
    (should= (str "Rental Record for Fred\n"
                  "\tPlan 9 from Outer Space\t2.0\n"
```

```
                    "\t8 1/2\t2.0\n"
                    "\tEraserhead\t3.5\n"
                    "You owed 7.5\n"
                    "You earned 3 frequent renter points\n")
            (make-statement
              (make-rental-order
                @customer
                [(make-rental
                   (make-movie "Plan 9 from Outer Space" :regular)
                   1)
                 (make-rental
                   (make-movie "8 1/2", :regular)
                   2)
                 (make-rental
                   (make-movie "Eraserhead" :regular)
                   3)]))))))
```

From these tests, you should be able to determine what this application does. Customers rent videos for a certain number of days. The price and the reward points are apparently calculated based upon the type of the video and the number of days they are rented. There seem to be three types of videos: :regular, :new-release, and :childrens.

Here is the code that passes these tests:

```
(defn make-customer [name]
  {:name name})

(defn make-movie [title type]
  {:title title
   :type type})

(defn make-rental [movie days]
  {:movie movie
   :days days})

(defn make-rental-order [customer rentals]
  {:customer customer
   :rentals rentals})
```

```
(defn determine-amount [rental]
  (let [{:keys [movie days]} rental
        type (:type movie)]
    (condp = type
      :regular
      (if (> days 2)
        (+ 2.0 (* (- days 2) 1.5))
        2.0)

      :new-release
      (* 3.0 days)

      :childrens
      (if (> days 3)
        (+ 1.5 (* (- days 3) 1.5))
        1.5))))

(defn determine-points [rental]
  (let [{:keys [movie days]} rental
        type (:type movie)]
    (if (and (= type :new-release)
             (> days 1))
      2
      1)))

(defn make-detail [rental]
  (let [title (:title (:movie rental))
        price (determine-amount rental)]
    (format "\t%s\t%.1f" title price)))

(defn make-details [rentals]
  (map make-detail rentals))

(defn make-footer [rentals]
  (let [owed (reduce + (map determine-amount rentals))
        points (reduce + (map determine-points rentals))]
    (format
      "\nYou owed %.1f\nYou earned %d frequent renter points\n"
      owed points)))
```

```
(defn make-statement [rental-order]
  (let [{:keys [name]} (:customer rental-order)
        {:keys [rentals]} rental-order
        header (format "Rental Record for %s\n" name)
        details (string/join "\n" (make-details rentals))
        footer (make-footer rentals)]
    (str header details footer)))
```

If you read the first edition of *Refactoring*, this should look pretty familiar. In essence, we have a simple report generator that calculates and formats a statement for a rental order.

The very first thing you should have noticed is the horrific SRP violation in the tests. Those tests couple the business rules with the construction and formatting of the statement. If someone from marketing decides to make even a trivial change to the statement format, all the tests will fail.

Consider, for example, the effects of changing the statement to begin with the words "Rental Statement for" instead of "Rental Record for."

This SRP violation makes the tests very fragile. To fix this we need to separate the tests that specify the format of the report from the tests that specify the business rules.

To do this I'm going to split the tests into three different modules: one for testing the calculations, another for the formatting, and the last for integration.

Here is the `statement-calculator` test. From now on, I'll include all the ns[24] statements so that you can see the names of the modules and their source code dependencies.

```
(ns video-store.statement-calculator-spec
  (:require [speclj.core :refer :all]
            [video-store.statement-calculator :refer :all]))
```

---

24. ns stands for namespace. These statements generally appear at the start of every Clojure module and define the module's name and its dependencies.

```
(declare customer)

(describe "Rental Statement Calculation"
  (with customer (make-customer "Fred"))

  (it "makes statement for a single new release"
    (should= {:customer-name "Fred"
              :movies [{:title "The Cell"
                        :price 9.0}]
              :owed 9.0
              :points 2}
             (make-statement-data
               (make-rental-order
                 @customer
                 [(make-rental
                    (make-movie "The Cell" :new-release)
                    3)]))))

  (it "makes statement for two new releases"
    (should= {:customer-name "Fred",
              :movies [{:title "The Cell", :price 9.0}
                       {:title "The Tigger Movie", :price 9.0}],
              :owed 18.0,
              :points 4}
             (make-statement-data
               (make-rental-order
                 @customer
                 [(make-rental
                    (make-movie "The Cell" :new-release)
                    3)
                  (make-rental
                    (make-movie "The Tigger Movie" :new-release)
                    3)]))))

  (it "makes statement for one childrens movie"
    (should= {:customer-name "Fred",
              :movies [{:title "The Tigger Movie", :price 1.5}],
              :owed 1.5,
```

```
          :points 1}
       (make-statement-data
         (make-rental-order
           @customer
           [(make-rental
               (make-movie "The Tigger Movie" :childrens)
               3)]))))

  (it "makes statement for several regular movies"
    (should= {:customer-name "Fred",
             :movies [{:title "Plan 9 from Outer Space",
                      :price 2.0}
                     {:title "8 1/2", :price 2.0}
                     {:title "Eraserhead", :price 3.5}],
             :owed 7.5,
             :points 3}
       (make-statement-data
         (make-rental-order
           @customer
           [(make-rental
               (make-movie "Plan 9 from Outer Space"
                            :regular)
             1)
            (make-rental
               (make-movie "8 1/2", :regular)
             2)
            (make-rental
               (make-movie "Eraserhead" :regular)
             3)]))))))
```

What we've done here is replace the formatted rental statement with a
data structure that contains all the data that goes into the statement. This
allows us to separate the formatting from the calculation, as shown in the
statement-calculator implementation:

```
(ns video-store.statement-calculator)

(defn make-customer [name]
  {:name name})
```

```
(defn make-movie [title type]
  {:title title
   :type type})

(defn make-rental [movie days]
  {:movie movie
   :days days})

(defn make-rental-order [customer rentals]
  {:customer customer
   :rentals rentals})

(defn determine-amount [rental]
  (let [{:keys [movie days]} rental
        type (:type movie)]
    (condp = type
      :regular
      (if (> days 2)
        (+ 2.0 (* (- days 2) 1.5))
        2.0)

      :new-release
      (* 3.0 days)

      :childrens
      (if (> days 3)
        (+ 1.5 (* (- days 3) 1.5))
        1.5))))

(defn determine-points [rental]
  (let [{:keys [movie days]} rental
        type (:type movie)]
    (if (and (= type :new-release)
             (> days 1))
      2
      1)))
```

```
(defn make-statement-data [rental-order]
  (let [{:keys [name]} (:customer rental-order)
        {:keys [rentals]} rental-order]
    {:customer-name name
     :movies (for [rental rentals]
                 {:title (:title (:movie rental))
                  :price (determine-amount rental)})
     :owed (reduce + (map determine-amount rentals))
     :points (reduce + (map determine-points rentals))}))
```

This is a bit simpler than before and is nicely encapsulated. Notice the ns statement shows that this module has no source code dependencies. Everything in the module is about the calculation of the data that goes into the statement. However, there is nothing here that hints at the formatting of the statement.

The formatting test is quite simple:

```
(ns video-store.statement-formatter-spec
  (:require [speclj.core :refer :all]
            [video-store.statement-formatter :refer :all]))


(describe "Rental Statement Format"
  (it "Formats a rental statement"
    (should= (str "Rental Record for CUSTOMER\n"
                  "\tMOVIE\t9.9\n"
                  "You owed 100.0\n"
                  "You earned 99 frequent renter points\n")
             (format-rental-statement
               {:customer-name "CUSTOMER"
                :movies [{:title "MOVIE"
                          :price 9.9}]
                :owed 100.0
                :points 99}))))
```

This should be self-explanatory. We're just making sure that we can format the data produced by the `statement-calculator` module. The implementation is also very simple:

```
(ns video-store.statement-formatter)

(defn format-rental-statement [statement-data]
  (let [customer-name (:customer-name statement-data)
        movies (:movies statement-data)
        owed (:owed statement-data)
        points (:points statement-data)]
    (str
      (format "Rental Record for %s\n" customer-name)
      (apply str
             (for [movie movies]
               (format "\t%s\t%.1f\n"
                       (:title movie)
                       (:price movie))))
      (format "You owed %.1f\n" owed)
      (format "You earned %d frequent renter points\n" points))))
```

Again, we have a nicely encapsulated module with no source code dependencies.

To make sure that both of these modules work together as they should, I added a simple integration test:

```
(ns video-store.integration-specs
  (:require [speclj.core :refer :all]
            [video-store.statement-formatter :refer :all]
            [video-store.statement-calculator :refer :all]))

(describe "Integration Tests"
  (it "formats a statement for several regular movies"
    (should= (str "Rental Record for Fred\n"
```

```
              "\tPlan 9 from Outer Space\t2.0\n"
              "\t8 1/2\t2.0\n"
              "\tEraserhead\t3.5\n"
              "You owed 7.5\n"
              "You earned 3 frequent renter points\n")
          (format-rental-statement
            (make-statement-data
              (make-rental-order
                (make-customer "Fred")
                [(make-rental
                  (make-movie
                    "Plan 9 from Outer Space" :regular)
                  1)
                (make-rental
                  (make-movie "8 1/2", :regular)
                  2)
                (make-rental
                  (make-movie "Eraserhead" :regular)
                  3)])))))))
```

This is much better from an SRP point of view. If the marketing folks make trivial changes to the format of the report, only the formatting and integration tests will break. None of the calculation tests will break. That might not seem like a big win in a toy example like this. But in a real-world application where the tests would number in the thousands, this is a very big win indeed.

We are also protected from business rule changes. If the finance people decide they need to change the way prices are calculated, the formatting test will be immune, and only the calculation and integration tests will be affected.

A DIP Violation

While all this winning was going on, did you happen to notice the DIP violation? You might have missed it because it's not in the production code. It's in the integration test.

Look at the ns statement. Do you see those two lines that mention the statement-formatter and the statement-calculator? Those lines create source code dependencies on the concrete implementations of those modules. That's a high-level policy depending on a concrete low-level detail. That's a definitional DIP violation.

Perhaps this puzzles you. How can a test be a high-level policy? Aren't tests as low level as you can get? Aren't they the ultimate details?

Yes, that's true. But integration tests in particular are stand-ins for high-level policy. Look at that integration test again. It does precisely what the high-level policy of the application would have to do. It calls make-statement-data and passes the result to format-rental-statement. And since both of those functions are concrete implementations, our high-level production code will have the same DIP violation as our integration test.

Do we always pay attention to the DIP in our tests? It is always wise to be aware. It may not always be wise to force compliance. Some tests are best left coupled to low-level implementations. However, if you want your test suites to be robust and flexible and if you don't want a hundred tests to break when you change one small thing in the production code, then keeping an eye on the coupling between your tests and the production code is a good idea.[25]

But perhaps you are still not convinced. So let's add a new feature. Sometimes we want the statement to be displayed on a text terminal, and sometimes we want it on a browser. So we need text and HTML versions of format-rental-statement.

Let's also add one more new feature. Some of our stores are offering a "buy two, get one free" policy. So, if you rent three videos, you will only be charged for the two most expensive ones.

---

25. I spend a lot of time on this topic in my book *Clean Craftsmanship* (Addison-Wesley, 2021).

If we were implementing this in an OO language, we would likely be tempted to create two new abstract classes or interfaces. The StatementFormatter abstraction would have a format-rental-statement method that would be implemented in both the TextFormatter and HTMLFormatter implementations. Likewise, the StatementPolicy abstraction would implement the make-statement-data function in both NormalPolicy and BuyTwoGetOneFreePolicy.

We can easily mimic this design by using any one of the three approaches that we discussed in the section on the OCP. We could build vtables for the two abstractions. Or we could use defprotocol and defrecord to build actual Java interfaces and implementations. Or, finally, we could use multi-methods.

Let's see what the multi-method approach looks like. Keep in mind that this is a child-sized problem posing as an adult situation. What you'll see me do here is meant to show how much larger problems can be designed and partitioned.

In the end, as shown in Figure 12.6, I split the whole system up into eleven modules, three of which are tests.

Figure 12.6 looks like a UML diagram for an OO solution. The dependency inversion should be obvious. The order-processing module is the highest-level policy. It depends upon two abstractions. The statement-formatter is an interface, whereas the statement-policy is an abstract class with one implemented method.

If you are confused at my use of OO vernacular to describe a functional program in Clojure, you shouldn't be. The OO words I'm using have very direct analogies in the functional world.

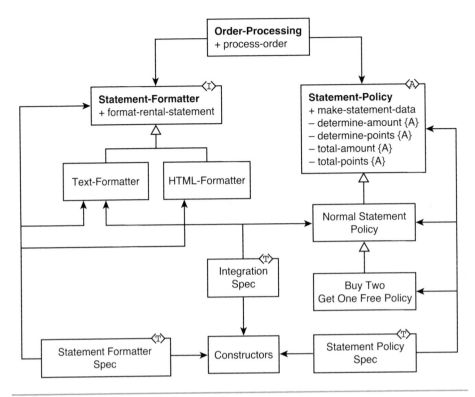

Figure 12.6. Splitting the Video Store application into modules

The statement-formatter interface is implemented by the text-formatter and the HTML-formatter. The statement-policy abstract class is implemented by the normal-statement-policy. The buy-two-get-one-free-policy implementation derives from normal-statement-policy but overrides one of its methods. The mechanisms behind all this "inheritance" will become clear in a moment.

The tests appear at the bottom. They are marked with <T>. They use a little utility module named constructors that knows how to build the basic data structures. Then each uses its particular portion of the production code to test what it needs.

Now let's look at the source code. Pay special attention to the ns statements and notice that they match the arrows on the UML diagram.

Let's begin with the constructors. They are pretty self-explanatory:

```
(ns video-store.constructors)

(defn make-customer [name]
  {:name name})

(defn make-movie [title type]
  {:title title
   :type type})

(defn make-rental [movie days]
  {:movie movie
   :days days})

(defn make-rental-order [customer rentals]
  {:customer customer
   :rentals rentals})
```

The constructors have no outgoing dependencies in the ns statement and simply build plain old Clojure data structures.

The integration test is in the integration-specs module:

```
(ns video-store.integration-specs
  (:require [speclj.core :refer :all]
            [video-store.constructors :refer :all]
            [video-store.text-statement-formatter :refer :all]
            [video-store.normal-statement-policy :refer :all]
            [video-store.order-processing :refer :all]))

(declare rental-order)

(describe "Integration Tests"
  (with rental-order (make-rental-order
                       (make-customer "Fred")
                       [(make-rental
                          (make-movie
                            "Plan 9 from Outer Space"
                            :regular)
```

```
                      1)
                     (make-rental
                       (make-movie "8 1/2", :regular)
                       2)
                     (make-rental
                       (make-movie "Eraserhead" :regular)
                       3)]))
    (it "formats a text statement"
      (should= (str "Rental Record for Fred\n"
                  "\tPlan 9 from Outer Space\t2.0\n"
                  "\t8 1/2\t2.0\n"
                  "\tEraserhead\t3.5\n"
                  "You owed 7.5\n"
                  "You earned 3 frequent renter points\n")
            (process-order
              (make-normal-policy)
              (make-text-formatter)
              @rental-order)))))
```

This is pretty much the same as before, except that the ns statement has all the explicit source code dependencies. This test still violates the DIP, but only because it must call the make-normal-policy and make-text-formatter constructors within the corresponding modules. I suppose I could have used an *Abstract Factory*[26] to break those last dependencies; but it didn't seem worth the effort for a test that tests integration.

The other two tests are more specific. Pay special attention to the fact that their source code dependencies only pull in what they need:

```
(ns video-store.statement-formatter-spec
  (:require [speclj.core :refer :all]
            [video-store.statement-formatter :refer :all]
            [video-store.text-statement-formatter :refer :all]
            [video-store.html-statement-formatter :refer :all]))

(declare statement-data)
```

---

26. See Chapter 16, "Design Patterns Review."

```
(describe "Rental Statement Format"
  (with statement-data {:customer-name "CUSTOMER"
                        :movies [{:title "MOVIE"
                                  :price 9.9}]
                        :owed 100.0
                        :points 99})
  (it "Formats a text rental statement"
    (should= (str "Rental Record for CUSTOMER\n"
             "\tMOVIE\t9.9\n"
             "You owed 100.0\n"
             "You earned 99 frequent renter points\n")
       (format-rental-statement
         (make-text-formatter)
         @statement-data
         )))

  (it "Formats an html rental statement"
    (should= (str
             "<h1>Rental Record for CUSTOMER</h1>"
             "<table>"
             "<tr><td>MOVIE</td><td>9.9</td></tr>"
             "</table>"
             "You owed 100.0<br>"
             "You earned <b>99</b> frequent renter points")
       (format-rental-statement
         (make-html-formatter)
         @statement-data))))
```

The statement-formatter-spec tests the two different formats. The format is specified by the first argument of the format-rental-statement function. That argument is created by the make-text-formatter and make-html-formatter functions, which are implemented in the appropriate modules, as you'll see.

The last test is the statement-policy-spec:

```
(ns video-store.statement-policy-spec
  (:require
    [speclj.core :refer :all]
```

```
        [video-store.constructors :refer :all]
        [video-store.statement-policy :refer :all]
        [video-store.normal-statement-policy :refer :all]
        [video-store.buy-two-get-one-free-policy :refer :all]))

(declare customer normal-policy formatter)
(declare new-release-1 new-release-2 childrens)
(declare regular-1 regular-2 regular-3)

(describe "Rental Statement Calculation"
  (with customer (make-customer "CUSTOMER"))
  (with normal-policy (make-normal-policy))
  (with new-release-1 (make-movie "new release 1" :new-release))
  (with new-release-2 (make-movie "new release 2" :new-release))
  (with childrens (make-movie "childrens" :childrens))
  (with regular-1 (make-movie "regular 1" :regular))
  (with regular-2 (make-movie "regular 2" :regular))
  (with regular-3 (make-movie "regular 3" :regular))
  (context "normal policy"
    (it "makes statement for a single new release"
      (should= {:customer-name "CUSTOMER"
                :movies [{:title "new release 1"
                          :price 9.0}]
                :owed 9.0
                :points 2}
               (make-statement-data
                 @normal-policy
                 (make-rental-order
                   @customer
                   [(make-rental @new-release-1 3)]))))

    (it "makes statement for two new releases"
      (should= {:customer-name "CUSTOMER",
                :movies [{:title "new release 1", :price 9.0}
                         {:title "new release 2", :price 9.0}],
                :owed 18.0,
                :points 4}
               (make-statement-data
                 @normal-policy
```

```
        (make-rental-order
          @customer
          [(make-rental @new-release-1 3)
           (make-rental @new-release-2 3)])))))

  (it "makes statement for one childrens movie"
    (should= {:customer-name "CUSTOMER",
              :movies [{:title "childrens", :price 1.5}],
              :owed 1.5,
              :points 1}
             (make-statement-data
               @normal-policy
               (make-rental-order
                 @customer
                 [(make-rental @childrens 3)]))))

  (it "makes statement for several regular movies"
    (should= {:customer-name "CUSTOMER",
              :movies [{:title "regular 1", :price 2.0}
                       {:title "regular 2", :price 2.0}
                       {:title "regular 3", :price 3.5}],
              :owed 7.5,
              :points 3}
             (make-statement-data
               @normal-policy
               (make-rental-order
                 @customer
                 [(make-rental @regular-1 1)
                  (make-rental @regular-2 2)
                  (make-rental @regular-3 3)]))))))

(context "Buy two get one free policy"
  (it "makes statement for several regular movies"
    (should= {:customer-name "CUSTOMER",
              :movies [{:title "regular 1", :price 2.0}
                       {:title "regular 2", :price 2.0}
                       {:title "new release 1", :price 3.0}],
              :owed 5.0,
              :points 3}
```

```
            (make-statement-data
              (make-buy-two-get-one-free-policy)
              (make-rental-order
                @customer
                [(make-rental @regular-1 1)
                 (make-rental @regular-2 1)
                 (make-rental @new-release-1 1)]))))))))
```

The statement-policy-spec tests the various pricing rules. You've seen the first batch already. The last test checks the buy two, get one free policy used by some stores. Notice that the policy is passed into the make-statement-data function and is created by the make-normal-policy and make-buy-two-get-one-free-policy functions.

Now, on to the production code. We begin with the order-processing module:

```
(ns video-store.order-processing
  (:require [video-store.statement-formatter :refer :all]
            [video-store.statement-policy :refer :all]))

(defn process-order [policy formatter order]
  (->> order
       (make-statement-data policy)
       (format-rental-statement formatter)))
```

There's not much to it. Notice the source code dependencies only refer to the statement-formatter interface and the statement-policy abstraction.

The statement-formatter interface is very simple:

```
(ns video-store.statement-formatter)

(defmulti format-rental-statement
            (fn [formatter statement-data]
               (:type formatter)))
```

The defmulti statement is roughly equivalent to creating an abstract method in Java or C#. Since this module has nothing but one abstract method, it is roughly equivalent to an interface. The dispatcher function is trivial; it just returns the :type of the formatter.

The statement-policy abstraction is a bit more interesting:

```
(ns video-store.statement-policy)

(defn- policy-movie-dispatch [policy rental]
  [(:type policy) (-> rental :movie :type)])

(defmulti determine-amount policy-movie-dispatch)
(defmulti determine-points policy-movie-dispatch)
(defmulti total-amount (fn [policy _rentals] (:type policy)))
(defmulti total-points (fn [policy _rentals] (:type policy)))

(defn make-statement-data [policy rental-order]
  (let [{:keys [name]} (:customer rental-order)
        {:keys [rentals]} rental-order]
    {:customer-name name
     :movies (for [rental rentals]
               {:title (:title (:movie rental))
                :price (determine-amount policy rental)})
     :owed (total-amount policy rentals)
     :points (total-points policy rentals)}))
```

The statement-policy module has four abstract methods and one implemented method. Notice how it uses the Template Method[27] pattern. Notice also that the determine-amount and determine-points functions use a dispatch code that is a tuple. That's pretty interesting. It means that we can dispatch those functions based upon two degrees of freedom instead of one. That's something that's hard to do in most OO languages. We'll see it used shortly.

But first let's look at the text-statement-formatter implementation:

```
(ns video-store.text-statement-formatter
  (:require [video-store.statement-formatter :refer :all]))
```

---

27. See Chapter 17, "Wa-Tor."

```
(defn make-text-formatter [] {:type ::text})

(defmethod format-rental-statement
            ::text
            [_formatter statement-data]
  (let [customer-name (:customer-name statement-data)
        movies (:movies statement-data)
        owed (:owed statement-data)
        points (:points statement-data)]
    (str
      (format "Rental Record for %s\n" customer-name)
      (apply str
             (for [movie movies]
               (format "\t%s\t%.1f\n"
                 (:title movie)
                 (:price movie))))
      (format "You owed %.1f\n" owed)
      (format "You earned %d frequent renter points\n" points))))
```

This shouldn't be much of a surprise. I just moved the code over here without much change. Notice the make-text-formatter function at the top.

The html-statement-formatter shouldn't be very surprising either:

```
(ns video-store.html-statement-formatter
  (:require [video-store.statement-formatter :refer :all]))

(defn make-html-formatter [] {:type ::html})

(defmethod format-rental-statement ::html
  [formatter statement-data]
  (let [customer-name (:customer-name statement-data)
        movies (:movies statement-data)
        owed (:owed statement-data)
        points (:points statement-data)]
    (str
      (format "<h1>Rental Record for %s</h1>" customer-name)
      "<table>"
```

```
(apply str
       (for [movie movies]
         (format "<tr><td>%s</td><td>%.1f</td></tr>"
                 (:title movie) (:price movie))))
"</table>"
(format "You owed %.1f<br>" owed)
(format "You earned <b>%d</b> frequent renter points"
        points)))))
```

The more interesting modules are the two policy modules. Let's begin
with normal-statement-policy:

```
(ns video-store.normal-statement-policy
  (:require [video-store.statement-policy :refer :all]))

(defn make-normal-policy [] {:type ::normal})

(defmethod determine-amount [::normal :regular] [_policy rental]
  (let [days (:days rental)]
    (if (> days 2)
      (+ 2.0 (* (- days 2) 1.5))
      2.0)))

(defmethod determine-amount
           [::normal :childrens]
           [_policy rental]
  (let [days (:days rental)]
    (if (> days 3)
      (+ 1.5 (* (- days 3) 1.5))
      1.5)))

(defmethod determine-amount
           [::normal :new-release]
           [_policy rental]
  (* 3.0 (:days rental)))

(defmethod determine-points [::normal :regular] [_policy _rental]
  1)
```

```
(defmethod determine-points
           [::normal :new-release]
           [_policy rental]
  (if (> (:days rental) 1) 2 1))

(defmethod determine-points
           [::normal :childrens]
           [_policy _rental]
  1)

(defmethod total-amount ::normal [policy rentals]
  (reduce + (map #(determine-amount policy %) rentals)))

(defmethod total-points ::normal [policy rentals]
  (reduce + (map #(determine-points policy %) rentals)))
```

That's different, isn't it? Look carefully at those defmethod statements. We've dispatched on both the policy type and the movie type. This isolates the business rules really well.

You might be worried that the two degrees of freedom will create an N*M problem, leading to a proliferation of the "determine" functions. You'll see how I handle that in a minute.

Notice the make-normal-policy constructor at the top that was used by our tests.

Now let's look at the buy-two-get-one-free-policy module:

```
(ns video-store.buy-two-get-one-free-policy
  (:require [video-store.statement-policy :refer :all]
            [video-store.normal-statement-policy :as normal]))

(derive ::buy-two-get-one-free ::normal/normal)

(defn make-buy-two-get-one-free-policy []
  {:type ::buy-two-get-one-free})
```

```
(defmethod total-amount
          ::buy-two-get-one-free
          [policy rentals]
  (let [amounts (map #(determine-amount policy %) rentals)]
    (if (> (count amounts) 2)
      (reduce + (drop 1 (sort amounts)))
      (reduce + amounts))))
```

Surprise, surprise! Look at that derive statement. This is Clojure's way of allowing you to create ISA[28] hierarchies. This statement says that a ::buy-two-get-one-free[29] policy is a :normal policy. The multi-method dispatching mechanism uses hierarchies like this to resolve which defmethod to dispatch to.

What this says to the compiler is that it should use the :normal implementations unless overridden by a specific ::buy-two-get-one-free implementation.

Thus, our module only has to override the total-amount function in order to subtract the least expensive movie if three or more are rented.

CONCLUSION

OK, that's it. We've chopped this system up into 11 modules. Each module is nicely encapsulated. We have inverted the most important source code dependencies so that high-level policies do not depend upon low-level details.

The overall structure looks a lot like an OO program, and yet it is entirely functional.

Nice.

---

28. Take care to avoid LSP violations!

29. Once again, don't worry about the double colons. They are just a way to scope keywords into a namespace.

FUNCTIONAL PRAGMATICS

13

TESTS

Throughout this book, you've seen many of the unit tests I have written. In virtually every case, I used the TDD[1] discipline of writing my tests and code in a tight loop, with the tests a few seconds ahead of the code.

For the most part, those tests were written using a framework called speclj[2] (pronounced "speckle"), written by Micah Martin and others. It is very similar to the RSpec framework that is popular in Ruby.

I have been practicing TDD for well over 20 years now. I've used it in Java, C#, C, C++, Ruby, Python, Lua, Clojure, and a variety of other languages. What I have learned in those decades is that the language does not matter to the discipline. The discipline is the same regardless of the language.

The fact that Clojure is a functional language does not change my testing strategy, nor affect my use of the TDD discipline. I write my Clojure programs test-first the way I write my Java programs test-first. The paradigm doesn't matter. The discipline is universal.

BUT WHAT ABOUT THE REPL?

Lots of functional programmers say they don't need TDD because they test everything in the REPL. I do lots of experimenting in the REPL too; but in most cases, I encode what I've learned into a test. Tests, like diamonds, are forever. Experiments in the REPL aren't there the morning after.

WHAT ABOUT MOCKS?

Mocking is a technique used by TDD practitioners to encapsulate their tests away from large swaths of the system. In effect, they create objects,

---

1. I have written a great deal about this discipline in *Clean Craftsmanship* (Addison-Wesley, 2021), *Clean Code* (Pearson, 2008), and *Agile Software Development: Principles, Patterns, and Practices* (Pearson, 2002). There is also a vast amount of information available on the Web. One of the best books on the topic is *Growing Object-Oriented Software, Guided by Tests* by Steve Freeman and Nat Pryce (Addison-Wesley, 2010).

2. https://github.com/slagyr/speclj

called *mocks*,[3] that represent those swaths and use the LSP to substitute the mocks in for them.

Since the LSP is viewed as an OO principle, and since mocks in OO languages are based on polymorphic interfaces, it has become something of an urban myth that functional languages do not support mocks.

But as we have seen, the LSP works just as well in a functional language as it does in an OO language, and polymorphic interfaces are generally very easy to create. Thus, the ability to write mocks, in all their various forms, is not at all impeded in a functional language.

As an example, here is a test from my more-speech[4] application that employs a couple of mocks:

```
(it "adds an unrooted article id to a tab"
  (let [message-id 1
        messages {message-id {:tags []}}
        event-context (atom {:text-event-map messages})]
    (reset! ui-context {:event-context event-context})
    (with-redefs [swing-util/add-id-to-tab (stub :add-id-to-tab)
                  swing-util/relaunch (stub :relaunch)]
      (add-article-to-tab 1 "tab" nil)
      (should-have-invoked :relaunch)
      (should-have-invoked :add-id-to-tab
                           {:with ["tab" :selected 1]}))))
```

Don't worry too much about what this test does. Just look down at the with-redefs statement. This test mocks the swing-util/add-id-to-tab and swing-util/relaunch functions to use named stubs. Those stubs are perfect no-ops. They accept any number of arguments and return nothing

---

3. They are more formally referred to as *test-doubles*, but in this context, I'll continue to use the colloquial vernacular.

4. https://github.com/unclebob/more-speech

at all.[5] But they do remember what happened to them.[6] So, down at the bottom, we see that the :relaunch stub should have been called, and the :add-id-to-tab stub should have been called with three arguments: "tab", :selected, and 1.

PROPERTY-BASED TESTING

One cannot hang out with functional programmers without eventually hearing about QuickCheck and property-based testing. Unfortunately, the topic often arises as a counterargument to TDD. I'm not going to try to support or refute that argument. Instead, I want to show you how very powerful property-based testing is within the TDD discipline.

First of all, what is property-based testing? *Property-based testing* is a verification and diagnostic technique that employs the random generation of inputs and a very powerful strategy of defect isolation.

Let's say that I've just written a function that computes the prime factors of a given integer:

```
(defn factors-of [n]
  (loop [factors [] n n divisor 2]
    (if (> n 1)
      (cond
        (> divisor (Math/sqrt n))
        (conj factors n)
        (= 0 (mod n divisor))
        (recur (conj factors divisor)
               (quot n divisor)
               divisor)
        :else
        (recur factors n (inc divisor)))
      factors)))
```

---

5. There are ways to get them to return values, but that's beyond the scope here. Check the speclj docs (https://github.com/slagyr/speclj) if you are interested.

6. Which technically makes them spies.

Let's also say that I wrote this function using TDD. Here are my tests:

```
(defn power2 [n]
  (apply * (repeat n 2N)))

(describe "factor primes"
  (it "factors 1 -> []"
    (should= [] (factors-of 1)))
  (it "factors 2 -> [2]"
    (should= [2] (factors-of 2)))
  (it "factors 3 -> [3]"
    (should= [3] (factors-of 3)))
  (it "factors 4 -> [2 2]"
    (should= [2 2] (factors-of 4)))
  (it "factors 5 -> [5]"
    (should= [5] (factors-of 5)))
  (it "factors 6 -> [2 3]"
    (should= [2 3] (factors-of 6)))
  (it "factors 7 -> [7]"
    (should= [7] (factors-of 7)))
  (it "factors 8 -> [2 2 2]"
    (should= [2 2 2] (factors-of 8)))
  (it "factors 9 -> [3 3]"
    (should= [3 3] (factors-of 9)))
  (it "factors lots"
    (should= [2 2 3 3 5 7 11 11 13]
             (factors-of (* 2 2 3 3 5 7 11 11 13))))
  (it "factors Euler 3"
    (should= [71 839 1471 6857] (factors-of 600851475143)))

  (it "factors mersenne 2^31-1"
    (should= [2147483647] (factors-of (dec (power2 31))))))
```

Pretty cool, right? But how certain am I that this function actually works? I mean, how do I know that there isn't some horrible corner case where the function fails unexpectedly?

Of course, I may never be perfectly sure about this; but there are some things I can do to make myself a lot more comfortable. One property of the output is that the product of all the factors will equal the input. So why don't I generate a thousand random integers and make sure that the prime factors of each multiply together to equal them.

I can do that like so:

```
(def gen-inputs (gen/large-integer* {:min 1 :max 1E9}))

(declare n)[7]

(describe "properties"
  (it "multiplies out properly"
    (should-be
      :result
      (tc/quick-check
        1000
        (prop/for-all
          [n gen-inputs]
          (let [factors (factors-of n)]
            (= n (reduce * factors)))))))))
```

Here I'm using test.check,[8] the property-based testing framework in Clojure that mimics the behavior of QuickCheck. The idea is pretty simple. I've got a generator up there named gen-inputs. It will generate random integers between 1 and a billion. That ought to be a good enough range.

The test tells QuickCheck to run 1,000 times. For each integer, it calculates the prime factors, multiplies them all together, and makes sure that the product equals the input. Nice.

The tc/quick-check function returns a map with the results. The :result element of that map will be true if all the checks passed; and that's what the should-be :result asserts.

---

7. A forward declaration of n.

8. https://clojure.org/guides/test_check_beginner

There is another property of the prime factors: They should all be prime. So let's write a function that tests for primality:

```
(defn is-prime? [n]
  (if (= 2 n)
    true
    (loop [candidates (range 2 (inc (Math/sqrt n)))]
      (if (empty? candidates)
        true
        (if (zero? (rem n (first candidates)))
          false
          (recur (rest candidates)))))))
```

That's a pretty traditional, if horribly inefficient, algorithm. Inefficient or not, we can use it to write the property test for the primality of all the factors:

```
(describe "factors"
  (it "they are all prime"
    (should-be
      :result
      (tc/quick-check
        1000
        (prop/for-all
          [n gen-inputs]
          (let [factors (factors-of n)]
            (every? is-prime? factors)))))))
```

OK. So now we know that this function returns a list of integers, each of which is prime, and that when multiplied together equal the input. That's kind of the definition of prime factors.

So this is nice. I can randomly generate a bunch of inputs and then apply property checks to the outputs.

A DIAGNOSTIC TECHNIQUE

But I called property-based testing a diagnostic technique, didn't I? So let's look at a more interesting example and I'll show you want I mean.

Remember our Video Store example from the preceding chapter? Let's do some property-based testing on that.

First of all, remember that we wrote a function called make-statement-data that took a policy and a rental-order and generated the statement-data that we then fed into one of our formatters? So here's the type specification of the rental-order using clojure.spec:

```
(s/def ::name string?)
(s/def ::customer (s/keys :req-un [name]))
(s/def ::title string?)
(s/def ::type #{:regular :childrens :new-release})
(s/def ::movie (s/keys :req-un [::title ::type]))
(s/def ::days pos-int?)
(s/def ::rental (s/keys :req-un [::days ::movie]))
(s/def ::rentals (s/coll-of ::rental))
(s/def ::rental-order (s/keys :req-un [::customer ::rentals]))
```

That's not too hard to read. From the bottom up:

- A :rental-order is a map with two elements: :customer and :rentals.
- The :rentals element is a collection of :rental items.
- A :rental is a map with :days and :movie elements.
- A :days element is a positive integer.
- A :movie element is a map with a :title and :type.
- A :type is one of :regular, :childrens, or :new-release.
- A :title is a string.

- A :customer is a map with a single :name element.
- A :name is a string.

With this type specification in place, we can write a generator that produces rental orders that conform to the type. So first, here are the generators:

```
(def gen-customer-name
  (gen/such-that not-empty gen/string-alphanumeric))

(def gen-customer
  (gen/fmap (fn [name] {:name name}) gen-customer-name))

(def gen-days (gen/elements (range 1 100)))

(def gen-movie-type
  (gen/elements [:regular :childrens :new-release]))

(def gen-movie
  (gen/fmap (fn [[title type]] {:title title :type type})
            (gen/tuple gen/string-alphanumeric gen-movie-type)))

(def gen-rental
  (gen/fmap (fn [[movie days]] {:movie movie :days days})
            (gen/tuple gen-movie gen-days)))

(def gen-rentals
  (gen/such-that not-empty (gen/vector gen-rental)))

(def gen-rental-order
  (gen/fmap (fn [[customer rentals]]
              {:customer customer :rentals rentals})
            (gen/tuple gen-customer gen-rentals)))

(def gen-policy (gen/elements
                  [(make-normal-policy)
                   (make-buy-two-get-one-free-policy)]))
```

I'm not going to explain the ins and outs of `clojure.check` here, but I will walk through what the generators do.

- `gen-policy` randomly selects one of the two policies.
- `gen-rental-order` creates a map from `gen-customer` and `gen-rentals`.
- `gen-rentals` creates a vector from `gen-rentals` and ensures that it is not empty.
- `gen-rental` creates a map from `gen-movie` and `gen-days`.
- `gen-movie` creates a map from `gen/string-alphanumeric` and `gen-movie-type`.
- `gen-movie-type` selects from among the three types.
- `gen-days` selects between integers from 1 to 100.
- `gen-customer` creates a map with a name from `gen-customer-name`.
- `gen-customer-name` generates a nonempty alphanumeric string.

Do you notice an eerie similarity between the type specification and the generator? So do I. Here are a few sample outputs from the generator:

```
[
 {:customer {:name "5Q"},
  :rentals [{:movie {:title "", :type :new-release}, :days 52}]}

 {:customer {:name "3"},
  :rentals [{:movie {:title "", :type :new-release}, :days 51}]}

 {:customer {:name "XA"},
  :rentals [{:movie {:title "r", :type :regular}, :days 82}
            {:movie {:title "", :type :childrens}, :days 60}]}

 {:customer {:name "4v"},
  :rentals [{:movie {:title "3", :type :childrens}, :days 29}]}

 {:customer {:name "0rT"},
  :rentals [{:movie {:title "", :type :regular}, :days 42}
            {:movie {:title "94Y", :type :regular}, :days 34}
```

```
                    {:movie {:title "D5", :type :new-release},
                            :days 58}]}

{:customer {:name "ZFAK"},
 :rentals [{:movie {:title "H8", :type :regular}, :days 92}
           {:movie {:title "d6WS8", :type :regular}, :days 59}
           {:movie {:title "d", :type :regular}, :days 53}
           {:movie {:title "Yj8b7", :type :regular}, :days 58}
           {:movie {:title "Z2q70", :type :childrens},
                            :days 9}]}

{:customer {:name "njGB0h"},
 :rentals [{:movie {:title "zk3UaE", :type :regular},
                            :days 53}]}

{:customer {:name "wD"},
 :rentals [{:movie {:title "51L", :type :childrens},
                     :days 17}]}

{:customer {:name "2J5nzN"},
 :rentals [{:movie {:title "", :type :regular}, :days 64}
           {:movie {:title "sA17jv", :type :regular}, :days 85}
           {:movie {:title "27E41n", :type :new-release},
                            :days 85}
           {:movie {:title "Z20", :type :new-release}, :days 68}
           {:movie {:title "8j5B7h6S", :type :regular},
                            :days 76}
           {:movie {:title "vg", :type :childrens}, :days 30}]}

{:customer {:name "wk"},
 :rentals [{:movie {:title "Kq6wbGG", :type :childrens},
                            :days 43}
           {:movie {:title "3S2DvUwv", :type :childrens},
                            :days 76}
           {:movie {:title "fdGW", :type :childrens}, :days 42}
           {:movie {:title "aS28X3P", :type :childrens},
                            :days 18}
           {:movie {:title "p", :type :childrens}, :days 83}
           {:movie {:title "xgC", :type :regular}, :days 84}
```

```
          {:movie {:title "CQoY", :type :childrens}, :days 23}
          {:movie {:title "38jWmKlhq", :type :regular},
                   :days 96}
          {:movie {:title "Liz8T", :type :regular}, :days 56}]}
    ]
```

Just a bunch of random data that conforms nicely to the type of a rental-order. But let's check that:

```
(describe "Quick check statement policy"
  (it "generates valid rental orders"
    (should-be
      :result
      (tc/quick-check
        100
        (prop/for-all
          [rental-order gen-rental-order]
          (nil?
            (s/explain-data
              ::constructors/rental-order
              rental-order))))))))
```

This is a nice little quick-check that generates 100 random rental-order objects and runs them through the clojure.spec/explain-data function. That function makes sure that each rental order conforms to the ::constructors/rental-order spec that we saw above. If it does, it returns nil, which passes the quick-check.

Now, does make-statement-data create a valid statement-data object? Let's check that using the same strategy as above:

```
(s/def ::customer-name string?)
(s/def ::title string?)
(s/def ::price pos?)
(s/def ::movie (s/keys :req-un [::title ::price]))
(s/def ::movies (s/coll-of ::movie))
(s/def ::owed pos?)
(s/def ::points pos-int?)
```

```
(s/def ::statement-data (s/keys :req-un [::customer-name
                                         ::movies
                                         ::owed
                                         ::points]))

(it "produces valid statement data"
  (should-be
    :result
    (tc/quick-check
      100
      (prop/for-all
        [rental-order gen-rental-order
         policy gen-policy]
        (nil?
          (s/explain-data
            ::policy/statement-data
            (make-statement-data policy rental-order)))))))
```

So here we see the clojure.spec for the statement-data, and the quick-check that makes sure that the output of make-statement-data conforms to it. Nice.

With all this passing, we can be pretty sure that the generator is generating valid rental orders. So now let's get on with the property checks.

One property we could check is to make sure that when make-statement-data converts a rental-order into a statement-data the :owed member of the statement-data object is the sum of all the movies itemized in that object.

The quick-check for this might be as follows:

```
(it "statement data totals are consistent under all policies"
  (should-be
    :result
    (tc/quick-check
      100
      (prop/for-all
        [rental-order gen-rental-order
```

```
       policy gen-policy]
      (let [statement-data (make-statement-data
                            policy rental-order)
            prices (map :price (:movies statement-data))
            owed (:owed statement-data)]
        (= owed (reduce + prices)))))))
```

This quick-check has a bug in it. Can you spot it?

Here's the output when I run it:

```
{:shrunk
 {:total-nodes-visited 45,
  :depth 14,
  :pass? false,
  :result false,
  :result-data nil,
  :time-shrinking-ms 3,
  :smallest
    [{:customer {:name "0"},
      :rentals [{:movie {:title "", :type :regular}, :days 1}
                {:movie {:title "", :type :regular}, :days 1}
                {:movie {:title "", :type :regular}, :days 1}]}
     {:type
      :video-store.
        buy-two-get-one-free-policy/buy-two-get-one-free}]},
  :failed-after-ms 0,
  :num-tests 7,
  :seed 1672092997135,
  :fail
   [{:customer {:name "4s7u"},
     :rentals
     [{:movie {:title "i7jiVAd", :type :childrens}, :days 85}
      {:movie {:title "7MQM", :type :new-release}, :days 26}
      {:movie {:title "qlS4S", :type :new-release}, :days 99}
      {:movie {:title "X", :type :regular}, :days 87}
      {:movie {:title "w1cRbM", :type :regular}, :days 11}
      {:movie {:title "7Hb4lO5", :type :regular}, :days 63}
      {:movie {:title "xWc", :type :childrens}, :days 41}]}]
```

```
   {:type
     :video-store.
       buy-two-get-one-free-policy/buy-two-get-one-free}],
 :result false,
 :result-data nil,
 :failing-size 6,
 :pass? false}
```

Yes, I know this looks awful; but this is where the real magic of quick-check shines through, so bear with me.

First of all, do you see that top element named :shrunk? That's a big clue to what is going on here. When quick-check finds an error, it begins hunting for the smallest randomly generated input that continues to produce that error.

So look at the :fail element. That's the rental-order that caused the initial failure. Now look at the :smallest element within the :shrunk element. The quick-check function managed to shrink the rental-order down while preserving the failure. That's the smallest rental-order that it could find that failed.

And why did it fail? Notice that there are three movies. Notice also that the policy is buy-two-get-one-free. Ah, of course, under that policy the sum of the movies is *not* equal to the :owed element.

It's that shrinking behavior that makes property-based testing a diagnostic technique.

FUNCTIONAL

So why are tools like quick-check not more popular in OO languages? Perhaps it's because they work best with pure functions. I imagine it's possible to set up generators and test properties in a mutable system, but it's likely a lot more complicated than in an immutable system.

14 GUI

Over the years, I have used two different GUI frameworks in functional programs. The first is named Quil,[1] and it is based upon the popular Java framework named Processing.[2] The second is SeeSaw,[3] which is based upon the old Java Swing[4] framework.

Quil is "functional," which makes it fun and easy to use in a "functional" program. SeeSaw is not functional at all. Indeed, it depends very strongly on mutable state that you must continuously update. This makes it a royal pain to use in a functional program. The difference is startling.

One of the first programs I wrote using Quil was spacewar. I've mentioned it a few times in this book. If you'd like to see the program in action, you can go to https://github.com/unclebob/spacewar where there is a ClojureScript version you can run in your browser. I did not write spacewar to be used in ClojureScript; but Mike Fikes ported it over in a day or so. It actually works better in my browser than it does in native Clojure on my laptop.

TURTLE-GRAPHICS IN QUIL

Walking through the source code of spacewar is beyond the scope of this book. However, there is a simpler Quil program that I wrote awhile back that is the perfect size. It's turtle-graphics.[5]

Turtle graphics[6] are a simple set of commands that were invented for the Logo language in the late 1960s. Those commands controlled a robot called a *turtle*. The robot sat on a large piece of paper and had a pen that

---

1. www.quil.info

2. https://processing.org

3. https://github.com/clj-commons/seesaw

4. https://en.wikipedia.org/wiki/Swing_(Java)

5. https://github.com/unclebob/turtle-graphics

6. https://en.wikipedia.org/wiki/Turtle_graphics

could be raised and lowered onto the paper. The robot could be told to move forward or backward a certain distance, or to turn a number of degrees left or right.

Figure 14.1 is a picture of the inventor, Seymour Papert, with one of his turtles.

Figure 14.1. Seymour Papert with one of his turtles[7]

So, for example, if you'd like to draw a square, you might issue these commands:

```
Pen down
Forward 10
Right 90
Forward 10
Right 90
Forward 10
Right 90
Forward 10
Pen up.
```

7. Courtesy of MIT Museum.

The original idea was to introduce children to programming by showing them how to control the turtle to draw interesting shapes. I don't know how well this worked for children, but it turned out to be pretty useful for programmers who wanted to draw complex designs on the screen. I once used a Logo system with turtle graphics on the Commodore 64 to write a pretty elaborate Lunar Lander game.

Anyway, awhile back, I thought it would be fun to have a turtle graphics system in Clojure so that I could easily investigate some interesting mathematical and geometric puzzles.

My goal was not to create a turtle graphics console on which you would type commands. Instead, I wanted a turtle graphics API that I could use to write graphical functions in Clojure.

So, for example, I wanted to write a program like this:

```
(defn polygon [theta, len, n]
  (pen-down)
  (speed 1000)
  (dotimes [_ n]
    (forward len)
    (right theta)))

(defn turtle-script []
  (polygon 144 400 5))
```

That program draws the picture in Figure 14.2. (Notice the little turtle sitting on the left vertex of the star.)

The turtle-script function is the entry point for the turtle-graphics system. You put your drawing commands into it. In this case, I put a call to the polygon function into it.

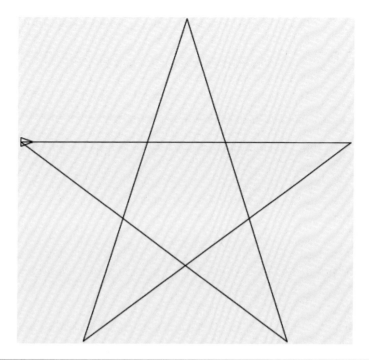

Figure 14.2. A star drawn using turtle graphics

Perhaps you've noticed that the `polygon` function does not appear to be functional because it doesn't produce a return value from its inputs. Instead, it has the side effect of drawing on the screen. Moreover, each of the commands mutates the state of the turtle. So `turtle-graphics` programs are not functional.

And yet, the `turtle-graphics` framework is "functional." Or rather, it is about as functional as a GUI program can be.[8] After all, the point of a GUI program is to mutate the state of the screen.

8. Although you might find this interesting: https://fsharpforfunandprofit.com/posts/13-ways-of-looking-at-a-turtle/.

The turtle-graphics framework begins by configuring and invoking Quil:

```
(defn ^:export -main [& args]
  (q/defsketch turtle-graphics
                :title "Turtle Graphics"
                :size [1000 1000]
                :setup setup
                :update update-state
                :draw draw-state
                :features [:keep-on-top]
                :middleware [m/fun-mode])
    args)
```

I'm not going to do a full tutorial on Quil here, but there are a few things I should point out. Take note of the :setup, :update, and :draw elements. Each points to a function.

The setup function will be called once at the start of the program.

The draw-state function will be called 60 times a second in order to refresh the screen. Everything that should be on the screen must be drawn by the draw function. The screen doesn't remember anything.

The update-state function will be called just before the draw-state function. This function is used to change the state of what is being drawn. Think of it as the function that moves the elements of the screen one 60th of a second into the future.

Think of this like a really simple loop:

```
(loop [state (setup)]
  (draw-state state)
  (recur (update-state state)))
```

If you think of this as a tail recursive loop, then the contents of the screen are the tail recursive values. So even though we are mutating the contents of the screen, we are doing so at the tail of the recursion where the mutation is harmless.[9] So, although not purely functional, it is as "functional" as any TCO[10] system can be.

Here's my setup function:

```
(defn setup []
  (q/frame-rate 60)
  (q/color-mode :rgb)
  (let [state {:turtle (turtle/make)
               :channel channel}]
    (async/go
      (turtle-script)
      (prn "Turtle script complete"))
    state))
```

This starts out pretty simple. It sets the frame rate to 60fps and the color mode to RGB, and it creates the state object that will be passed to update-state and draw-state.

The async/go function starts up a new lightweight thread in which our turtle-script will execute.

The state object is composed of a channel and the turtle. We'll talk about the channel later. For the moment, let's concentrate on the turtle:

```
(s/def ::position (s/tuple number? number?))
(s/def ::heading (s/and number? #(<= 0 % 360)))
(s/def ::velocity number?)
(s/def ::distance number?)
(s/def ::omega number?)
(s/def ::angle number?)
```

---

9. Mostly harmless.

10. Remember our discussion about tail call optimization back in Chapter 1.

```
(s/def ::weight (s/and pos? number?))
(s/def ::state #{:idle :busy})
(s/def ::pen #{:up :down})
(s/def ::pen-start (s/or :nil nil?
                        :pos (s/tuple number? number?)))
(s/def ::line-start (s/tuple number? number?))
(s/def ::line-end (s/tuple number? number?))
(s/def ::line (s/keys :req-un [::line-start ::line-end]))
(s/def ::lines (s/coll-of ::line))
(s/def ::visible boolean?)
(s/def ::speed (s/and int? pos?))
(s/def ::turtle (s/keys :req-un [::position
                                 ::heading
                                 ::velocity
                                 ::distance
                                 ::omega
                                 ::angle
                                 ::pen
                                 ::weight
                                 ::speed
                                 ::lines
                                 ::visible
                                 ::state]
                        :opt-un [::pen-start]))

(defn make []
  {:post [(s/assert ::turtle %)]}
  {:position [0.0 0.0]
   :heading 0.0
   :velocity 0.0
   :distance 0.0
   :omega 0.0
   :angle 0.0
   :pen :up
   :weight 1
   :speed 5
   :visible true
   :lines []
   :state :idle})
```

This shows the type specification of the turtle, followed by its constructor. Notice that the constructor checks the type as a :post condition. The elements of the turtle are mostly self-explanatory. There's the XY position, the angular heading, the velocity, the up/down state of the pen, the drawing weight of the pen, the visibility state, and so on. The other elements will come to light soon enough.

How do we draw the turtle?

```
(defn draw-state [state]
  (q/background 240)
  (q/with-translation
    [500 500]
    (let [{:keys [turtle]} state]
      (turtle/draw turtle))))
```

—Turtle module—

```
(defn draw [turtle]
  (when (= :down (:pen turtle))
    (q/stroke 0)
    (q/stroke-weight (:weight turtle))
    (q/line (:pen-start turtle) (:position turtle)))

  (doseq [line (:lines turtle)]
    (q/stroke-weight (:line-weight line))
    (q/line (:line-start line) (:line-end line)))

  (when (:visible turtle)
    (q/stroke-weight 1)
    (let [[x y] (:position turtle)
          heading (q/radians (:heading turtle))
          base-left (- (/ WIDTH 2))
          base-right (/ WIDTH 2)
          tip HEIGHT]
      (q/stroke 0)
      (q/with-translation
        [x y]
```

```
      (q/with-rotation
        [heading]
        (q/line 0 base-left 0 base-right)
        (q/line 0 base-left tip 0)
        (q/line 0 base-right tip 0))))))
```

The draw-state function, which is called by Quil 60 times each second, sets the background color of the screen to light gray, centers the drawing at (500, 500), and then calls turtle/draw, which draws the current line in progress and then all the other lines that were previously drawn. Finally, it draws the turtle itself. Notice how Quil helps with translation and rotation.

So how do we update the turtle state?

```
(defn update-state [{:keys [channel] :as state}]
  (let [turtle (:turtle state)
        turtle (turtle/update-turtle turtle)]
    (assoc state :turtle (handle-commands channel turtle))))
```

The update-state function calls turtle/update-turtle. Then it calls handle-commands, and there's that channel again. Let's look at update-turtle first:

```
(defn update-position
  [{:keys [position velocity heading distance] :as turtle}]
  (let [step (min (q/abs velocity) distance)
        distance (- distance step)
        step (if (neg? velocity) (- step) step)
        radians (q/radians heading)
        [x y] position
        vx (* step (Math/cos radians))
        vy (* step (Math/sin radians))
        position [(+ x vx) (+ y vy)]]
    (assoc turtle :position position
                  :distance distance
                  :velocity (if (zero? distance) 0.0 velocity))))

(defn update-heading [{:keys [heading omega angle] :as turtle}]
  (let [angle-step (min (q/abs omega) angle)
```

```
            angle (- angle angle-step)
            angle-step (if (neg? omega) (- angle-step) angle-step)
            heading (mod (+ heading angle-step) 360)]
        (assoc turtle :heading heading
                      :angle angle
                      :omega (if (zero? angle) 0.0 omega)))))

(defn make-line [{:keys [pen-start position weight]}]
  {:line-start pen-start
   :line-end position
   :line-weight weight})

(defn update-turtle [turtle]
  {:post [(s/assert ::turtle %)]}
  (if (= :idle (:state turtle))
    turtle
    (let [{:keys [distance
                  state
                  angle
                  lines
                  position
                  pen
                  pen-start] :as turtle}
          (-> turtle
              (update-position)
              (update-heading))
          done? (and (zero? distance)
                     (zero? angle))
          state (if done? :idle state)
          lines (if (and done? (= pen :down))
                  (conj lines (make-line turtle))
                  lines)
          pen-start (if (and done? (= pen :down))
                      position
                      pen-start)]
      (assoc turtle
             :state state
             :lines lines
             :pen-start pen-start))))
```

Notice that update-turtle has a :post condition that checks the type of the turtle after it has been updated. It's nice to know that when you update a big structure you haven't messed up some little part of it.

If the turtle's :state is :idle, meaning that it is neither moving nor rotating, then we don't make any changes. Otherwise, we update the position and heading of the turtle and then *destructure* its internals. We are done when the distance and angle remaining in the current animated motion are zero. And if we are done, we set the :state to :idle.

If we are done and the pen is down, then we add the line in progress to the list of previous lines, and we update the pen-start to the current position to prepare for the next line.

Updating the position and heading are simple functions that do the necessary trig calculations to place the turtle in the proper position and orientation. They both use the turtle's :velocity to adjust how big a step they take at each update.

Now on to handling the commands:

```
(defn handle-commands [channel turtle]
  (loop [turtle turtle]
    (let [command (if (= :idle (:state turtle))
                    (async/poll! channel)
                    nil)]
      (if (nil? command)
        turtle
        (recur (turtle/handle-command turtle command))))))
```

If the turtle is :idle, then we are ready for a command. So we poll the channel. If there is a command on the channel, we process it by calling turtle/handle-command, and then repeat until no commands are left on the channel.

Handling each command is pretty straightforward:

```
(defn pen-down [{:keys [pen position pen-start] :as turtle}]
  (assoc turtle :pen :down
              :pen-start (if (= :up pen) position pen-start)))

(defn pen-up [{:keys [pen lines] :as turtle}]
  (if (= :up pen)
    turtle
    (let [new-line (make-line turtle)
          lines (conj lines new-line)]
      (assoc turtle :pen :up
                  :pen-start nil
                  :lines lines))))

(defn forward [turtle [distance]]
  (assoc turtle :velocity (:speed turtle)
              :distance distance
              :state :busy))

(defn back [turtle [distance]]
  (assoc turtle :velocity (- (:speed turtle))
              :distance distance
              :state :busy))

(defn right [turtle [angle]]
  (assoc turtle :omega (* 2 (:speed turtle))
              :angle angle
              :state :busy))

(defn left [turtle [angle]]
  (assoc turtle :omega (* -2 (:speed turtle))
              :angle angle
              :state :busy))

(defn hide [turtle]
  (assoc turtle :visible false))
```

```
(defn show [turtle]
  (assoc turtle :visible true))

(defn weight [turtle [weight]]
  (assoc turtle :weight weight))

(defn speed [turtle [speed]]
  (assoc turtle :speed speed))

(defn handle-command [turtle [cmd & args]]
  (condp = cmd
    :forward (forward turtle args)
    :back (back turtle args)
    :right (right turtle args)
    :left (left turtle args)
    :pen-down (pen-down turtle)
    :pen-up (pen-up turtle)
    :hide (hide turtle)
    :show (show turtle)
    :weight (weight turtle args)
    :speed (speed turtle args)
    :else turtle))
```

We simply translate the command tokens into function calls. Not really
rocket science. The command functions manage the state of the turtle.
Take for instance, the forward command. It sets the turtle's :state to
:busy, sets the turtle's :velocity, and sets the :distance it must move
before going :idle again.

OK, we're almost done. Now all we need to do is look at the way the
turtle-script function sends commands to the channel:

```
(def channel (async/chan))
(defn forward [distance] (async/>!! channel [:forward distance]))
(defn back [distance] (async/>!! channel [:back distance]))
(defn right [angle] (async/>!! channel [:right angle]))
(defn left [angle] (async/>!! channel [:left angle]))
(defn pen-up [] (async/>!! channel [:pen-up]))
```

```
(defn pen-down [] (async/>!! channel [:pen-down]))
(defn hide [] (async/>!! channel [:hide]))
(defn show [] (async/>!! channel [:show]))
(defn weight [weight] (async/>!! channel [:weight weight]))
(defn speed [speed] (async/>!! channel [:speed speed]))
```

The async/>!! function sends its argument to the channel. If the channel is full, it waits. That really wasn't very surprising, was it?

And with that, we can put all the turtle graphics commands we like into the turtle-script function and watch the turtle dance around the screen drawing our pretty pictures.

You can see this framework in action in the videos at www.youtube.com /@Cleancoders; specifically, *The Euler Project*, episodes 2.3, 2.2, 5, and 9.

15 CONCURRENCY

KOHNKE

FINISH

Concurrency in functional programs is substantially less complicated than it is in programs that support mutable state. The reason, as I said back in Chapter 1, is that you can't have concurrent update problems if you don't do updates. I also said that this means you can't have race conditions.

These "facts" remove much of the complication of dealing with multiple threads. Threads simply cannot interfere with one another if they are composed of pure functions.

Or can they?

While comforting, those "facts" are not precisely true. The purpose of this chapter is to show how multithreaded "functional" programs can still have race conditions.

To examine this, let's set up some interacting finite state machines. One of my favorite examples is the making of a telephone call in the 1960s. The sequence of events looked roughly like Figure 15.1.

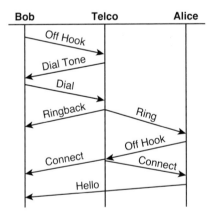

Figure 15.1. A message sequence chart of a telephone call

This is a *message sequence chart*. Time is on the vertical axis, and all messages are angled because they all take time to send.

You may be unfamiliar with the telephony nomenclature I used here. Indeed, if you were born after the year 2000, you may be unfamiliar with telephones in general. So, for the sake of history and nostalgia, let me walk you through the process.

Bob wants to place a call to Alice. Bob lifts the telephone receiver off its hook[1] and holds it to his ear. The telephone company (telco) sends a dial tone[2] to the receiver. Upon hearing that tone, Bob dials[3] Alice's number. The telco then sends a ringing voltage[4] to Alice's phone and a ringback[5] tone to Bob's receiver. Alice hears the ringing of her phone and lifts the receiver off the hook. The telco connects Bob to Alice, and Alice says "Hello" to Bob.

There are three finite state machines running in this scenario: Bob, telco, and Alice. Bob and Alice run separate instances of the User state machine[6] shown in Figure 15.2.

The Telco state machine is shown in Figure 15.3.

In these diagrams, the -> symbol means to send the corresponding event to the other state machine.

---

1. Telephones in the early 20th century had a hook that the receiver hung on. By the 1960s, the hook had been replaced by a cradle that the receiver sat in; but it was still called the hook.

2. This was a very recognizable sound that meant that the telephone system was ready for you to dial the number you wanted to call.

3. The verb *dial* means to enter the telephone number. In the early 1960s, this was accomplished by using a rotary dial on the face of the telephone.

4. 90 volts in the United States.

5. Another very distinct sound that was meant to entertain the caller while waiting for the called phone to be answered.

6. These state machines are abbreviated to keep them simple. In reality, all the states would have transitions back to Idle.

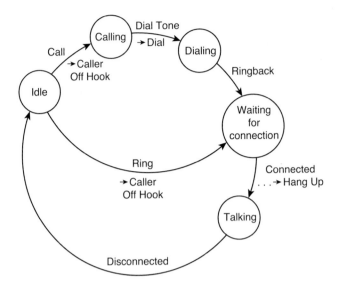

Figure 15.2. The User state machine

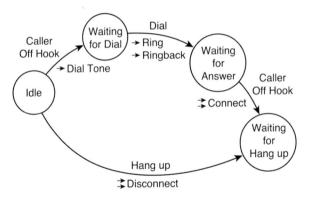

Figure 15.3. The Telco state machine

So when Bob decides to make a call (the call event from the Idle state) the User state machine sends the off-hook event to the Telco. When the Telco is in the Waiting for Dial state and receives the Dial event from the User, it sends the Ring and Ringback events to the appropriate User state machines.

If you study these diagrams carefully, you should be able to see how the state machines and messages interact to allow Bob to call Alice.

We can write these state machines in Clojure quite simply:

```
(def user-sm
  {:idle {:call [:calling caller-off-hook]
          :ring [:waiting-for-connection callee-off-hook]
          :disconnect [:idle nil]}
   :calling {:dialtone [:dialing dial]}
   :dialing {:ringback [:waiting-for-connection nil]}
   :waiting-for-connection {:connected [:talking talk]}
   :talking {:disconnect [:idle nil]}})

(def telco-sm
  {:idle {:caller-off-hook [:waiting-for-dial dialtone]
          :hangup [:idle nil]}
   :waiting-for-dial {:dial [:waiting-for-answer ring]}
   :waiting-for-answer {:callee-off-hook
                         [:waiting-for-hangup connect]}
   :waiting-for-hangup {:hangup [:idle disconnect]}})
```

Each state machine is simply a hash map of states, each of which contains a hash map of events that specify the new state and the action to be performed.

So when the user-sm is in the :idle state and it gets a :call event, it transitions to the :calling state and calls the caller-off-hook function.

These state machines can be executed by the following transition function:

```
(defn transition [machine-agent event event-data]
  (swap! log conj (str (:name machine-agent) "<-" event))
  (let [state (:state machine-agent)
        sm (:machine machine-agent)
```

```
        result (get-in⁷ sm [state event]))]
  (if (nil? result)
    (do
      (swap! log conj "TILT!")
      machine-agent)
    (do

      (when (second result)
        ((second result) machine-agent event-data))
      (assoc machine-agent :state (first result)))))))
```

The log variable is an atom that is simply used to accumulate a set
of logging statements so that we can watch the operation of the state
machines. Notice that this function takes the machine-agent and returns
it with the new state in place. This means we can use it with Clojure's
agent STM facility.

An agent is initialized with a data structure and then serializes all updates
to that data structure, thereby eliminating all concurrent update issues.
Here are the functions that create the two different agents:

```
(defn make-user-agent [name]
  (agent {:state :idle :name name :machine user-sm}))

(defn make-telco-agent [name]
  (agent {:state :idle :name name :machine telco-sm}))
```

We send events to our agents by using the agent's send function:

```
(send caller transition :call [telco caller callee])
```

In this example, we are sending the transition function to the caller
agent. The send function returns immediately and queues up the transition
function to be executed in the agent's thread. The arguments to the

---

7. The get-in function returns an element from a nested map. (get-in {:a {:b 2}} [:a :b])
   returns 2.

transition function are the event (:call) and the data that should be passed to the action function. In this case, the data is a list of the three agents that represent the finite state machines in the system.

The action functions are as follows:

```
(defn caller-off-hook
  [sm-agent [telco caller callee :as call-data]]
  (swap! log conj (str  (:name @caller) " goes off hook."))
  (send telco transition :caller-off-hook call-data))

(defn dial [sm-agent [telco caller callee :as call-data]]
  (swap! log conj (str (:name @caller) " dials"))
  (send telco transition :dial call-data))

(defn callee-off-hook
  [sm-agent [telco caller callee :as call-data]]
  (swap! log conj (str (:name @callee) " goes off hook"))
  (send telco transition :callee-off-hook call-data))

(defn talk [sm-agent [telco caller callee :as call-data]]
  (swap! log conj (str (:name sm-agent) " talks."))
  (Thread/sleep 10)
  (swap! log conj (str (:name sm-agent) " hangs up."))
  (send telco transition :hangup call-data))

(defn dialtone [sm-agent [telco caller callee :as call-data]]
  (swap! log conj (str "dialtone to " (:name @caller)))
  (send caller transition :dialtone call-data))

(defn ring [sm-agent [telco caller callee :as call-data]]
  (swap! log conj (str "telco rings " (:name @callee)))
  (send callee transition :ring call-data)
  (send caller transition :ringback call-data))

(defn connect [sm-agent [telco caller callee :as call-data]]
  (swap! log conj "telco connects")
  (send caller transition :connected call-data)
  (send callee transition :connected call-data))
```

```
(defn disconnect [sm-agent [telco caller callee :as call-data]]
  (swap! log conj "disconnect")
  (send callee transition :disconnect call-data)
  (send caller transition :disconnect call-data))
```

The second argument in each of the action functions is *destructured*.[8] So, for example, the call-data sent to caller-off-hook is a list, the first element of which will be placed in telco, the second in caller, the third in callee, and the whole list in call-data.

Given this implementation, we should be able to make a call between Bob and Alice by executing the following code. I have written it in the form of a test:

```
(it "should make and receive call"
  (let [caller (make-user "Bob")
        callee (make-user "Alice")
        telco (make-telco "telco")]
    (reset! log [])
    (send caller transition :call [telco caller callee])
    (Thread/sleep 100)
    (prn @log)
    (should= :idle (:state @caller))
    (should= :idle (:state @callee))
    (should= :idle (:state @telco))))
```

This test passes, which means that all the state machines returned to the idle state by the time 100ms had passed. The log output looks like this:

```
"Bob<-:call" "Bob goes off hook"
"telco<-:caller-off-hook" "dialtone to Bob"
"Bob<-:dialtone" "Bob dials"
"telco<-:dial" "telco rings Alice"
"Alice<-:ring" "Alice goes off hook"
"Bob<-:ringback"
```

---

8. In short, destructuring is a convenient way of breaking a complex data element into named components. See the Clojure documentation for more details.

```
"telco<-:callee-off-hook" "telco connects"
"Bob<-:connected" "Bob talks"
"Alice<-:connected" "Alice talks"
"Bob hangs up"
"Alice hangs up"
"telco<-:hangup" "disconnect"
"Alice<-:disconnect"
"Bob<-:disconnect"
"telco<-:hangup"
```

You can see how the threads interleaved with one another, while all three finite state machines worked together to drive the call to a successful completion.

The three agents have mutable state; but there can be no concurrent update problems because the agents serialize their operations. So no race conditions, right?

Not so fast there, Newt. Let's investigate another scenario.

What I'm about to show you in Figure 15.4, is a race condition that existed in the telephone system in the '60s.[9] Once again, we begin with Bob calling Alice. But this time Alice is just about to call Bob.

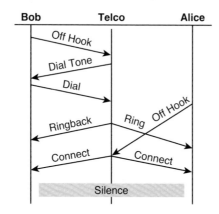

Figure 15.4. The race condition in the telephone system

9. It probably still exists today if you use landlines.

Do you see what went wrong? Those crossed lines are the problem. That's a race condition. The telco tried to ring Alice's phone; but before it could make the sound, Alice picked up the receiver in order to call Bob. From the point of view of the telco, everything is fine. It rang the phone and Alice picked up. So the telco happily connects Bob and Alice. But Alice is sitting there waiting for a dial tone; and Bob is confused because nobody has said hello and the ringback tone has stopped.

The most likely outcome is that both parties hang up without talking to each other. Alternatively, Alice might say something and Bob might respond, and they'd get into the comic routine of who called who.

Can we make our state machines emulate this fault? Here's the setup, once again posed as a test:

```
(it "should race"
  (let [caller (make-user "Bob")
        callee (make-user "Alice")
        telco1 (make-telco "telco1")
        telco2 (make-telco "telco2")]
    (reset! log [])
    (send caller transition :call [telco1 caller callee])
    (send callee transition :call [telco2 callee caller])
    (Thread/sleep 100)
    (prn @log)
    (should= :idle (:state @caller))
    (should= :idle (:state @callee))
    (should= :idle (:state @telco1))
    (should= :idle (:state @telco2))))
```

Notice that we now have four state machines: one for Bob, one for Alice, and one telco for each of the two calls. The test fails. After 100ms, the state machines have not returned to the Idle state.

So, what does the log tell us?

```
"Bob<-:call" "Bob goes off hook"
"telco1<-:caller-off-hook"
```

```
"Alice<-:call" "Alice goes off hook"
"telco2<-:caller-off-hook"
"dialtone to Bob"
"Bob<-:dialtone" "Bob dials"
"telco1<-:dial" "telco rings Alice"
"Bob<-:ringback"
"Alice<-:ring" "TILT!" …
```

This took me several tries, because the window for that particular race condition is pretty narrow. But there it is. See that TILT!? That's what our transition function puts in the log if it is ever asked to make an invalid transition. Alice is still in the :calling state waiting for the :dialtone event, and has no way to deal with the :ring event.

The bottom line is that race conditions are still possible even though concurrent updates are not. That's because it is always possible to construct interacting state machines that get out of sync with one another.

CONCLUSION

Somewhere around the turn of the century, Moore's law died. Clock rates hit a maximum of about 3GHz and then just stopped increasing. To drive more throughput, hardware engineers started putting more processors on their chips. We went through the dual-core stage and the quad-core stage—and we thought we were going to see a doubling in cores every other year or so. We started to fret about the possibility of dealing with machines that had 32, or 64, or 128 cores.

This is about the time functional languages started to gain in popularity. The thought was that since functional programs don't mutate data, multicore operations would be made much simpler. If you are working with pure functions, it is theoretically easy to spread those functions out over a plethora of cores.

But Moore's law wasn't done dying. It died for clock speed a few years before it died for component density. So, for the past decade or more, our processors have been quad core (don't talk to me about hyperthreading); and that is not likely to change. This has decreased the fear of the 128-core processor and lessened the urgency behind functional programming.

And that's probably a good thing because, as this chapter has shown, the reasoning was somewhat faulty to begin with. Race conditions might be more common in threads that have mutable variables, but in any system where there are concurrent finite state machines, the possibility exists that race conditions might drive them out of sync with one another.

DESIGN PATTERNS

The idea of design patterns[1] was one of the most profound in the software industry. It ranks up there with structured programming, object-oriented programming, and functional programming. It told us that applications consist, in part, of repeatable and reusable elements. Those elements solved problems common to many, if not all, applications.

Of course, like all good ideas in software, design patterns have been misunderstood, overused, abused, and even discarded as archaic or specific to only very narrow contexts. This is a shame, because design patterns are eminently useful.

---

1. The definitive work on this topic was Erich Gamma, Richard Helm, Ralph Johnson, and John Vlissides, *Design Patterns: Elements of Reusable Object-Oriented Software* (Addison-Wesley, 1994).

DESIGN PATTERNS REVIEW

A *design pattern* is a named solution to a common problem in a particular context. Yes, I know, another word salad. So let me tell you a story.

Long ago, in a decade far, far away, I was a prolific writer on a social network called comp.object.[2] In this group, we debated issues of OO design.

One day someone posed a simple problem and suggested that we all solve it in our own way and then debate the result. The problem was:

Given a switch and a light, make the switch turn the light on.

The debates raged for months.

The simplest solution was, of course, Figure 16.1.

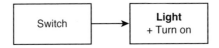

Figure 16.1.   The simplest solution for the switch and the light

The Switch class[3] calls the TurnOn method of the Light class.

The objection to this was that the Switch class could be used to turn on other things like Fans or Televisions. Therefore, the Switch class should not know about the Light class. An abstraction should be imposed between the two, as shown in Figure 16.2.

Now the Switch class uses an interface named Switchable. The Light class implements Switchable.

This solves the problem. Now we could have any number of devices controlled by the Switch. This solution is one of the simplest expressions

---

2. A newsgroup within the vast array of newsgroups transmitted by Network News Transport Protocol (NNTP) over Unix-to-Unix copy (UUCP) and the Internet.

3. Remember, this was an OO forum. Don't get hung up on the word *class*.

of the DIP, the OCP, and the LSP. It also has a name. It's called *Abstract Server*.[4]

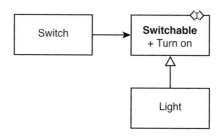

Figure 16.2. The Abstract Server

If we were on a team discussing how to protect our Switch class from being explicitly coupled to our Light class, someone on the team could pipe up and say, "We could use an Abstract Server." If all the team members knew that name and what it implied, they could quickly decide whether that solution was appropriate or not.

That's a design pattern, a named solution to a problem in a particular context. The value of design patterns is that the names and the solutions are canonical, and therefore, people who are familiar with that canon can understand one another simply by using the name. You say "Abstract Server" and I immediately understand that you mean "impose an interface between the client and the server."

But what about the context part of the design pattern? Well, let's go back to our team. Someone has just suggested using the Abstract Server pattern. Another team member says, "No, you don't understand, we don't own the Light class; it's part of a third-party library, so we can't alter it to implement an interface."

So, the context of the problem is that we want to decouple Switch from Light, but we can't modify Light. So someone else on the team says, "Well, we could use an *Adapter*."

---

4. Robert C. Martin, *Agile Software Development: Principles, Patterns, and Practices* (Pearson, 2002), 318.

If you were on the team and didn't know what the Adapter pattern was, you wouldn't understand their suggestion. But if you were aware of the design patterns canon, you could swiftly assess the suggestion. Again, the benefit of design patterns is knowing the names and the canonical forms so that you can quickly apply them.

The Adapter pattern looks like Figure 16.3.

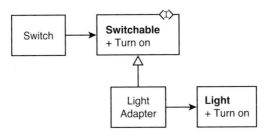

Figure 16.3.   The object form of the Adapter pattern

The LightAdapter implements the Switchable interface and forwards the TurnOn call to the Light. Even before this is drawn on the whiteboard, everyone on the team can see it in their minds because they know the design patterns canon. So they all nod in agreement with the idea.

Just as they are about to move on to the next issue, someone on the team says, "Wait, which form of the Adapter should we use?"

It turns out that the canonical name for a design pattern does not necessarily describe a single solution. Some of the patterns have multiple forms. The Adapter is one such pattern. It could look like Figure 16.3, or it could look like Figure 16.4.

The former is called the *object* form of the Adapter because the LightAdapter is its own object. The latter is the *class* form of the Adapter because the LightAdapter is a subclass of Light.

The team members debate the two forms for a moment and come to the decision that the class form of the Adapter is sufficient for the moment and will relieve them of the complication of constructing a separate LightAdapter object.

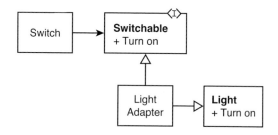

Figure 16.4. The class form of the Adapter pattern

PATTERNS IN FUNCTIONAL PROGRAMMING

Among the strange rumors we have heard over the years is that design patterns are hacks to get around the problems created by OO languages and that in functional languages they are not necessary.

As you'll see in the pages that follow, there are indeed aspects of certain design patterns that appear to be workarounds for certain inadequacies in OO languages; but this is hardly applicable to all design patterns. Moreover, even those particular design patterns have a more general form in which they are applicable in functional languages.

ABSTRACT SERVER

So, what does the Abstract Server look like in a functional language?

Consider the Switch/Light problem again. Here's how we might express it in Clojure:

```clojure
(defn turn-on-light []
  ;turn on the bloody light!
  )

(defn engage-switch []
  ;Some other stuff. . .
  (turn-on-light))
```

OK, that's not rocket science. However, the original problem is immediately evident. Our engage-switch function has a direct dependency on turn-on-light, which means we can't use it to turn on a fan or a television or anything else. So, what should we do?

We can use the Abstract Server pattern, of course. All we need to do is insert an abstract interface between the engage-switch function and the turn-on-light function. We could do that by simply passing a function argument. Let's call this the *function* form of the Abstract Server:

```clojure
(defn engage-switch [turn-on-function]
  ;Some other stuff. . .
  (turn-on-function))
```

That works in the simplest case. But let's make the problem just a bit more interesting. Let's say that our engage-switch function must turn the light both on and off at various times. Perhaps it's part of some home security system with special timers for the lights. This changes the original problem to look like this:

```clojure
(defn turn-on-light []
  ;turn on the bloody light!
  )

(defn turn-off-light []
  ;Criminy! just turn it off!
  )
```

```
(defn engage-switch []
  ;Some other stuff...
  (turn-on-light)
  ;Some more other stuff...
  (turn-off-light))
```

Now the `engage-switch` function is twice as coupled to the light. We could use the same function form of the Abstract Server, but it's a bit ugly passing in two arguments. So let's pass in a single vtable argument. We'll call this the *vtable* form of the Abstract Server:

```
(defn make-switchable-light []
  {:on turn-on-light
   :off turn-off-light})

(defn engage-switch [switchable]
  ;Some other stuff...
  ((:on switchable))
  ;Some more other stuff...
  ((:off switchable)))
```

Yeah, that's actually pretty nice. And since Clojure is a dynamically typed language, we don't have the problem that an inheritance or implements relationship would cause.

Of course, we could have solved this with the *multi-method* form of the Abstract Server pattern:

```
(defmulti turn-on :type)
(defmulti turn-off :type)

(defmethod turn-on :light [switchable]
  (turn-on-light))

(defmethod turn-off :light [switchable]
  (turn-off-light))

(defn engage-switch [switchable]
  ;Some other stuff...
```

```
(turn-on switchable)
;Some more other stuff...
(turn-off switchable))
```

I tested this using the following test:

```
(describe "switch/light"
  (with-stubs)
  (it "turns light on and off"
    (with-redefs [turn-on-light (stub :turn-on-light)
                  turn-off-light (stub :turn-off-light)]
      (engage-switch {:type :light})
      (should-have-invoked :turn-on-light)
      (should-have-invoked :turn-off-light))))
```

The two stubs mock out the target functions. We invoke the engage-switch function with the {:type :light} argument. Then we test that the two target functions were, in fact, called.

I'll leave the *protocol/record* form of the Abstract Server pattern as an exercise. At this point, it should be clear that the pattern is both applicable and useful in a functional language.

Adapter

The Adapter pattern is used whenever you have a client who wants to use a server, but the interface that the client expects and the interface that the server expresses are incompatible.

As an example, let's suppose that we have the engage-switch function from the preceding discussion, but we want to pass it a third-party :variable-light. The turn-on-light function of the :variable-light accepts an argument for the intensity of the light: 0 for off and 100 for full on.

The interface of the :variable-light does not match the expectation of the engage-switch function. So we need an Adapter.

Perhaps the simplest form of the Adapter might look like this:

```
(defn turn-on-light [intensity]
  ;Turn it on with intensity.
  )

(defmulti turn-on :type)
(defmulti turn-off :type)

(defmethod turn-on :variable-light [switchable]
  (turn-on-light 100))

(defmethod turn-off :variable-light [switchable]
  (turn-on-light 0))

(defn engage-switch [switchable]
  ;Some other stuff...
  (turn-on switchable)
  ;Some more other stuff...
  (turn-off switchable))
```

I tested this with the following test:

```
(describe "Adapter"
  (with-stubs)
  (it "turns light on and off"
    (with-redefs [turn-on-light (stub :turn-on-light)]
      (engage-switch {:type :variable-light})
      (should-have-invoked :turn-on-light {:times 1 :with [100]})
      (should-have-invoked :turn-on-light {:times 1 :with [0]}))))
```

If I were to draw this structure in the UML, I'd likely draw something like Figure 16.5.

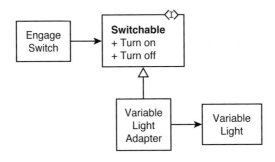

Figure 16.5. The object form of the Adapter pattern

The `defmulti` functions correspond to the `Switchable` interface. The `{:type :variable-light}` object, coupled to the two `defmethod` functions, corresponds to the `VariableLightAdapter`. The `EngageSwitch` and `VariableLight` "classes" correspond to the two functions that we are trying to adapt.

Perhaps you don't find this convincing. After all, it's just a simple little program with a couple of `defmulti` functions. There's no obvious OO structure like that shown in the UML. So let's impose that structure by splitting up the source files.

We begin with the `switchable` interface. In the `ns` statement, I used the convention that `turn-on-light` was the overall namespace for the project that contains the `switchable` namespace:

```
(ns turn-on-light.switchable)

(defmulti turn-on :type)
(defmulti turn-off :type)
```

This is a polymorphic interface. Notice that it has no source code dependencies. Also, keep in mind that the `ns` statement in Clojure has the same kind of source file requirement that Java has for classes. The source file and the namespace have to have corresponding names.[5] So, as we move the elements of this code into separate namespaces, we are also moving them into separate source files.

Next, let's see the engage-switch and variable-light namespaces:

```
(ns turn-on-light.engage-switch
  (:require [turn-on-light.switchable :as s]))

(defn engage-switch [switchable]
  ;Some other stuff...
  (s/turn-on switchable)
  ;Some more other stuff...
  (s/turn-off switchable))
```

```
(ns turn-on-light.variable-light)

(defn turn-on-light [intensity]
  ;Turn it on with intensity.
  )
```

No real surprises here. The engage-switch namespace depends upon the switchable interface. The variable-light namespace has no outgoing source code dependencies.

The variable-light-adapter namespace connects the switchable interface to the variable-light. Notice the make-adapter constructor. The tests will use that:

```
(ns turn-on-light.variable-light-adapter
  (:require [turn-on-light.switchable :as s]
            [turn-on-light.variable-light :as v-l]))
```

---

5. In particular, the turn-on-light.switchable namespace must be in a file named switchable.clj within a directory named turn_on_light.

```
(defn make-adapter []
  {:type :variable-light})

(defmethod s/turn-on :variable-light [switchable]
  (v-l/turn-on-light 100))

(defmethod s/turn-off :variable-light [switchable]
  (v-l/turn-on-light 0))
```

And lastly, the test ties everything together in a nice, neat little ball by depending upon all the concrete namespaces:

```
(ns turn-on-light.turn-on-spec
  (:require [speclj.core :refer :all]
            [turn-on-light.engage-switch :refer :all]
            [turn-on-light.variable-light :as v-l]
            [turn-on-light.variable-light-adapter
               :as v-l-adapter]))

(describe "Adapter"
  (with-stubs)
  (it "turns light on and off"
    (with-redefs [v-l/turn-on-light (stub :turn-on-light)]
      (engage-switch (v-l-adapter/make-adapter))
      (should-have-invoked :turn-on-light
                           {:times 1 :with [100]})
      (should-have-invoked :turn-on-light
                           {:times 1 :with [0]}))))
```

Look through those source code dependencies and compare them to the UML diagram, and you'll see that they match perfectly.

So which form of the Adapter pattern was this? We might call it the multi-method form; but it is also the object form.

Would it be possible, in Clojure, to build the class form of the Adapter pattern? No, because Clojure does not have inheritance of implementation, and that's what the class form of the Adapter pattern depends upon.

So, although the Adapter pattern is not language specific, there are forms that are. It would not be possible, for example, to create the multi-method form of the Adapter pattern in Java.

IS THAT REALLY AN ADAPTER OBJECT?

Perhaps you think that since the only data element in the variable-light-adapter is the :type, it is not really worthy of being called an object. OK then, here is a different version of the variable-light-adapter that you might find more convincing:

```
(ns turn-on-light.variable-light-adapter
  (:require [turn-on-light.switchable :as s]
            [turn-on-light.variable-light :as v-l]))

(defn make-adapter [min-intensity max-intensity]
  {:type :variable-light
   :min-intensity min-intensity
   :max-intensity max-intensity})

(defmethod s/turn-on :variable-light [variable-light]
  (v-l/turn-on-light (:max-intensity variable-light)))

(defmethod s/turn-off :variable-light [variable-light]
  (v-l/turn-on-light (:min-intensity variable-light)))
```

```
(ns turn-on-light.turn-on-spec
  (:require [speclj.core :refer :all]
            [turn-on-light.engage-switch :refer :all]
            [turn-on-light.variable-light :as v-l]
            [turn-on-light.variable-light-adapter
              :as v-l-adapter]))
```

```
(describe "Adapter"
  (with-stubs)
  (it "turns light on and off"
    (with-redefs [v-l/turn-on-light (stub :turn-on-light)]
      (engage-switch (v-l-adapter/make-adapter 5 90))
      (should-have-invoked :turn-on-light
                           {:times 1 :with [90]})
      (should-have-invoked :turn-on-light
                           {:times 1 :with [5]})))))
```

By now, you should be convinced that this is the Adapter pattern, right out of the GOF[6] book. You should also be expecting that many of the other GOF patterns can be expressed in functional languages like Clojure. And, perhaps more importantly, you should be thinking about namespace/source file structures as part of the design and architecture of functional programs.

COMMAND

Of all the design patterns in the GOF book, *Command* is the one that intrigues me the most. Not because it is complicated, but because it is *simple*. Very, very simple.

---

6. *GOF* is the affectionate name we gave to the *Design Patterns* book back in the '90s. It stands for "Gang of Four" because there were four authors: Erich Gamma, John Vlissides, Ralph Johnson, and Richard Helm.

As an aside, this is also what intrigues me about Clojure. As I said in the introduction to this book, Clojure is semantically rich but syntactically trivial. Well, the Command pattern has the same attributes. Its richness is in its outrageous simplicity.

In C++, we might write the Command pattern as follows:

```
class Command {
  public:
    virtual void execute() = 0;
};
```

That's it. Just one abstract class (interface) with a single, pure, virtual (abstract) function. So simple. But there are just so many interesting things you can do with this pattern. For a deep dive into this richness, see the corresponding chapter in *Agile Software Development: Principles, Patterns, and Practices*.[7]

In a functional language like Clojure, you might think that this pattern just disappears. After all, if you want to pass a command to some other function, you can just pass the command function. You don't need to make an object out of it, because in functional languages, functions *are* objects:

```
(ns command.core)

(defn execute []
  )

(defn some-app [command]
  ;Some other stuff. . .
  (command)⁸
  ;Some more other stuff. . .
  )
```

---

7. Martin, *Agile Software Development*, p. 181.

8. The careful reader will recognize that the command, as it is written, is not a pure (referentially transparent) function. It should be clear, however, that pure functions can be passed in the manner shown.

```
(ns command.core-spec
  (:require [speclj.core :refer :all]
            [command.core :refer :all]))

(describe "command"
  (with-stubs)
  (it "executes the command"
    (with-redefs [execute (stub :execute)]
      (some-app execute)
      (should-have-invoked :execute))))
```

As you can see, the test passes the execute function to some-app, and the some-app function invokes that command. No big deal.

Now, what if you wanted to create the command with a data element that will get passed as an argument to the execute function? In C++, we'd do that this way (pardon the inline functions):

```
class CommandWithArgument : public Command {
  public:
    CommandWithArgument(int argument)
    :argument(argument)
    {}

    virtual void execute()
    {theFunctionToExecute(argument);}

  private:
    int argument;

    void theFunctionToExecute(int argument)
    {
      //do something with that argument!
    }
};
```

In Clojure we'd do it like this, once again demonstrating that functions, in functional languages, are actually objects:

```
(describe "command"
  (with-stubs)
  (it "executes the command"
    (with-redefs [execute (stub :execute)]
      (some-app (partial execute :the-argument))
      (should-have-invoked :execute {:with [:the-argument]})))))


  ─────


(defn execute [argument]
  )

(defn some-app [command]
  ;Some other stuff. . .
  (command)
  ;Some more other stuff. . .
  )
```

UNDO

One of the more useful variations of the Command pattern can be seen in the following C++ code:

```
class UndoableCommand : public Command {
  public:
    virtual void undo() = 0;
};
```

That undo() function opens up so many interesting possibilities.

Long ago, I worked on a GUI application that was an analog of AutoCAD. It was a drawing tool for architectural floor plans, roof plans, property line plans, and so on. The GUI was a typical palette/canvas.

Users clicked in the palette to select the function they wanted, such as *Add a Room*, and then they'd click in the canvas for placement and size.

Every click in the palette caused the appropriate derivative of the UndoableCommand to be instantiated and executed. The execution managed the mouse/keyboard gestures in the canvas and then made the appropriate modifications to the internal data model. Thus, there was an UndoableCommand derivative for every different function that the palette could offer.

When an UndoableCommand had finished execution, it was pushed onto the *undo* stack. Whenever the user clicked on the *undo* icon in the palette, the UndoableCommand on the top of the *undo* stack was popped off and its undo function was called.

As an UndoableCommand object executed, it recorded what it did in such a way that the undo function could reverse those changes. In C++, that recording was kept in the member variables of the particular UndoableCommand object itself:

```
class AddRoomCommand : public UndoableCommand {
  public:
    virtual void execute() {
      // manage canvas events to add room
      // record what was done in theAddedRoom
    }

    virtual void undo() {
      // remove theAddedRoom from the canvas
    }

  private:
    Room* theAddedRoom;
};
```

This is not functional, because the AddRoomCommand object is mutable. But in a functional language, we can simply have the execute function create a new instance of UndoableCommand. Something like this:

```
(ns command.undoable-command)

(defmulti execute :type)
(defmulti undo :type)
```

―――――

```
(ns command.add-room-command
  (:require [command.undoable-command :as uc]))

(defn add-room []
  ;stuff that adds rooms to the canvas
  ;and returns the added room
  )

(defn delete-room [room]
  ;stuff that deletes the specified room from the canvas
  )

(defn make-add-room-command []
  {:type :add-room-command})

(defmethod uc/execute :add-room-command [command]
  (assoc (make-add-room-command) :the-added-room (add-room)))

(defmethod uc/undo :add-room-command [command]
  (delete-room (:the-added-room command)))
```

―――――

```
(ns command.core
  (:require [command.undoable-command :as uc]
            [command.add-room-command :as ar]))
```

```
(defn gui-app [actions]
  (loop [actions actions
         undo-list (list)]
    (if (empty? actions)
      :DONE
      (condp = (first actions)
        :add-room-action
        (let [executed-command (uc/execute
                                  (ar/make-add-room-command))]
          (recur (rest actions)
                 (conj undo-list executed-command)))

        :undo-action
        (let [command-to-undo (first undo-list)]
          (uc/undo command-to-undo)
          (recur (rest actions)
                 (rest undo-list)))
        :TILT))))
```

```
(ns command.core-spec
  (:require [speclj.core :refer :all]
            [command.core :refer :all]
            [command.add-room-command :as ar]))

(describe "command"
  (with-stubs)
  (it "executes the command"
    (with-redefs [ar/add-room (stub :add-room {:return :a-room})
                  ar/delete-room (stub :delete-room)]
      (gui-app [:add-room-action :undo-action])
      (should-have-invoked :add-room)
      (should-have-invoked :delete-room {:with [:a-room]}))))
```

We create the undoable-command interface using defmulti functions. We implement that interface in the add-room-command namespace, and we simulate the GUI in the gui-app function of the command.core namespace.

The test stubs out the low-level functions of the add-room-command and makes sure they are called correctly. It calls the gui-app with a list of palette-actions.

The two methods of the add-room-command are polymorphically dispatched. That might not seem necessary for the execute case, since the gui-app has just created the add-room-command object. But were we to add more commands to this system, the polymorphic dispatch of execute would become more necessary.

The polymorphic dispatch of undo is clearly necessary, even in this small example, because by the time the :undo-action is received from the palette, we have no idea which command is being undone.

Here, again, we see that as we add complexity to the application, the canonical form of the GOF pattern begins to assert itself. With the single method command, we could get away with using plain old functions (function objects, really). But when the application needed a richer kind of command, we fell back on the GOF style.

COMPOSITE

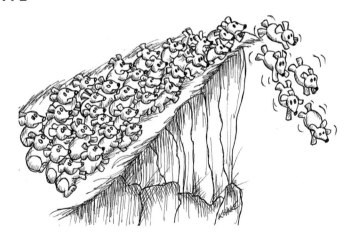

Composite continues the theme of semantic richness and syntactic triviality. It is a wonderful example of the old handle/body approach that

I first read about in one of Jim Coplien's books.[9] The structure of the Composite pattern is depicted in the UML in Figure 16.6.

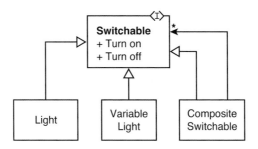

Figure 16.6. The Composite pattern

Our old friend the Switchable interface is implemented by our other old friends, the Light and the VariableLight. The CompositeSwitchable also implements Switchable and contains a list of other instances of Switchable.

The implementation of TurnOn and TurnOff in the CompositeSwitchable simply propagates calls of the same functions to all the instances in the list. Thus, when you call TurnOn on an instance of a CompositeSwitchable, it will call TurnOn on all the Switchable instances it contains.

In Java, we might implement CompositeSwitchable as follows:

```java
public class CompositeSwitchable implements Switchable {
  private List<Switchable> switchables = new ArrayList<>();

  public void addSwitchable(Switchable s) {
    switchables.add(s):
  }

  public void turnOn() {
    for (var s : switchables)
      s.turnOn();
  }
```

9. James O. Coplien, *Advanced C++ Programming Styles and Idioms* (Addison-Wesley, 1991).

```
  public void turnOff() {
    for (var s : switchables)
      s.turnOff();
  }
}
```

In a functional language, like Clojure, the temptation is to avoid the Composite pattern and simply use the map or doseq function, as you can see in the test below:

```
(ns composite-example.switchable)

(defmulti turn-on :type)
(defmulti turn-off :type)


_____


(ns composite-example.light
  (:require [composite-example.switchable :as s]))

(defn make-light [] {:type :light})

(defn turn-on-light [])
(defn turn-off-light [])

(defmethod s/turn-on :light [switchable]
  (turn-on-light))

(defmethod s/turn-off :light [switchable]
  (turn-off-light))


_____


(ns composite-example.variable-light
  (:require [composite-example.switchable :as s]))

(defn make-variable-light [] {:type :variable-light})

(defn set-light-intensity [intensity])
```

```
(defmethod s/turn-on :variable-light [switchable]
  (set-light-intensity 100))

(defmethod s/turn-off :variable-light [switchable]
  (set-light-intensity 0))
```

```
(ns composite-example.core-spec
  (:require [speclj.core :refer :all]
           [composite-example
            [light :as l]
            [variable-light :as v]
            [switchable :as s]]))

(describe "composite-switchable"
  (with-stubs)
  (it "turns all on"
    (with-redefs
      [l/turn-on-light (stub :turn-on-light)
       v/set-light-intensity (stub :set-light-intensity)]
      (let [switchables [(l/make-light) (v/make-variable-light)]]
        (doseq [s-able switchables] (s/turn-on s-able))
        (should-have-invoked :turn-on-light)
        (should-have-invoked :set-light-intensity
                             {:with [100]})))))
```

This accomplishes the goal of turning on all the lights, but it does so at the expense of externalizing the plurality of the lights. The point of the Composite pattern is to hide that plurality. So let's use the actual Composite pattern:

```
(ns composite-example.composite-switchable
  (:require [composite-example.switchable :as s]))

(defn make-composite-switchable []
  {:type :composite-switchable
   :switchables []})
```

```
(defn add [composite-switchable switchable]
  (update composite-switchable :switchables conj switchable))

(defmethod s/turn-on :composite-switchable [c-switchable]
  (doseq [s-able (:switchables c-switchable)]
    (s/turn-on s-able)))

(defmethod s/turn-off :composite-switchable [c-switchable]
  (doseq [s-able (:switchables c-switchable)]
    (s/turn-off s-able)))
```

```
(ns composite-example.core-spec
  (:require [speclj.core :refer :all]
           [composite-example
            [light :as l]
            [variable-light :as v]
            [switchable :as s]
            [composite-switchable :as cs]]))

(describe "composite-switchable"
  (with-stubs)
  (it "turns all on"
    (with-redefs
      [l/turn-on-light (stub :turn-on-light)
       v/set-light-intensity (stub :set-light-intensity)]
      (let [group (-> (cs/make-composite-switchable)
                      (cs/add (l/make-light))
                      (cs/add (v/make-variable-light)))]
        (s/turn-on group)
        (should-have-invoked :turn-on-light)
        (should-have-invoked :set-light-intensity
                          {:with [100]})))))
```

The composite-switchable implements the switchable interface. The add function is functional in that it returns a new composite-switchable with the argument added to the :switchables list. The turn-on and turn-off methods use doseq to iterate through the :switchables list and propagate the appropriate function call. Finally, the test creates the composite-switchable, adds a light and variable-light, and then invokes turn-on. And we see both lights turned on appropriately.

FUNCTIONAL?

At this point, you might be thinking that this is all well and good for objects that have side effects, like lights and variable lights. Indeed, the entire switchable interface is oriented around the side effect of turning something on or off. So is this pattern only for objects with side effects?

Let's consider a shape abstraction that looks like this:

```
(ns composite-example.shape
  (:require [clojure.spec.alpha :as s]))

(s/def ::type keyword?)
(s/def ::shape-type (s/keys :req [::type]))

(defmulti translate (fn [shape dx dy] (::type shape)))
(defmulti scale (fn [shape factor] (::type shape)))
```

It's a straightforward interface with two methods: translate and scale. I also added a type specification for safety's sake. (This would be a good time to brush up on the double-colon syntax of namespaced keywords.) Every shape will be a map that has a ::shape/type element.

The circle and square implementations are also pretty straightforward, including their type specifications:

```
(ns composite-example.circle
  (:require [clojure.spec.alpha :as s]
            [composite-example.shape :as shape]))

(s/def ::center (s/tuple number? number?))
(s/def ::radius number?)
```

```clojure
(s/def ::circle (s/keys :req [::shape/type
                              ::radius
                              ::center]))

(defn make-circle [center radius]
  {:post [(s/valid? ::circle %)]}
  {::shape/type ::circle
   ::center center
   ::radius radius})

(defmethod shape/translate ::circle [circle dx dy]
  {:pre [(s/valid? ::circle circle)
         (number? dx) (number? dy)]
   :post [(s/valid? ::circle %)]}
  (let [[x y] (::center circle)]
    (assoc circle ::center [(+ x dx) (+ y dy)])))

(defmethod shape/scale ::circle [circle factor]
  {:pre [(s/valid? ::circle circle)
         (number? factor)]
   :post [(s/valid? ::circle %)]}
  (let [radius (::radius circle)]
    (assoc circle ::radius (* radius factor))))
```

```clojure
(ns composite-example.square
  (:require [clojure.spec.alpha :as s]
            [composite-example.shape :as shape]))

(s/def ::top-left (s/tuple number? number?))
(s/def ::side number?)
(s/def ::square (s/keys :req [::shape/type
                             ::side
                             ::top-left]))

(defn make-square [top-left side]
  {:post [(s/valid? ::square %)]}
  {::shape/type ::square
```

```
    ::top-left top-left
    ::side side})

(defmethod shape/translate ::square [square dx dy]
  {:pre [(s/valid? ::square square)
         (number? dx) (number? dy)]
   :post [(s/assert ::square %)]}
  (let [[x y] (::top-left square)]
    (assoc square ::top-left [(+ x dx) (+ y dy)])))

(defmethod shape/scale ::square [square factor]
  {:pre [(s/valid? ::square square)
         (number? factor)]
   :post [(s/valid? ::square %)]}
  (let [side (::side square)]
    (assoc square ::side (* side factor))))
```

Notice the :pre and :post conditions on the methods. I'm using these to check the types coming into and going out of the functions. You could rightly be concerned about the runtime penalty of all those checks. I'd either globally disable[10] them, or strategically comment them out once I was happy that my types were being managed properly.

Notice that the translate and scale functions return new shape instances. They are fully functional in their behavior.

So, now let's look at composite-shape:

```
(ns composite-example.composite-shape
  (:require [clojure.spec.alpha :as s]
            [composite-example.shape :as shape]))

(s/def ::shapes (s/coll-of ::shape/shape-type))
(s/def ::composite-shape (s/keys :req [::shape/type
                                       ::shapes]))
```

---

10. There is a compile-time switch that disables all asserts, including :pre and :post.

```
(defn make []
  {:post [(s/assert ::composite-shape %)]}
  {::shape/type ::composite-shape
   ::shapes []})

(defn add [cs shape]
  {:pre [(s/valid? ::composite-shape cs)
         (s/valid? ::shape/shape-type shape)]
   :post [(s/valid? ::composite-shape %)]}
  (update cs ::shapes conj shape))

(defmethod shape/translate ::composite-shape [cs dx dy]
  {:pre [(s/valid? ::composite-shape cs)
         (number? dx) (number? dy)]
   :post [(s/valid? ::composite-shape %)]}
  (let [translated-shapes (map #(shape/translate % dx dy)
                              (::shapes cs))]
    (assoc cs ::shapes translated-shapes)))

(defmethod shape/scale ::composite-shape [cs factor]
  {:pre [(s/valid? ::composite-shape cs)
         (number? factor)]
   :post [(s/valid? ::composite-shape %)]}
  (let [scaled-shapes (map #(shape/scale % factor)
                          (::shapes cs))]
    (assoc cs ::shapes scaled-shapes)))
```

We've seen this pattern before in the light/variable-light example. This time, however, the composite-shape returns a new composite-shape with the new shape instances. And so it is functional.

For those of you who are curious, here are the tests I used:

```
(ns composite-example.core-spec
  (:require [speclj.core :refer :all]
            [composite-example
```

```
                        [square :as square]
                        [shape :as shape]
                        [circle :as circle]
                        [composite-shape :as cs]]]))

    (describe "square"
      (it "translates"
        (let [s (square/make-square [3 4] 1)
              translated-square (shape/translate s 1 1)]
          (should= [4 5] (::square/top-left translated-square))
          (should= 1 (::square/side translated-square))))

      (it "scales"
        (let [s (square/make-square [1 2] 2)
              scaled-square (shape/scale s 5)]
          (should= [1 2] (::square/top-left scaled-square))
          (should= 10 (::square/side scaled-square)))))

    (describe "circle"
      (it "translates"
        (let [c (circle/make-circle [3 4] 10)
              translated-circle (shape/translate c 2 3)]
          (should= [5 7] (::circle/center translated-circle))
          (should= 10 (::circle/radius translated-circle))))

      (it "scales"
        (let [c (circle/make-circle [1 2] 2)
              scaled-circle (shape/scale c 5)]
          (should= [1 2] (::circle/center scaled-circle))
          (should= 10 (::circle/radius scaled-circle)))))

    (describe "composite shape"
      (it "translates"
        (let [cs (-> (cs/make)
                     (cs/add (square/make-square [0 0] 1))
```

```
                  (cs/add (circle/make-circle [10 10] 10)))
            translated-cs (shape/translate cs 3 4)]
      (should= #{{::shape/type ::square/square
                  ::square/top-left [3 4]
                  ::square/side 1}
                 {::shape/type ::circle/circle
                  ::circle/center [13 14]
                  ::circle/radius 10}}
              (set (::cs/shapes translated-cs)))))

  (it "scales"
    (let [cs (-> (cs/make)
                 (cs/add (square/make-square [0 0] 1))
                 (cs/add (circle/make-circle [10 10] 10)))
          scaled-cs (shape/scale cs 12)]
      (should= #{{::shape/type ::square/square
                  ::square/top-left [0 0]
                  ::square/side 12}
                 {::shape/type ::circle/circle
                  ::circle/center [10 10]
                  ::circle/radius 120}}
              (set (::cs/shapes scaled-cs))))))
```

You may have noticed that as we proceed in these chapters, I'm using more of the nuanced features of Clojure. This is intentional. I expect that as you read this book, you will have a good Clojure reference nearby, so I'm giving you a series of opportunities to look things up and get more familiar with the language.

As we have seen, Composite is yet another GOF pattern that fits well into the functional world. Once we start taking advantage of polymorphic dispatch, with either vtables, multi-methods, or protocol/record structures, the GOF patterns fit right in, more or less as the GOF described them.

DECORATOR

Yet another of the handle/body patterns is *Decorator*. The Decorator pattern is a way to add functionality to a type model without directly modifying the type model.

For example, let's continue with our shape project. We have a shape type model that supports circle and square subtypes. Within that type model, so long as it conforms to the LSP, we can translate and scale any of the subtypes of shape without knowing the explicit subtype we are manipulating.

Now let's add a new, optional functionality: a journaled-shape. A journaled-shape is a shape that remembers the operations that have been performed on it since its creation. We want to be able to keep journals on squares and circles; but only certain squares and circles. We don't want every circle and square to be journaled, because the memory and processing penalty is too high.

Now, of course, we could implement this by adding a :journaled? flag to the shape abstraction and then putting an if statement in the circle and square implementations. But that's messy. What we really want is a way to add this functionality without changing the shape abstraction or any of its subtypes, including `circle`, `square`, and `composite-shape` (the OCP).

Enter the Decorator pattern. The UML looks like Figure 16.7.

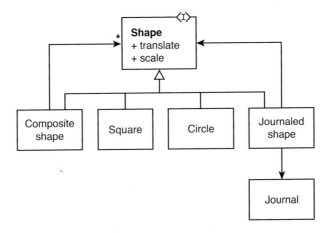

Figure 16.7. The Decorator pattern

I've included the `composite-shape` because it is currently part of the `shape` type model. The `journaled-shape` is the Decorator. The `journaled-shape` derives from `shape` and holds a reference to a `shape`. When `translate` or `scale` is called on a `journaled-shape` it creates an entry in the journal and then delegates the call to the contained shape.

Here's the Clojure implementation:

```
(ns decorator-example.journaled-shape
  (:require [decorator-example.shape :as shape]
            [clojure.spec.alpha :as s]))

(s/def ::journal-entry
      (s/or :translate (s/tuple #{:translate}[11] number? number?)
            :scale (s/tuple #{:scale} number?)))
```

---

11. A set can be used as a function that tests for membership.

```
(s/def ::journal (s/coll-of ::journal-entry))
(s/def ::shape ::shape/shape-type)
(s/def ::journaled-shape (s/and
                              (s/keys :req [::shape/type
                                            ::journal
                                            ::shape])
                          #(= ::journaled-shape
                              (::shape/type %))))

(defn make [shape]
  {:post [(s/valid? ::journaled-shape %)]}
  {::shape/type ::journaled-shape
   ::journal []
   ::shape shape})

(defmethod shape/translate ::journaled-shape [js dx dy]
  {:pre [(s/valid? ::journaled-shape js)
         (number? dx) (number? dy)]
   :post [(s/valid? ::journaled-shape %)]}
  (-> js (update ::journal conj [:translate dx dy])
     (assoc ::shape (shape/translate (::shape js) dx dy))))

(defmethod shape/scale ::journaled-shape [js factor]
  {:pre [(s/valid? ::journaled-shape js)
         (number? factor)]
   :post [(s/valid? ::journaled-shape %)]}
  (-> js (update ::journal conj [:scale factor])
     (assoc ::shape (shape/scale (::shape js) factor))))
```

The ::journaled-shape object has ::shape and ::journal fields. The ::journal field is a collection of ::journal-entry tuples that are of the form [:translate dx dy] or [:scale factor] where dx, dy, and factor are numbers. The ::shape field must contain a valid shape.

The make constructor creates a valid journaled-shape (as checked by the :post condition).

The translate and scale functions add the appropriate journal entry to the ::journal and then delegate their respective functions to the ::shape, returning a new journaled-shape with the updated ::journal and the modified ::shape.

Here's the test. I only tested the journaled-shape with a square because if it works for square, it will work for every shape:

```
(describe "journaled shape decorator"
  (it "journals scale and translate operations"
    (let [jsd (-> (js/make (square/make-square [0 0] 1))
                  (shape/translate 2 3)
                  (shape/scale 5))]
      (should= [[:translate 2 3] [:scale 5]]
               (::js/journal jsd))
      (should= {::shape/type ::square/square
                ::square/top-left [2 3]
                ::square/side 5}
               (::js/shape jsd)))))
```

We make a journaled-shape with a square in it. We translate and scale it, and then we make sure the ::journal has recorded the translate and scale calls and that the square has the translated and scaled values.

Once again, I've included the type specifications just to give you a challenge and to demonstrate how they can be used. Frankly, however, I think the tests do an adequate job of checking the types; so in real life, I doubt I would use such detailed type specifications for this kind of small problem. On the other hand, it is kind of nice to see the types all spelled out like that.

In any case, notice that the journaled-shape Decorator will work for any shape, including a composite-shape. So we have effectively added a new functionality to the type model without making any changes to the existing element of that type model. That's the OCP at work.

VISITOR

Oh, no! Not the. . . *Visitor*! Yes, we're going to investigate the much-maligned Visitor pattern. Visitor is not one of the handle/body patterns. It has its own unique structure that, as we'll see, is complicated by certain language choices.

The purpose of the Visitor pattern is similar to that of the Decorator pattern. We want to add a new function to an existing type model without changing that type model (the OCP). The Decorator is appropriate when the new function is independent of the other subtypes in the type model. Look back at the `journaled-shape` to verify this constraint. The journaling was independent of whether the contained shape was a `circle` or a `square`. The `journaled-shape` Decorator never knew the subtype of the contained `shape`.

We use the Visitor pattern when the function we wish to add is *dependent* upon the subtypes in the type model.

So, for example, what if we wanted to add a function to our shape abstraction for converting the shape to a string for serialization purposes? We could add a `to-string` function to the `shape` interface. Easy-peasy.

But wait! What if one of our customers wanted the shapes in XML? I suppose we could add a `to-xml` function as well as the `to-string` function.

But, wait again! What if another of our customers wanted the shapes in JSON, and yet another wanted them in YAML, and. . .

At some point, you realize that there is no end to these data formats and that customers are going to continually ask you for more and more and more. And you don't want to pollute the shape interface with all those horrible methods.

The Visitor pattern gives us a way out of this dilemma. The UML looks something like Figure 16.8.

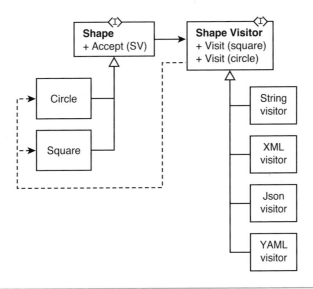

Figure 16.8. The Visitor pattern

The first thing I want to point out is the 90-degree rotation of the Shape subtypes into methods in the ShapeVisitor. Each of the subtypes, Square and Circle, is the type of the argument of a visit function in the ShapeVisitor. I call the subtype-to-method transformation a 90-degree rotation because it pleases some neurons in my hindbrain.

We see our Shape abstraction and all its subtypes over on the left. On the right, we see the ShapeVisitor hierarchy. The pattern adds the accept function to the Shape interface. That function takes a single argument, which is a ShapeVisitor. This violates the OCP, but only once.

In Java, the implementation of the accept function is trivial:

```
void accept(ShapeVisitor v) {
  v.visit(this);
}
```

If you've never studied the Visitor pattern before, then this might be a little difficult to follow. So take your time and walk through this with me.

Let's say we want a JSON string for some Shape we've got. In Java, or C++ or other similar languages, here's how we'd get it:

```
Shape s = // get a shape without knowing the subtype
ShapeVisitor v = new JsonVisitor();
s.accept(v);
String json = v.getJson();
```

We get a Shape object from somewhere. We create the JsonVisitor. We pass the JsonVisitor to our Shape using the accept method. The accept method polymorphically dispatches to the proper subtype of Shape—let's say it's a Square. The accept method of Square calls visit(this) on the JsonVisitor. The type of this is Square, so the visit(Square s) function of the JsonVisitor is called. That function generates the JSON string for the Square and saves it in a member variable of the JsonVisitor. The getJson() function returns the contents of that member variable.

You may have to read that over a few times to follow it. This is a technique called *double-dispatch*. The first dispatch deploys to the subtype of the Shape, so now we know the type of that subtype. The second dispatch deploys to the proper subtype of the visitor passing along the true type of the subtype.

If you followed all of that, you can see that each of the derivatives of the ShapeVisitor is a new "method" of the Shape type model, but the only thing we had to add to Shape was the accept method. So ~(the OCP). You should also now understand why we couldn't use a Decorator. The new functions depend strongly on the subtypes. You can't make a JSON string for a Square if you don't know it's a Square.

Now, I told you all that so I could tell you this. All that horrible complexity is there because of a language constraint. Yes, yes. . . this is where all those design pattern naysayers actually do have a point. The Visitor pattern is as complex as it is because of a particular language feature.

What feature is that? *Closed classes.*

To Close, or to Clojure?

In languages like C++ and Java, we create classes that are *closed*. What that means is that we cannot add a new method to a class by putting that new method's declaration in a new source file. If we want to add a new method to a class, in a closed language, we have to open the source file of that class and add the method *within* the definition of that class.

Clojure does not have this constraint. Neither, to some extent, does C#. Indeed, many languages allow you to add methods to classes without changing the source file that contains the declaration of those classes.

The reason Clojure does not have this constraint is that classes are not a feature of the language. We create them by convention, not by syntax.

So, wait, does that mean we don't need the Decorator or Visitor pattern in Clojure? No, it doesn't mean that at all. Indeed, as we saw, we still need the Decorator in its GOF form. How else would you do the journaled-shape?

However, the GOF form of the Visitor is not necessary in languages that have open classes. Or rather, some of the details of the GOF form are not necessary.

So let me show you this particular Visitor in Clojure. First, the tests:

```
(ns visitor-example.core-spec
  (:require [speclj.core :refer :all]
            [visitor-example
             [square :as square]
             [json-shape-visitor :as jv]
             [circle :as circle]]))

(describe "shape-visitor"
  (it "makes json square"
    (should= "{\"top-left\": [0,0], \"side\": 1}"
             (jv/to-json (square/make [0 0] 1))))

  (it "makes json circle"
    (should= "{\"center\": [3,4], \"radius\": 1}"
             (jv/to-json (circle/make [3 4] 1)))))
```

This shouldn't be too surprising; although you should pay special attention to the source code dependencies. This test needs pretty much everything.

Now let's remember what the shape type model looks like. Just to keep things simple, I've removed all the clojure.spec type specifications:

```
(ns visitor-example.shape)

(defmulti translate (fn [shape dx dy] (::type shape)))
(defmulti scale (fn [shape factor] (::type shape)))
```

```
(ns visitor-example.square
  (:require
    [visitor-example.shape :as shape]))

(defn make [top-left side]
  {::shape/type ::square
```

```
    ::top-left top-left
    ::side side})

(defmethod shape/translate ::square [square dx dy]
  (let [[x y] (::top-left square)]
    (assoc square ::top-left [(+ x dx) (+ y dy)])))

(defmethod shape/scale ::square [square factor]
  (let [side (::side square)]
    (assoc square ::side (* side factor))))
```

```
(ns visitor-example.circle
  (:require
    [visitor-example.shape :as shape]))

(defn make [center radius]
  {::shape/type ::circle
   ::center center
   ::radius radius})

(defmethod shape/translate ::circle [circle dx dy]
  (let [[x y] (::center circle)]
    (assoc circle ::center [(+ x dx) (+ y dy)])))

(defmethod shape/scale ::circle [circle factor]
  (let [radius (::radius circle)]
    (assoc circle ::radius (* radius factor))))
```

That should all look pretty familiar. Now for the `json-shape-visitor`:

```
(ns visitor-example.json-shape-visitor
  (:require [visitor-example
             [shape :as shape]
             [circle :as circle]
             [square :as square]]))

(defmulti to-json ::shape/type)
```

```
(defmethod to-json ::square/square [square]
  (let [{:keys [::square/top-left¹² ::square/side]} square
        [x y] top-left]
    (format "{\"top-left\": [%s,%s], \"side\": %s}" x y side)))

(defmethod to-json ::circle/circle [circle]
  (let [{:keys [::circle/center ::circle/radius]} circle
        [x y] center]
    (format "{\"center\": [%s,%s], \"radius\": %s}" x y radius)))
```

Look at this carefully. That `defmulti` in the `json-shape-visitor` adds the `to-json` method directly into the `shape` type model. You probably understand it well enough at this point; but do you see *why* this is a Visitor?

Can you see the 90-degree rotation from subtypes to functions?

Just like the Java version of the Visitor, all the subtypes for the `to-json` operation are gathered into the `json-shape-visitor` module.

If you follow all the source code dependencies and compare them to the UML diagram, you'll see that they are all there. The only things missing are the `ShapeVisitor` interface and the dual dispatch. Those were just there to get around the fact that languages like C++ and Java have closed classes.

This tells us that the GOF got this pattern a bit wrong. The dual dispatch is ancillary to the Visitor pattern and is only necessary in languages with closed classes.

THE 90-DEGREE PROBLEM

But wait. That 90-degree rotation has a problem. Whenever you have a module that has methods for each of the subtypes of some type model, that module must be changed whenever the type model is changed. For example, if we were to add a `triangle` to our shape hierarchy, our

---

12. The namespaced keyword *destructuring* creates a local var named for the local part of the key—
    top-left in this case.

`json-shape-visitor` would need a `::triangle/triangle` defmethod of `to-json`. This violates the OCP.

This is also a problem because it violates the *Dependency Rule* of *Clean Architecture*[13] by forcing higher-level modules to have source code dependencies upon lower-level modules across an architectural boundary.[14] This is shown in the UML in Figure 16.9.

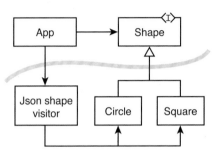

Figure 16.9. Violation of the Dependency Rule

In general, we want the `shape` implementations to be plug-ins to the `App`. But the `json-shape-visitor` thwarts that because the only way for our `App` to emit JSON is to invoke the `json-shape-visitor`, which depends directly on `circle` and `square`.

In Java, C#, and C++, we can solve this by using an *abstract factory*, which the `App` could use to instantiate the `visitor` object without depending directly upon it.

In Clojure, we have another—and much better—option. We can just separate the interface of the `json-shape-visitor` from its implementation as follows:

```
(ns visitor-example.json-shape-visitor
  (:require [visitor-example
            [shape :as shape]]))
```

---

13. Robert C. Martin, *Clean Architecture* (Pearson, 2017), p. 203.

14. Martin, *Clean Architecture*, p. 159.

```
(defmulti to-json ::shape/type)
```

_____

```
(ns visitor-example.json-shape-visitor-implementation
  (:require [visitor-example
              [json-shape-visitor :as v]
              [circle :as circle]
              [square :as square]]))

(defmethod v/to-json ::square/square [square]
  (let [{:keys [::square/top-left ::square/side]} square
        [x y] top-left]
    (format "{\"top-left\": [%s,%s], \"side\": %s}" x y side)))

(defmethod v/to-json ::circle/circle [circle]
  (let [{:keys [::circle/center ::circle/radius]} circle
        [x y] center]
    (format "{\"center\": [%s,%s], \"radius\": %s}" x y radius)))
```

The trick to this is to make sure that the json-shape-visitor-implementation module is required by main so that the defmethods are properly registered with the defmulti:

```
(ns visitor-example.main
  (:require [visitor-example
              [json-shape-visitor-implementation]]))
```

Typically, main is invoked before any part of the application, and thus, the application does not have a source code dependency on main.[15] Unfortunately, my tests do not have access to a true main, so the dependency has to be included:

```
(ns visitor-example.core-spec
  (:require [speclj.core :refer :all]
              [visitor-example
```

_____

15. Martin, *Clean Architecture*, p. 231.

```
          [square :as square]
          [json-shape-visitor :as jv]
          [circle :as circle]
          [main]]]))

(describe "shape-visitor"
  (it "makes json square"
    (should= "{\"top-left\": [0,0], \"side\": 1}"
             (jv/to-json (square/make [0 0] 1))))

  (it "makes json circle"
    (should= "{\"center\": [3,4], \"radius\": 1}"
             (jv/to-json (circle/make [3 4] 1)))))
```

So there it is, a functional, and architecturally competent, Visitor in
Clojure. As the UML in Figure 16.10 shows, all the dependencies cross
the architectural boundary pointing to the higher-level (abstract) side of
that boundary. Hallelujah!

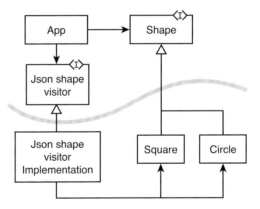

Figure 16.10. Functional and architecturally competent Visitor

So the Visitor pattern is a case where the GOF form was polluted by the
language constraints of the day. In 1995, when the GOF book was
published, closed classes were considered a necessary attribute of statically
typed languages and were therefore almost ubiquitous.

ABSTRACT FACTORY

The DIP advises us to avoid source code dependencies upon things that are both volatile and concrete. So we create abstract structures and try to route our dependencies upon them. However, when we create instances of objects, we often have to violate that advice; and this can cause architectural difficulties, as shown by the UML in Figure 16.11.

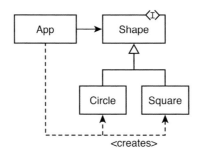

Figure 16.11. DIP violation due to creation

The App in Figure 16.11 uses the Shape interface. Everything it needs to do can be done through that interface, with one exception. The App must create instances of the Circle and Square derivatives; and that forces the App to hang source code dependencies upon the corresponding modules.

We've actually seen this situation in our previous examples. Consider, for example, the code from the tests from the `visitor-example` earlier in this chapter. Notice that the test requires source code dependencies upon `square` and `circle` for the sole purpose of calling those `make` functions:

```
(ns visitor-example.core-spec
  (:require [speclj.core :refer :all]
            [visitor-example
             [square :as square]
             [json-shape-visitor :as jv]
             [circle :as circle]]))

(describe "shape-visitor"
  (it "makes json square"
    (should= "{\"top-left\": [0,0], \"side\": 1}"
             (jv/to-json (square/make [0 0] 1))))

  (it "makes json circle"
    (should= "{\"center\": [3,4], \"radius\": 1}"
             (jv/to-json (circle/make [3 4] 1)))))
```

Perhaps this seems a small price to pay. But if, as shown in Figure 16.12, we add an architectural boundary to that UML diagram, the true cost becomes clear.

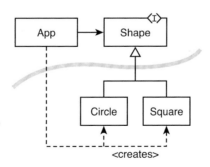

Figure 16.12. Violation of the Dependency Rule across the architectural boundary

Here we can see that the *Dependency Rule* of *Clean Architecture*[16] has been violated by that <creates> dependency. That rule states that all source code dependencies that cross an architectural boundary must point toward the higher-level side of that boundary. The Circle and Square modules are low-level details that are plug-ins to the App. Thus, to preserve the architecture, we need to somehow deal with those <creates> dependencies.

The *Abstract Factory* pattern provides a good solution. It looks like Figure 16.13.

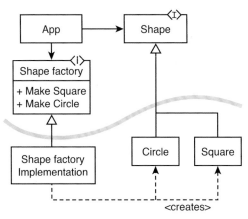

Figure 16.13.   Abstract Factory pattern resolves Dependency Rule

All the source code dependencies that cross the boundary now point toward the higher-level side, so the Dependency Rule violation has been resolved. The Circle and Square can still be independent plug-ins to the App. The App can still create Circle and Square instances but indirectly through the ShapeFactory interface, which inverts the source code dependency (the DIP).

This is easy to implement in Clojure. All we need is the shape-factory interface and its implementation:

```
(ns abstract-factory-example.shape-factory)

(defmulti make-circle
  (fn [factory center radius] (::type factory)))
```

---

16. Robert C. Martin, *Clean Architecture* (Pearson, 2017).

```
(defmulti make-square
  (fn [factory top-left side] (::type factory)))
```

_____

```
(ns abstract-factory-example.shape-factory-implementation
  (:require [abstract-factory-example
              [shape-factory :as factory]
              [square :as square]
              [circle :as circle]]))

(defn make []
  {::factory/type ::implementation})

(defmethod factory/make-square ::implementation
  [factory top-left side]
  (square/make top-left side))

(defmethod factory/make-circle ::implementation
  [factory center radius]
  (circle/make center radius))
```

And with that, we can write a test that simulates our App:

```
(ns abstract-factory-example.core-spec
  (:require [speclj.core :refer :all]
            [abstract-factory-example
              [shape :as shape]
              [shape-factory :as factory]
              [main :as main]]))

(describe "Shape Factory"
  (before-all (main/init))
  (it "creates a square"
    (let [square (factory/make-square
                   @main/shape-factory
                   [100 100] 10)]
      (should= "Square top-left: [100,100] side: 10"
               (shape/to-string square)))))
```

```
(it "creates a circle"
    (let [circle (factory/make-circle
                     @main/shape-factory
                     [100 100] 10)]
        (should= "Circle center: [100,100] radius: 10"
                 (shape/to-string circle)))))
```

The first thing to notice about this test is that it has no source file dependencies on `circle` or `square`. It depends only on the two interfaces: `shape` and `shape-factory`. That was our architectural goal.

But what is that `main` dependency? Do you see the `(before-all (main/init))` line at the start of the test? That tells the test runner to call `(main/init)` before any of the tests. This simulates the `main` module initializing everything before starting the App.

Here's `main`:

```
(ns abstract-factory-example.main
   (:require [abstract-factory-example
             [shape-factory-implementation :as imp]]))

(def shape-factory (atom nil))

(defn init[]
   (reset! shape-factory (imp/make)))
```

Oh, HO! We've got a global atom named `shape-factory`! And that atom is being initialized to the `shape-factory-implementation` by the `init` function.

So, looking back at the test, we see that the `make-circle` and `make-square` methods were passing the dereferenced atom.

Setting a global like this is a pretty common strategy for dealing with factories. The main program creates the concrete factory implementations and then loads it into a global that everyone can access. In a statically typed language, that global would have the type of the interface ShapeFactory. In dynamically typed languages, no such type declaration is required.

90 Degrees Again

Look at that UML diagram in Figure 16.13 again. Do you see the 90-degree rotation in the ShapeFactory? You can see it in the shape-factory code too. The ShapeFactory (and the shape-factory) have methods that correspond to the subtypes of Shape.

The problem that this caused for Visitor is also present here, although in a slightly different form. Whenever a new subtype of shape is added, the shape-factory must be modified. That violates the OCP because we must modify a module on the high-level side of the architectural boundary. If the OCP matters at all, it matters most especially across such boundaries. Study that UML diagram until you see what I mean.

We can resolve this problem by replacing the 90-degree rotation with a single method that takes an opaque token. Something like this:

```
(ns abstract-factory-example.shape-factory)

(defmulti make (fn [factory type & args] (::type factory)))
```

```
(ns abstract-factory-example.shape-factory-implementation
  (:require [abstract-factory-example
             [shape-factory :as factory]
             [square :as square]
             [circle :as circle]]))

(defn make []
  {::factory/type ::implementation})

(defmethod factory/make ::implementation
```

```clojure
  [factory type & args]
  (condp = type
    :square (apply square/make args)
    :circle (apply circle/make args)))
```

```clojure
(ns abstract-factory-example.core-spec
  (:require [speclj.core :refer :all]
            [abstract-factory-example
             [shape :as shape]
             [shape-factory :as factory]
             [main :as main]]))

(describe "Shape Factory"
  (before-all (main/init))
  (it "creates a square"
    (let [square (factory/make
                   @main/shape-factory
                   :square
                   [100 100] 10)]
      (should= "Square top-left: [100,100] side: 10"
               (shape/to-string square)))))

  (it "creates a circle"
    (let [circle (factory/make
                   @main/shape-factory
                   :circle
                   [100 100] 10)]
      (should= "Circle center: [100,100] radius: 10"
               (shape/to-string circle)))))
```

Notice that the argument passed into shape-factory/make is opaque. That is, it is not defined by any of the other modules, including—and especially—the square and circle modules. The :square and :circle keywords are not namespaced, nor are they declared anywhere. They are simply opaque values that happen to have names. I might as well have used 1 for square and 2 for circle, or used "square" and "circle" strings.

This opacity is the key to this solution. If we ever need to add a `triangle` subtype, nothing above the boundary line will have to change (the OCP).

TYPE SAFETY?

In a statically typed language, like Java, this technique abandons type safety. Opaque values cannot be type safe. There is no way, for example, to use an `enum` in Java to solve this issue.

In Clojure, we aren't concerned about static type safety, but what about dynamic type specifications? We're out of luck there too. There is no way to gain an advantage by using `clojure.spec` since all errors, either with or without `clojure.spec`, will be runtime errors.

For example, nothing stops me from calling `shape-factory/make` with `:sqare` (intentionally misspelled). The `condp` in `shape-factory-implementation` will simply throw an exception. If I were to set up some type constraint in `clojure.spec` forcing the `type` argument of `shape-factory/make` to be either `:square` or `:circle`, it would still just throw a runtime exception.

There is no escape from this in any language. Whether in Java, C++, Ruby, Clojure, or C#, if you want to maintain the OCP across architectural boundaries (and you usually do), then at some point across that boundary you are going to have to abandon type safety and rely on runtime exceptions. This is just simply software physics.

CONCLUSION

I'll leave the rest of the GOF patterns, and any other patterns you might be familiar with, as an exercise. By now, I'm pretty sure you understand that functional languages that have facilities similar to Clojure are as OO as Java, C#, Ruby, and Python, and that the patterns described in the GOF book generally apply so long as the constraint of immutability is enforced.

And as for *Singleton*: Just create one.

POSTSCRIPT: OO POISON?

I thought it wise to revisit here my hope and goal from the introduction. By now, it should be clear that functional programming and OOP are compatible and mutually beneficial styles.

The design pattern examples that I have presented so far are not unusual. Clojure programmers frequently use defmulti and defmethod to express polymorphism. They typically use maps to express encapsulated data structures (i.e., objects). They often even build constructors for those objects. They might not realize it, but they are building OO programs.

What might seem unusual to some functional programmers, and even to some Clojure programmers, is the way I have organized the source files and namespaces. That organization is so reminiscent of Java, C++, C#, Ruby, and even Python that it screams "OO" to folks who'd thought that they'd left OO behind many long years ago.

It should be very clear by now that Clojure is every bit as object oriented as Java, C++, C#, Python, and Ruby. Clojure is also as functional as F#, Scala, Elixir, and (dare I say it?) Haskell.

Let's examine the OO claim just a bit.

Clojure does not have inheritance; but it does have at least three very effective mechanisms of polymorphism. At least two of those mechanisms support open classes.

Clojure does not have `public/private/protected` modifiers; but it does have namespaced keywords and dynamic type specification, which allows encapsulation to be strongly expressed and dynamically, if not statically, enforced. Clojure also has private functions (created with `defn-`) that can only be seen within the containing source file.

Clojure supports, but does not enforce, a source file and namespace structure that affords the same architectural partitioning we find so familiar in any of the (so-called) enterprise languages.

And so Clojure is an OO/functional[17] language. As are, to one extent or another, languages like Scala, Elixir, and F#, to name just a few. And, since that is true, the OO mindset is still a perfectly valid way of modeling applications in those languages.

We can still describe our functional programs using interfaces and classes, types and subtypes. We can still partition the source files and manage their dependencies in order to create robust, independently deployable and independently developable architectures. Nothing in that regard has changed at all.

What *has* changed is the extra constraint that functional programming places upon us, which is the elimination, or at least the strong sequestration,

---

17. OOFL? FOOL? Hmm, perhaps we should avoid the acronyms.

of side effects. Our classes and modules will strongly prefer immutable, as opposed to mutable, objects. But they are still objects, and they can still be expressed and organized as classes that implement interfaces.

And that means that the vast majority of the design principles and design patterns that we found so helpful in OO languages still apply, and are still useful, in functional languages like Clojure and others.

VI

CASE STUDY

17 WA-TOR

In the final chapter of this book, you and I are going to play a little game about a little game. The little game our little game will be about is called *Wa-Tor*; a simple little cellular automaton described by A. K. Dewdney in the December 1984 issue of *Scientific American*.[1] The game you and I are going to play is to *pretend* that Wa-Tor is an enterprise-level application requiring significant effort in architecture and design.

I mean, honestly, I could hack together Wa-Tor in a few hours and walk away happy. But for this chapter, I want us to really think about the issues as though this were a 50 mega line of code (LOC) monster.

So what is Wa-Tor?[2] The Wikipedia article referenced in the footnote should give you all the information you need to understand it in the required depth (which is not much). But essentially, Wa-Tor is a typical predator/prey simulation using fish and sharks. The fish move around randomly and occasionally reproduce. The sharks also move around randomly but will eat a fish if one is adjacent. Sharks will occasionally reproduce if they eat enough fish. Sharks will die if they do not eat a fish before they starve.

The world that the fish and sharks live in has no land; it's all water. Moreover, the top meets the bottom and the left meets the right, so the world is topologically a torus. Thus, Wa-Tor stands for WAter TORus.

We'll talk more about the features of the program later. For the moment, what are the architectural and design considerations?

Let's start with the basics. SRP. Who are the actors—whom do we want to keep separate?

In most large enterprise systems, there are many different actors. But in this little app, there are only two to worry about. There are the user experience (UX) designers, who will undoubtedly change their minds a dozen or so

---

1. Alas, *SciAm*, I knew it well. . .

2. https://en.wikipedia.org/wiki/Wa-Tor

times before they actually like what they see on the screen. And then there are the modelers who will also likely fiddle with the internal shark/fish behavior and might possibly add more animals to the mix.

So we start out with Figure 17.1, a very obvious and very traditional partitioning.

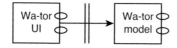

Figure 17.1. The obvious and traditional partitioning of Wa-Tor

The WatorUI component is lower level[3] than the WatorModel component. According to the Dependency Rule, this means that the source code dependencies must cross the architectural boundary pointing toward the WatorModel. Because of this, the WatorUI will be a plug-in to the WatorModel.

There are only two components[4] and one boundary in this partitioning so far. In larger systems, we would see many more boundaries and many more components within each.

Let's focus on the model first.[5] What kinds of classes are we going to need?

Yes, I said classes. We may be using a functional language, but if you've learned anything in this book so far, it is that functional design and OO design are two sides of the same coin.

So, at first blush, I think the object model looks something like Figure 17.2.

---

3. The definition of high and low "level" that I'm using here is "distance from I/O." See Robert C. Martin, *Clean Architecture* (Pearson, 2017), p. 183.

4. See Martin, *Clean Architecture*, p. 93.

5. http://wiki.c2.com/?ModelFirst

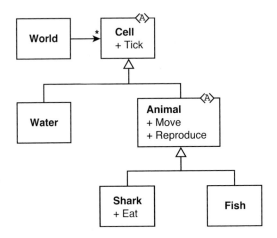

Figure 17.2.   Initial object model of Wa-Tor

The world contains a bunch of cells. Each cell can process a tick[6] of time. I guessed that cell is abstract rather than an interface because I expect that there will be concrete functions at this level.

Each cell can be water, or an animal that can move and reproduce. The two possible subtypes of animal are fish and sharks that can eat.

Let's see if we can code this. No tests yet, because we haven't defined any behavior:

```
(ns wator.cell)

(defmulti tick ::type)
```

```
(ns wator.water
  (:require [wator
             [cell :as cell]]))

(defn make [] {::cell/type ::water})
```

---

6. Dewdney called these *chronons*.

```
(defmethod cell/tick ::water [water]
  )
```

_____

```
(ns wator.animal)

(defmulti move ::type)
(defmulti reproduce ::type)

(defn tick [animal]
  )
```

_____

```
(ns wator.fish
  (:require [wator
            [cell :as cell]
            [animal :as animal]]))

(defn make [] {::cell/type ::fish})

(defmethod cell/tick ::fish [fish]
  (animal/tick fish)
  )

(defmethod animal/move ::fish [fish]
  )

(defmethod animal/reproduce ::fish [fish]
  )
```

_____

```
(ns wator.shark
  (:require [wator
            [cell :as cell]
            [animal :as animal]]))
```

```
(defmethod cell/tick ::shark [shark]
  (animal/tick shark)
  )

(defmethod animal/move ::shark [shark]
  )

(defmethod animal/reproduce ::shark [shark]
  )

(defn eat [shark]
  )
```

This looks pretty standard. The cell module looks like an interface so far. The water module implements it trivially. The dangling parentheses are there to remind me that I want to add something to that function.

The animal module *does not* implement tick, but it does have a function named tick that can be called by its subtypes. I put this in as a guess. It's a bit of hubris, I suppose; but I have a feeling that it'll be necessary.[7]

The fish trivially implements both the cell and animal. This actually looks more like multiple inheritance than the UML diagram. On the other hand, there's no inheritance anywhere in this code, so. . .

Finally, shark also trivially implements both cell and animal and adds its own eat function.

I didn't code the world because I don't know enough to even start. However, there are a few issues that I think the world will have to deal with. We don't want the world to depend upon the GUI, and yet the GUI is going to put a lot of constraints on the world. For example, it seems to me that the GUI is going to tell us the size of the world. I also think that since the GUI is likely to repaint the screen N times per second, the GUI will define *time*.

---

7. Yeah, I know. You Aren't Gonna Need It (YAGNI). Well, we'll see.

But let's set all that aside for the time being. Enough of this up-front design. Let's see if we can code some of the behavior.

What is the behavior of water? We ask our modelers, and they tell us that a water cell will randomly evolve into a fish cell if given enough time. Here's my implementation of that rule:

```
(ns wator.core-spec
  (:require [speclj.core :refer :all]
            [wator
             [cell :as cell]
             [water :as water]
             [fish :as fish]]))

(describe "Wator"
  (with-stubs)
  (context "Water"
    (it "usually remains water"
        (with-redefs [rand (stub :rand {:return 0.0})]
          (let [water (water/make)
                evolved (cell/tick water)]
            (should= ::water/water (::cell/type evolved)))))

    (it "occasionally evolves into a fish"
      (with-redefs [rand (stub :rand {:return 1.0})]
        (let [water (water/make)
              evolved (cell/tick water)]
          (should= ::fish/fish (::cell/type evolved)))))))
```

———

```
(ns wator.water
  (:require [wator
             [cell :as cell]
             [fish :as fish]
             [config :as config]]))

(defn make [] {::cell/type ::water})
```

```
(defmethod cell/tick ::water [water]
  (if (> (rand) config/water-evolution-rate)
    (fish/make)
    water))
```

———

```
(ns wator.config)

(def water-evolution-rate 0.99999)
```

So, right away we see the "functional" nature of this program.[8] The
return value of tick is a new cell. I don't know if that water-evolution-
rate is correct. The modelers haven't told us what the rate should be. So
I just guessed. I expect that they'll wait until they see how the model
behaves and then tell us to change it.

So far, I haven't specified any dynamic types. It seems a bit early for that.
But I'm pretty sure it's coming.

Anyway, let's see if we can make a fish move.

Wait. How do you move a fish? Where is the fish? Does the fish know
its location, or is that something the world knows?

The cells are arranged in a two-dimensional rectangular Cartesian grid
that wraps left to right and top to bottom. So the location of a cell is the
tuple [x y]. The world could hold the cells in a two-dimensioned array,
or in a map keyed by the position tuple.

I like using maps for things like this, so let's make a world full of water cells:

```
(context "world"
  (it "creates a world full of water cells"
    (let [world (world/make 2 2)
```

———

8. Almost. The (rand) invocation is impure.

```
      cells (:cells world)
      positions (set (keys cells))]
  (should= #{[0 0] [0 1]
             [1 0] [1 1]} positions)
  (should (every? #(= ::water/water (::cell/type %))
                  (vals cells))))))
```

———

```
(ns wator.world
  (:require [wator
             [water :as water]]))

(defn make [w h]
  (let [locs (for [x (range w) y (range h)] [x y])
        loc-water (interleave locs (repeat (water/make)))
        cells (apply hash-map loc-water)]
    {:cells cells}))
```

Did you catch the use of the lazy list of water cells passed into `interleave`? Now we should be able to put a `fish` in the world and move it around. Here's my first try at a test:

```
(context "animal"
  (it "moves"
    (let [fish (fish/make)
          world (-> (world/make 3 3)
                    (world/set-cell [1 1] fish))
          [loc cell] (animal/move fish [1 1] world)]
      (should= cell fish)
      (should (#{[0 0] [0 1] [0 2]
                 [1 0] [1 2]
                 [2 0] [2 1] [2 2]}
               loc)))))
```

This is pretty straightforward. We create a 3-by-3 world with a `fish` in the center. Then we move the `fish`. Finally, we make sure it's still a `fish` and that its destination is one of the neighboring cells.

I made a ton of design decisions while composing this test. Those kinds of decisions are why the last *D* in *TDD* often stands for *design*. I'll walk you through those decisions in a moment, but first let me show you the code that passes this test:

```
(ns wator.world
  (:require [wator
             [water :as water]]))

(defn make [w h] . . .)

(defn set-cell [world loc cell]
  (assoc-in world [:cells loc] cell))


_____


(ns wator.animal
  (:require [wator
             [cell :as cell]]))

(defmulti move (fn [animal & args] (::cell/type animal)))
(defmulti reproduce (fn [animal & args] (::cell/type animal)))

(defn tick [animal]
  )

(defn do-move [animal loc world]
  [[0 0] animal])


_____


(ns wator.fish
  (:require [wator
             [cell :as cell]
             [animal :as animal]]))

(defn make [] {::cell/type ::fish})
```

```
(defmethod cell/tick ::fish [fish]
  (animal/tick fish)
  )

(defmethod animal/move ::fish [fish loc world]
  (animal/do-move fish loc world))

(defmethod animal/reproduce ::fish [fish]
  )
```

When you see . . . in a method body, it means that there has been no change to that method since the last time I presented it.

There's nothing really astonishing here. I changed the defmulti definitions in animal to accept multiple arguments, and I created a default do-move method in animal that the subtypes can call if they like.[9] The implementation of do-move is degenerate and is there only to test the test.

So, on to the design decisions that I made while composing this test. My first problem was that an animal can't move if it can't see the world. So either every animal should hold a reference to the world, or the world should be a global atom, or the world should be passed in as an argument to the move function. I chose the latter because I feel a kind of mild disdain[10] for abandoning the functional paradigm and falling back on atoms and STM.

My next problem was that the animal does not know its location. So I need to pass the location of the animal into the move function along with the world.

Finally, and most importantly, I puzzled over what the move function should return. At first, I thought it should return the updated world. But this creates the following inconsistency problem.

---

9. This is kind of like implementing a method in a base class and allowing subclasses to either override it or not.

10. Perhaps that disdain is misplaced, but this IS a book about functional design, so. . .

Imagine the update process for the world. It begins at location [0 0] and walks through the world updating each cell in turn. Now imagine there is a fish at [0 0] and that the update moves it to [0 1]. But [0 1] is the cell that the world updates next. So that same fish moves *again*. A fish should not move twice in a single turn.

So the move function cannot update the world. Instead, the world is going to have to build up a new world from the old world, one cell at a time. I imagine we could do it something like this:[11]

```
(let [new-world-cells (apply hash-map
                       (map update-cell old-world-cells))]. . .)
```

So now let's actually implement the degenerate do-move function. What is the process for moving an animal? I think it's pretty simple. We just get the neighbors of the animal's location, determine which are valid destinations (i.e., are water), and then randomly choose from that list. So do-move should look like this:

```
(defn do-move [animal loc world]
  (let [neighbors (world/neighbors world loc)

        destinations (filter
                        #(water/is?
                          (world/get-cell world %))
                        neighbors)
        new-location (rand-nth destinations)]
    [new-location animal]))
```

Very pretty. We ask the world for the neighbors of the location, filter out any that aren't water, and then randomly choose one. Cool.

---

11. Remember that :cells holds a map, so the update-cell function will take [key val] pairs and return [key val] pairs.

I thought it best to make sure that all the torus math was nicely sequestered within world. I didn't want it leaking out into all the animals:

```
(defn wrap [world [x y]]
  (let [[w h] (::bounds world)]
    [(mod x w) (mod y h)])
  )


(defn neighbors [world loc]
  (let [[x y] loc
        neighbors (for [dx (range -1 2) dy (range -1 2)]
                    (wrap world [(+ x dx) (+ y dy)]))]
    (remove #(= loc %) neighbors)))
```

Are you ready for the stuff that's not pretty? The code above refused to compile, because (are you ready for this?) water depends upon fish (for the evolution), fish depends upon animal (for do-move), and animal depends upon water. That's a dependency cycle, and Clojure *hates* dependency cycles. See Figure 17.3.

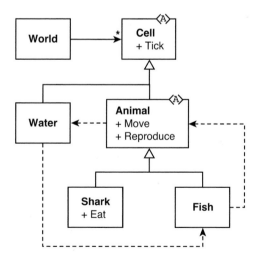

Figure 17.3. A dependency cycle

OK, take a deep breath. Remember, we're playing a game here. In a simple application like Wa-Tor, I would not be partitioning these files so ruthlessly. In fact, there's a good chance I'd just write the whole program in a single file and let the devil have his way with me. But we are pretending that this is a multi-mega-line enterprise application, and so we're going to be assiduously careful with all these source code dependencies. Right?

So the way we have to solve this is by falling back on something like the old C mechanism of declarations and implementations. See Figure 17.4.

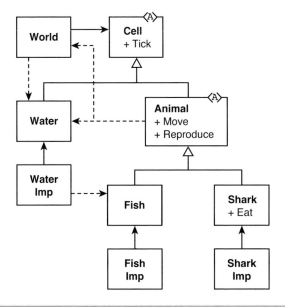

Figure 17.4.   Breaking the dependency cycle

By splitting water such that its fish dependency is in water-imp, and by making sure that water-imp depends upon water instead of the other way around (the DIP), the cycle is broken. I also split up fish and shark[12] for consistency. I'll probably have to split up animal pretty soon too.[13]

---

12. Actually, just fish. I split shark on the diagram but not in the code. YAGNI, YAGNI, YAGNI.

13. Future Uncle Bob: . . .nope.

So now the code looks like this:

```
(ns wator.world
  (:require [wator
             [water :as water]]))

(defn make [w h]
  (let [locs (for [x (range w) y (range h)] [x y])
        loc-water (interleave locs (repeat (water/make)))
        cells (apply hash-map loc-water)]
    {::cells cells
     ::bounds [w h]}))

(defn set-cell [world loc cell]
  (assoc-in world [::cells loc] cell))

(defn get-cell [world loc]
  (get-in world [::cells loc]))

; . . .


  _____


(ns wator.cell)

(defmulti tick ::type)


  _____


(ns wator.water
  (:require [wator
             [cell :as cell]]))

(defn make [] {::cell/type ::water})

(defn is? [cell]
  (= ::water (::cell/type cell)))


  _____
```

```
(ns wator.water-imp
  (:require [wator
             [cell :as cell]
             [water :as water]
             [fish :as fish]
             [config :as config]]))

(defmethod cell/tick ::water/water [water]
  (if (> (rand) config/water-evolution-rate)
    (fish/make)
    water))


  ————


(ns wator.animal
  (:require [wator
             [world :as world]
             [cell :as cell]
             [water :as water]]))

(defmulti move (fn [animal & args] (::cell/type animal)))
(defmulti reproduce (fn [animal & args] (::cell/type animal)))

(defn tick [animal]
  )

(defn do-move [animal loc world]
  (let [neighbors (world/neighbors world loc)
        destinations (filter #(water/is?
                                (world/get-cell world %))
                             neighbors)
        new-location (rand-nth destinations)]
    [new-location animal]))


  ———


(ns wator.fish
  (:require [wator
             [cell :as cell]]))
```

```
(defn make [] {::cell/type ::fish})
```

———

```
(ns wator.fish-imp
  (:require [wator
             [cell :as cell]
             [animal :as animal]
             [fish :as fish]]))

(defmethod cell/tick ::fish/fish [fish]
  (animal/tick fish)
  )

(defmethod animal/move ::fish/fish [fish loc world]
  (animal/do-move fish loc world))

(defmethod animal/reproduce ::fish/fish [fish]
  )
```

The shark isn't relevant yet, so I didn't show it.

The criterion for splitting water and fish is pretty easy to see. Any function that references a file outside of the direct type hierarchy gets put into the imp file. Pay special attention to the namespaces and the namespaced keywords. For example, notice that the defmethods in fish-imp will still be dispatched on ::fish/fish.

And just in case you thought I'd forgotten, here are the current tests:

```
(ns wator.core-spec
  (:require [speclj.core :refer :all]
             [wator
              [cell :as cell]
              [water :as water]
              [water-imp]
              [animal :as animal]
              [fish :as fish]
              [fish-imp]
              [world :as world]]))
```

```
(describe "Wator"
  (with-stubs)
  (context "Water"
    (it "usually remains water"
      (with-redefs [rand (stub :rand {:return 0.0})]
        (let [water (water/make)
              evolved (cell/tick water)]
          (should= ::water/water (::cell/type evolved)))))

    (it "occasionally evolves into a fish"
      (with-redefs [rand (stub :rand {:return 1.0})]
        (let [water (water/make)
              evolved (cell/tick water)]
          (should= ::fish/fish (::cell/type evolved))))))

  (context "world"
    (it "creates a world full of water cells"
      (let [world (world/make 2 2)
            cells (::world/cells world)
            positions (set (keys cells))]
        (should= #{[0 0] [0 1]
                   [1 0] [1 1]} positions)
        (should (every? #(= ::water/water (::cell/type %))
                        (vals cells)))))

    (it "makes neighbors"
      (let [world (world/make 5 5)]
        (should= [[0 0] [0 1] [0 2]
                  [1 0] [1 2]
                  [2 0] [2 1] [2 2]]
                 (world/neighbors world [1 1]))
        (should= [[4 4] [4 0] [4 1]
                  [0 4] [0 1]
                  [1 4] [1 0] [1 1]]
                 (world/neighbors world [0 0]))
        (should= [[3 3] [3 4] [3 0]
                  [4 3] [4 0]
```

```
                  [0 3] [0 4] [0 0]]
          (world/neighbors world [4 4]))))))

  (context "animal"
    (it "moves"
      (let [fish (fish/make)
            world (-> (world/make 3 3)
                      (world/set-cell [1 1] fish))
            [loc cell] (animal/move fish [1 1] world)]
        (should= cell fish)
        (should (#{[0 0] [0 1] [0 2]
                   [1 0] [1 2]
                   [2 0] [2 1] [2 2]}
                  loc))))))
```

Look at the :require up in the ns statement. Notice that we are requiring
the imps but not explicitly using them. Requiring them registers the
defmethods that they contain.

OK, now that we can move the fish, I'm pretty sure the sharks will move
too. So next we should try some reproduction. But before we do that, I'm
getting (pretend) concerned about the type system for the world. Let's get
that set up first:

```
(ns wator.world
  (:require [clojure.spec.alpha :as s]
            [wator
             [cell :as cell]
             [water :as water]]))

(s/def ::location (s/tuple int? int?))
(s/def ::cell #(contains? % ::cell/type))
(s/def ::cells (s/map-of ::location ::cell))
(s/def ::bounds ::location)
(s/def ::world (s/keys :req [::cells ::bounds]))

(defn make [w h]
  {:post [(s/valid? ::world %)]}
  …)
```

OK, that's better. Now, what do we need for reproduction? The modelers said that a `fish` will reproduce if it is next to a `water` cell and is above a certain age. The two daughter `fish` have their ages reset to zero. Otherwise, the `::age` of a `fish` increases with time.

Here are the tests:

```
(it "reproduces"
  (let [fish (-> (fish/make)
               (animal/set-age config/fish-reproduction-age))
       world (-> (world/make 3 3)
               (world/set-cell [1 1] fish))
       [loc1 cell1 loc2 cell2] (animal/reproduce
                                 fish [1 1] world)]
    (should= loc1 [1 1])
    (should (fish/is? cell1))
    (should= 0 (animal/age cell1))
    (should (#{[0 0] [0 1] [0 2]
              [1 0] [1 2]
              [2 0] [2 1] [2 2]}
            loc2))
    (should (fish/is? cell2))
    (should= 0 (animal/age cell2))))

(it "doesn't reproduce if there is no room"
  (let [fish (-> (fish/make)
               (animal/set-age config/fish-reproduction-age))
       world (-> (world/make 1 1)
               (world/set-cell [0 0] fish))
       failed (animal/reproduce fish [0 0] world)]
    (should-be-nil failed)))

(it "doesn't reproduce if too young"
    (let [fish (-> (fish/make)
                 (animal/set-age
                   (dec config/fish-reproduction-age)))
         world (-> (world/make 3 3)
```

```
                (world/set-cell [1 1] fish))
        failed (animal/reproduce fish [1 1] world)]
    (should-be-nil failed)))
```

Notice that if the `fish` reproduces, the return value contains both daughters. But if something goes wrong, we return `nil`. This is because I reckon that the high-level policy of a `fish` includes something like this:

```
(if-let [result (animal/reproduce …)]
  result
  (animal/move …))
```

Anyway, here's the abbreviated code that passes that test:

```
(ns wator.animal
  (:require [clojure.spec.alpha :as s]
            [wator
             [world :as world]
             [cell :as cell]
             [water :as water]
             [config :as config]]]))

(s/def ::age int?)
(s/def ::animal (s/keys :req [::age]))

(defmulti move (fn [animal & args] (::cell/type animal)))
(defmulti reproduce (fn [animal & args] (::cell/type animal)))
(defmulti make-child ::cell/type)

(defn make []
  {::age 0})

(defn age [animal]
  (::age animal))

(defn set-age [animal age]
  (assoc animal ::age age))

;. . .
```

```
(defn do-reproduce [animal loc world]
  (if (>= (age animal) config/fish-reproduction-age)
    (let [neighbors (world/neighbors world loc)
          birth-places (filter #(water/is? (world/get-cell world %))
                               neighbors)]
      (if (empty? birth-places)
        nil
        [loc (set-age animal 0)
         (rand-nth birth-places) (make-child animal)]]))
    nil))
```

```
(ns wator.fish
  (:require [clojure.spec.alpha :as s]
            [wator
             [cell :as cell]
             [animal :as animal]]]))

(s/def ::fish (s/and #(= ::fish (::cell/type %))
                     ::animal/animal))
(defn is? [cell]
  (= ::fish (::cell/type cell)))

(defn make []
  {:post [(s/valid? ::fish %)]}
  (merge {::cell/type ::fish}
         (animal/make)))

(defmethod animal/make-child ::fish [fish]
  (make))
```

_____

```
(ns wator.fish-imp
  (:require [wator
             [cell :as cell]
```

```
            [animal :as animal]
            [fish :as fish]]]))

; . . .

(defmethod animal/reproduce ::fish/fish [fish loc world]
  (animal/do-reproduce fish loc world))
```

Again, notice that I am deferring the fish/reproduce function to animal/do-reproduce. This allows me to specify the common behavior of reproduce in animal while allowing fish to override or augment it. I don't know if this will be necessary,[14] but it's pretty cheap to add and it eliminates the duplication in shark and fish.

SCRATCH THAT ITCH

I'm getting an itchy feeling that I should have implemented world/tick first. I've made a lot of decisions about the return values of move and reproduce based upon what I think world/tick is going to need. So let's switch gears and focus on that before we continue to add more, possibly errant, goop to the animals.

Here's the first test:

```
(it "moves a fish around each tick"
  (let [fish (fish/make)
        small-world (-> (world/make 1 2)
                        (world/set-cell [0 0] fish)
                        (world/tick))
        vacated-cell (world/get-cell small-world [0 0])
        occupied-cell (world/get-cell small-world [0 1])]
    (should (water/is? vacated-cell))
    (should (fish/is? occupied-cell))
    (should= 1 (animal/age occupied-cell))))
```

---

14. Yeah, I know, YAGNI and all that. But rules are meant to be broken.

It's pretty simple. We make a small-world with two cells, one of which is a fish. We call tick on that world, and then we make sure that the fish moves to the vacant cell and that it leaves water behind.

Next, I wrote a dummy implementation for tick, just to see the test pass:

```
(defn tick [world]
  (-> (make 2 1)
      (set-cell [0 0] (water/make))
      (set-cell [0 1] (animal/set-age (fish/make) 1))))
```

Lo and behold, this won't compile because world now depends upon fish, which depends upon animal, which depends back upon world. Sigh. Cyclic dependencies are the bane of source code structures that are thought through poorly.

But we know how to solve this. We simply have to invert a dependency (the DIP) by splitting world-imp out of world. The UML looks like Figure 17.5.

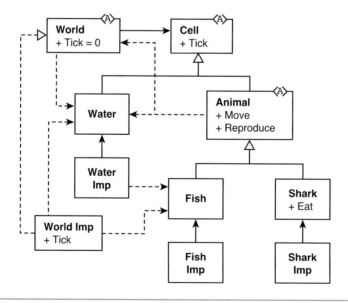

Figure 17.5. Breaking another dependency cycle

The =0 next to tick in the World class is my way of indicating that it is an abstract method. So here's the code:

```
(ns wator.world
  (:require [clojure.spec.alpha :as s]
            [wator
             [cell :as cell]
             [water :as water]]))

(s/def ::location (s/tuple int? int?))
(s/def ::cell #(contains? % ::cell/type))
(s/def ::cells (s/map-of ::location ::cell))
(s/def ::bounds ::location)
(s/def ::world (s/and (s/keys :req [::cells ::bounds])
                      #(= (::type %) ::world)))

(defmulti tick ::type)

(defn make [w h]
  {:post [(s/valid? ::world %)]}
  (let [locs (for [x (range w) y (range h)] [x y])
        loc-water (interleave locs (repeat (water/make)))
        cells (apply hash-map loc-water)]
    {::type ::world
     ::cells cells
     ::bounds [w h]}))

; . . .
```
_____

```
(ns wator.world-imp
  (:require [wator
             [world :as world :refer :all]
             [animal :as animal]
             [fish :as fish]
             [water :as water]]))
```

```
(defmethod world/tick ::world/world [world]
  (-> (make 2 1)
      (set-cell [0 0] (water/make))
      (set-cell [0 1] (animal/set-age (fish/make) 1))))
```

This passed the test once I added [world-imp] to the :require list in the test. Take note that tick is now a multi-method with only one implementation. That's the dependency inversion that we needed.

But now I'm bothered by that water dependency in world. There's a technical term for how I feel about it. That term is *icky*. That dependency is *wrong* somehow.

I need a shower. I resolve lots of issues while in the shower.

SHOWERS SOLVE PROBLEMS

OK, I'm back from my shower, and this is the conversation I had with myself while under the spray.

"Creating water in world is icky. I mean, I just split world in two because creating a fish led to a cycle. So creating water could lead to a cycle too. But wait, this is all about creation. Maybe what I need is a factory! Yeah, an Abstract Factory named cell-factory, and it will take opaque tokens like :fish and :water, and. . . (OH!). . . and :default-cell. Yeah, and. . . Wait, why do I need a whole new factory? Why can't world BE the factory? Yeah! That's the *Factory Method* pattern. That's the ticket!"

The UML for this (in Figure 17.6) is revealing.

An architectural boundary just appeared. All dependencies cross it going toward the high-level side, following the Dependency Rule. I may not use this boundary in the actual architecture, but it's there if I need it.

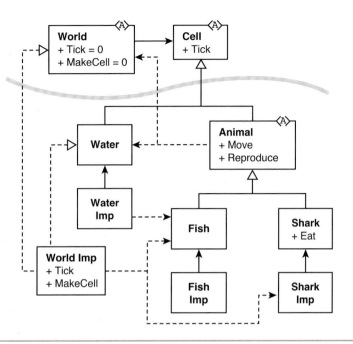

Figure 17.6. Wa-Tor with the Factory Method pattern

So now the code looks like this:

```clojure
(ns wator.world
  (:require [clojure.spec.alpha :as s]
            [wator
             [cell :as cell]
             [water :as water]]]))

(s/def ::location (s/tuple int? int?))
(s/def ::cell #(contains? % ::cell/type))
(s/def ::cells (s/map-of ::location ::cell))
(s/def ::bounds ::location)
(s/def ::world (s/and (s/keys :req [::cells ::bounds])
                      #(= (::type %) ::world)))

(defmulti tick ::type)
(defmulti make-cell (fn [factory-type cell-type] factory-type))
```

```
(defn make [w h]
  {:post [(s/valid? ::world %)]}
  (let [locs (for [x (range w) y (range h)] [x y])
        default-cell (make-cell ::world :default-cell)
        loc-water (interleave locs (repeat default-cell))
        cells (apply hash-map loc-water)]
    {::type ::world
     ::cells cells
     ::bounds [w h]}))
;. . .
```

```
(ns wator.world-imp
  (:require [wator
              [world :as world :refer :all]
              [animal :as animal]
              [fish :as fish]
                  [shark :as shark]
              [water :as water]]))

(defmethod world/tick ::world/world [world]
  (-> (make 2 1)
      (set-cell [0 0] (water/make))
      (set-cell [0 1] (animal/set-age (fish/make) 1))))

(defmethod world/make-cell ::world/world [world cell-type]
  (condp = cell-type
    :default-cell (water/make)
    :water (water/make)
    :fish (fish/make)
    :shark (shark/make)))
```

The `factory-type` in `make-cell` is simply passed in as ::world. That allows the `defmethod` ::world/world to resolve it.

I have high hopes for this change. And please note, this whole change was driven by one test that I made to pass using a dummy implementation in `tick`, reminding us yet again that TDD is a design technique.

OK, now let's make that dummy implementation fail. Here's the test that fails:

```
(it "moves a fish around each tick"
  (doseq [scenario
          [{:dimension [2 1] :starting [0 0] :ending [1 0]}
           {:dimension [2 1] :starting [1 0] :ending [0 0]}
           {:dimension [1 2] :starting [0 0] :ending [0 1]}
           {:dimension [1 2] :starting [0 1] :ending [0 0]}]]
    (let [fish (fish/make)
          {:keys [dimension starting ending]} scenario
          [h w] dimension
          small-world (-> (world/make h w)
                          (world/set-cell starting fish)
                          (world/tick))
          vacated-cell (world/get-cell small-world starting)
          occupied-cell (world/get-cell small-world ending)]
      (should (water/is? vacated-cell))
      (should (fish/is? occupied-cell))
      (should= 1 (animal/age occupied-cell)))))
```

I created the four possible 1-by-2 scenarios and made sure the world got updated properly after a tick.

Making this pass forced me to change the design yet again. The animal/move, animal/reproduce, and cell/tick functions must return a [from to] list in which each is a single-element map containing {loc cell}. Look at the world-imp and you'll see why:

```
(ns wator.world-imp
  . . .)


(defmethod world/tick ::world/world [world]
  (let [cells (::world/cells world)]
    (loop [locs (keys cells)
           new-cells {}
           moved-into #{}]
      (cond
```

```
(empty? locs)
(assoc world ::world/cells new-cells)

(contains? moved-into (first locs))
(recur (rest locs) new-cells moved-into)

:else
(let [loc (first locs)
      cell (get cells loc)
      [from to] (cell/tick cell loc world)
      new-cells (-> new-cells (merge from) (merge to))
      to-loc (first (keys to))]
  (recur (rest locs)
         new-cells
         (conj moved-into to-loc)))))))

; . . .
```

It turns out that every operation makes changes to either one or two cells. When an animal moves, reproduces, or eats, only two cells are involved. If an animal fails to move, or if it starves, only one cell is involved. In the first case the operation will return [from to], and in the second case it will return [nil to]. In either case, both from and to are merged[15] into new-cells.

Notice the moved-into argument of the loop. At first, I didn't have it there, and the tests failed because world/tick moved the fish to the remaining water cell. But then world/tick called cell/tick on the water cell, which replaced itself with water. When the new-cells were merged in, the water overwrote the fish.

So moved-into is a set of all the to cell locations. The cell/tick function should not be called on them because they've been moved into by a previous tick, and so the animal there has already been ticked.

---

15. merge is well behaved if you merge in a nil.

Quite a few changes had to be made throughout the structure to get this to work. So my "itch" from a few pages back was correct. It's a good thing I paid attention to it early enough to make the change doable:

```
(ns wator.cell)

(defmulti tick (fn [cell & args] (::type cell)))
```

———

```
(ns wator.water-imp
  (:require [wator
             [cell :as cell]
             [water :as water]
             [fish :as fish]
             [config :as config]]))

(defmethod cell/tick ::water/water [water loc world]
  (if (> (rand) config/water-evolution-rate)
    [nil {loc (fish/make)}]
    [nil {loc water}]))
```

———

```
(ns wator.animal . . .)

;. . .

(defn increment-age [animal]
  (update animal ::age inc))

(defn tick [animal loc world]
  (-> animal
      increment-age
      (move loc world)))
```

```
(defn do-move [animal loc world]
  (let [neighbors (world/neighbors world loc)
        destinations (filter #(water/is?
                                (world/get-cell world %))
                             neighbors)
        new-location (if (empty? destinations)
                       loc
                       (rand-nth destinations))]
    (if (= new-location loc)
      [nil {loc animal}]
      [{loc (water/make)} {new-location animal}])))

;. . .


_____


(ns wator.fish-imp . . .)

(defmethod cell/tick ::fish/fish [fish loc world]
  (animal/tick fish loc world)
  )

; . . .
```

And, of course, a few of the tests needed to change:

```
(ns wator.core-spec . . .)

(describe "Wator"
  (with-stubs)
  (context "Water"
    (it "usually remains water"
      (with-redefs [rand (stub :rand {:return 0.0})]
        (let [water (water/make)
              world (world/make 1 1)
              [from to] (cell/tick water [0 0] world)]
          (should-be-nil from)
          (should (water/is? (get to [0 0])))
          )))
```

```
(it "occasionally evolves into a fish"
  (with-redefs [rand (stub :rand {:return 1.0})]
    (let [water (water/make)
          world (world/make 1 1)
          [from to] (cell/tick water [0 0] world)]
      (should-be-nil from)
      (should (fish/is? (get to [0 0]))))))))
```

`;. . .`

```
(context "animal"
  (it "moves"
    (let [fish (fish/make)
          world (-> (world/make 3 3)
                    (world/set-cell [1 1] fish))
          [from to] (animal/move fish [1 1] world)
          loc (first (keys to))]
      (should (water/is? (get from [1 1])))
      (should (fish/is? (get to loc)))
      (should (#{[0 0] [0 1] [0 2]
                 [1 0] [1 2]
                 [2 0] [2 1] [2 2]}
               loc))))

  (it "doesn't move if there are no spaces"
    (let [fish (fish/make)
          world (-> (world/make 1 1)
                    (world/set-cell [0 0] fish))
          [from to] (animal/move fish [0 0] world)]
      (should (fish/is? (get to [0 0])))
      (should (nil? from)))
```

There's another scenario that I think will fail—two fish competing for the same spot:

```
(it "move two fish who compete for the same spot"
  (let [fish (fish/make)
        competitive-world (-> (world/make 3 1)
                              (world/set-cell [0 0] fish)
```

```
                    (world/set-cell [2 0] fish)
                    (world/tick))
        start-00 (world/get-cell competitive-world [0 0])
        start-20 (world/get-cell competitive-world [2 0])
        end-10 (world/get-cell competitive-world [1 0])]
    (should (fish/is? end-10))
    (should (or (fish/is? start-00)
                (fish/is? start-20)))
    (should (or (water/is? start-00)
                (water/is? start-20)))))
```

A simple 3-by-1 world with fish at either end. Only one of them can move into the center slot. The other will have to remain where it was. This test fails because the animal/move function does not know that a fish already moved into the target slot.

Solving this means somehow sending the moved-into list to animal/move. I hate the idea of adding yet another argument to animal/move, so perhaps we can squirrel this information away in the world that we pass to animal/move:

```
(ns wator.world-imp . . .)

(defmethod world/tick ::world/world [world]
  (let [cells (::world/cells world)]
    (loop [locs (keys cells)
           new-cells {}
           moved-into #{}]
      (cond
        (empty? locs)
        (assoc world ::world/cells new-cells)

        (contains? moved-into (first locs))
        (recur (rest locs) new-cells moved-into)

        :else
        (let [loc (first locs)
              cell (get cells loc)
```

```
              [from to] (cell/tick
                           cell loc
                           (assoc world :moved-into moved-into))
               new-cells (-> new-cells (merge from) (merge to))
               to-loc (first (keys to))
               to-cell (get to to-loc)
               moved-into (if (water/is? to-cell)
                              moved-into
                              (conj moved-into to-loc))]
           (recur (rest locs) new-cells moved-into))))))
```

———

```
(ns wator.animal . . .)

; . . .

(defn do-move [animal loc world]
  (let [neighbors (world/neighbors world loc)
        moved-into (get world :moved-into #{})
        available-neighbors (remove moved-into neighbors)
        destinations (filter #(water/is?
                                (world/get-cell world %))
                             available-neighbors)
        new-location (if (empty? destinations)
                         loc
                         (rand-nth destinations))]
    (if (= new-location loc)
      [nil {loc animal}]
      [{loc (water/make)} {new-location animal}])))
```

Note that I did not use a namespaced keyword for :moved-into. That's because I consider it to be tramp data that is not really part of the world and is just kind of hitching a ride. This feels a little dirty, but it works.[16]

Note that we only put locations into moved-into if the cell being moved in is not water.

---

16. Welcome to real-world engineering trade-offs.

IT'S TIME TO WILDLY REPRODUCE[17]

OK, let's see if we can fill the world with fish:

```
(it "fills the world with reproducing fish"
  (loop [world (-> (world/make 10 10)
                   (world/set-cell [5 5] (fish/make)))
         n 100]
    (if (zero? n)
      (let [cells (-> world ::world/cells vals)
            fishies (filter fish/is? cells)
            fish-count (count fishies)]
        (should (< 50 fish-count)))
      (recur (world/tick world) (dec n)))))
```

Nifty. Create a 10-by-10 `world`. Load it with one `fish`. Send it 100 `ticks`, and make sure there are more than 50 `fish`. I mean, the fish are moving around and reproducing like crazy in there!

Of course, this test fails; but only because we didn't call `reproduce` in `animal/tick`. So let's fix that:

```
(defn tick [animal loc world]
  (let [aged-animal (increment-age animal)
        reproduction (reproduce aged-animal loc world)]
    (if reproduction
      reproduction
      (move aged-animal loc world))))
```

Yup. Age the animal, then see if it will reproduce. If not, then move it. Simple. Easy.

Of course, I had to fix the fact that `reproduce` didn't use our new [from to] convention:

```
(defn do-reproduce [animal loc world]
  (if (>= (age animal) config/fish-reproduction-age)
```

---

17. Ugliness breeds ugliness.

```
(let [neighbors (world/neighbors world loc)
      birth-places (filter #(water/is?
                              (world/get-cell world %))
                            neighbors)]
  (if (empty? birth-places)
    nil
    [{loc (set-age animal 0)}
     {(rand-nth birth-places) (make-child animal)}]))
nil))
```

And that broke an earlier test:

```
(it "reproduces"
  (let [fish (-> (fish/make)
                 (animal/set-age config/fish-reproduction-age))
        world (-> (world/make 3 3)
                  (world/set-cell [1 1] fish))
        [from to] (animal/reproduce fish [1 1] world)
        from-loc (-> from keys first)
        from-cell (-> from vals first)
        to-loc (-> to keys first)
        to-cell (-> to vals first)]
    (should= from-loc [1 1])
    (should (fish/is? from-cell))
    (should= 0 (animal/age from-cell))
    (should (#{[0 0] [0 1] [0 2]
               [1 0] [1 2]
               [2 0] [2 1] [2 2]}
             to-loc))
    (should (fish/is? to-cell))
    (should= 0 (animal/age to-cell))))
```

But with that, the fish reproduce like. . . fish. That was pretty easy. I think our design is coming together.

WHAT ABOUT THE SHARKS?

I've neglected the shark class so far because its behavior is almost identical to fish and is mostly governed by the animal abstraction. But now let's see if we can get shark objects to move and reproduce.

This required me to flesh out the shark module and also make one small design change. I used the *Template Method* pattern to get the reproduction age of an animal. The tests hint at that change:

```
(context "animal"
  (it "moves"
    (doseq [scenario
            [{:constructor fish/make :tester fish/is?}
             {:constructor shark/make :tester shark/is?}]]
      (let [animal ((:constructor scenario))
            world (-> (world/make 3 3)
                      (world/set-cell [1 1] animal))
            [from to] (animal/move animal [1 1] world)
            loc (first (keys to))]
        (should (water/is? (get from [1 1])))
        (should ((:tester scenario) (get to loc)))
        (should (#{[0 0] [0 1] [0 2]
                   [1 0] [1 2]
                   [2 0] [2 1] [2 2]}
                 loc)))))

  (it "doesn't move if there are no spaces"
    (doseq [scenario
            [{:constructor fish/make :tester fish/is?}
             {:constructor shark/make :tester shark/is?}]]
      (let [animal ((:constructor scenario))
            world (-> (world/make 1 1)
                      (world/set-cell [0 0] animal))
            [from to] (animal/move animal [0 0] world)]
        (should ((:tester scenario) (get to [0 0])))
        (should (nil? from)))))
```

```
(it "reproduces"
  (doseq [scenario
            [{:constructor fish/make :tester fish/is?}
             {:constructor shark/make :tester shark/is?}]]
    (let [animal ((:constructor scenario))
          reproduction-age (animal/get-reproduction-age animal)
          animal (animal/set-age animal reproduction-age)
          world (-> (world/make 3 3)
                    (world/set-cell [1 1] animal))
          [from to] (animal/reproduce animal [1 1] world)
          from-loc (-> from keys first)
          from-cell (-> from vals first)
          to-loc (-> to keys first)
          to-cell (-> to vals first)]
      (should= from-loc [1 1])
      (should ((:tester scenario) from-cell))
      (should= 0 (animal/age from-cell))
      (should (#{[0 0] [0 1] [0 2]
                 [1 0] [1 2]
                 [2 0] [2 1] [2 2]}
                to-loc))
      (should ((:tester scenario) to-cell))
      (should= 0 (animal/age to-cell)))))

(it "doesn't reproduce if there is no room"
  (doseq [scenario
            [{:constructor fish/make :tester fish/is?}
             {:constructor shark/make :tester shark/is?}]]
    (let [animal ((:constructor scenario))
          reproduction-age (animal/get-reproduction-age animal)
          animal (animal/set-age animal reproduction-age)
          world (-> (world/make 1 1)
                    (world/set-cell [0 0] animal))
          failed (animal/reproduce animal [0 0] world)]
      (should-be-nil failed))))

(it "doesn't reproduce if too young"
  (doseq [scenario
            [{:constructor fish/make :tester fish/is?}
```

```
                      {:constructor shark/make :tester shark/is?}]]
      (let [animal ((:constructor scenario))
            reproduction-age (animal/get-reproduction-age animal)
            animal (animal/set-age animal (dec reproduction-age))
            world (-> (world/make 3 3)
                      (world/set-cell [1 1] animal))
            failed (animal/reproduce animal [1 1] world)]
        (should-be-nil failed)))))
```

```
(ns wator.animal …)

(defmulti move (fn [animal & args] (::cell/type animal)))
(defmulti reproduce (fn [animal & args] (::cell/type animal)))
(defmulti make-child ::cell/type)
(defmulti get-reproduction-age ::cell/type)

; . . .
```

```
(ns wator.fish . . .)

(defmethod animal/get-reproduction-age ::fish [fish]
  config/fish-reproduction-age)

; . . .
```

```
(ns wator.shark
  (:require [clojure.spec.alpha :as s]
            [wator
             [config :as config]
             [cell :as cell]
             [animal :as animal]]))
```

```
(s/def ::shark (s/and #(= ::shark (::cell/type %))
                      ::animal/animal))
(defn is? [cell]
  (= ::shark (::cell/type cell)))


(defn make []
  {:post [(s/valid? ::shark %)]}
  (merge {::cell/type ::shark}
         (animal/make)))


(defmethod animal/make-child ::shark [fish]
  (make))


(defmethod animal/get-reproduction-age ::shark [shark]
  config/shark-reproduction-age)


; . . .
```

So far, with the exception of the reproduction age, the behavior of both the shark and fish is "inherited" from (actually it is delegated to) animal. But the shark class has extra constraints that we need to implement now.

The modelers have told us that a shark only reproduces if its :health is above a certain threshold. The :health of a shark is increased by eating a fish, and it decreases with time. If the :health of a shark reaches zero, the shark starves, leaving behind water. When a shark reproduces, its :health is split between the two daughters.

OK, so let's test that the :health decreases with age:

```
(context "shark"
  (it "starts with some health"
    (let [shark (shark/make)]
      (should= config/shark-starting-health
               (shark/health shark))))

  (it "loses health with time"
    (let [small-world (-> (world/make 1 1)
```

```
                          (world/set-cell [0 0] (shark/make)))
              aged-world (world/tick small-world)
              aged-shark (world/get-cell aged-world [0 0])]
        (should= (dec config/shark-starting-health)
                 (shark/health aged-shark)))))))
```

_____

```
(ns wator.shark . . .)

(s/def ::health int?)
(s/def ::shark (s/and #(= ::shark (::cell/type %))
                      ::animal/animal
                      (s/keys :req [::health])))

(defn make []
  {:post [(s/valid? ::shark %)]}
  (merge {::cell/type ::shark
          ::health config/shark-starting-health}
         (animal/make)))

(defn health [shark]
  (::health shark))

(defn decrement-health [shark]
  (update shark ::health dec))

(defmethod cell/tick ::shark [shark loc world]
  (-> shark
      (decrement-health)
      (animal/tick loc world))
  )

; . . .
```

Pretty easy. We just added the ::health field to the ::shark spec and
shark/make, and then we decremented the ::health in the tick function
just before delegating the rest of the behavior to the superclass animal.

Now let's test that a shark will die when its ::health goes to zero:

```
(it "dies when health goes to zero"
     (let [sick-shark (-> (shark/make)
                          (shark/set-health 1))
           small-world (-> (world/make 1 1)
                           (world/set-cell [0 0] sick-shark))
           aged-world (world/tick small-world)
           dead-shark (world/get-cell aged-world [0 0])]
       (should (water/is? dead-shark))))
```

―――

```
(ns wator.shark . . .)

(defmethod cell/tick ::shark [shark loc world]
  (if (= 1 (health shark))
    [nil {loc (water/make)}]
    (-> shark
        (decrement-health)
        (animal/tick loc world))))

; . . .
```

Pretty easy. OK, so now let's test that sharks will eat when given the opportunity:

```
(it "eats when a fish is adjacent"
  (let [world (-> (world/make 2 1)
                  (world/set-cell [0 0] (fish/make))
                  (world/set-cell [1 0] (shark/make)))
        shark-ate-world (world/tick world)
        full-shark (world/get-cell shark-ate-world [0 0])
        where-shark-was (world/get-cell shark-ate-world [1 0])
        expected-health (+ config/shark-starting-health
                           config/shark-eating-health
                           -1)]
```

```
(should (shark/is? full-shark))
(should (water/is? where-shark-was))
(should= expected-health (shark/health full-shark))))
```

We create a 2-by-1 world with a shark next to a fish. After one tick, the shark should be where the fish was, and water should be where the shark was, and the shark's ::health should have increased.

Getting this to pass forced me to abandon the delegation to animal/tick because a shark should try to reproduce first, then try to eat next, and then finally try to move:

```
(ns wator.shark . . .)

(defn eat [shark loc world]
  (let [neighbors (world/neighbors world loc)
        fishy-neighbors (filter #(fish/is?
                                   (world/get-cell world %))
                                 neighbors)]
    (if (empty? fishy-neighbors)
      nil
      [{loc (water/make)}
       {(rand-nth fishy-neighbors) (feed shark)}]))
  )

(defmethod cell/tick ::shark [shark loc world]
  (if (= 1 (health shark))
    [nil {loc (water/make)}]
    (let [aged-shark (-> shark
                         (animal/increment-age)
                         (decrement-health))]
      (if-let [reproduction (animal/reproduce
                              aged-shark loc world)]
        reproduction
        (if-let [eaten (eat aged-shark loc world)]
          eaten
          (animal/move aged-shark loc world))))))
```

All this slipped in with little hassle. We've passed through the design bottleneck and are now reaping the benefits.

The modelers told us that a shark will only reproduce if its health is above a threshold. Let's test that. In fact, let's make that change first[18] and see which tests break:

```
(ns wator.shark . . .)

(defmethod animal/reproduce ::shark [shark loc world]
  (if (>= (health shark) config/shark-reproduction-health)
    (animal/do-reproduce shark loc world)
    nil))
```

As expected, the test for animal reproduction fails in the shark scenario. We can address this by putting a little hack in that test:

```
(it "reproduces"
  (doseq [scenario [{:constructor fish/make :tester fish/is?}
                    {:constructor
                      #(-> (shark/make)
                           (shark/set-health
                             (inc config/shark-reproduction-
                               health)))
                     :tester shark/is?}]]

; . . .
```

Yes, that's a bit ugly, but it does the job. I suppose I should add a test for checking the other side of that threshold:

```
(it "doesn't reproduce if not healthy enough"
  (let [shark (-> (shark/make)
                  (shark/set-health
```

---

18. TDD VIOLATION! ALERT! ALERT!

```
                    (dec config/shark-reproduction-health))
                  (animal/set-age config/shark-reproduction-age))
        world (-> (world/make 3 3)
                  (world/set-cell [1 1] shark))
        failed (animal/reproduce shark [1 1] world)]
    (should-be-nil failed)))
```

OK. One last thing. The health of the parent shark is split between the two daughter sharks:

```
(it "shares health with both daughters after reproduction"
  (let [initial-health (inc config/shark-reproduction-health)
        pregnant-shark (-> (shark/make)
                           (animal/set-age
                             (inc config/shark-reproduction-age))
                           (shark/set-health initial-health))
        world (-> (world/make 2 1)
                  (world/set-cell [0 0] pregnant-shark))
        new-world (world/tick world)
        daughter1 (world/get-cell new-world [0 0])
        daughter2 (world/get-cell new-world [1 0])
        expected-health (quot (dec initial-health) 2)]
    (should (shark/is? daughter1))
    (should (shark/is? daughter2))
    (should= expected-health (shark/health daughter1))
    (should= expected-health (shark/health daughter2))))
```

Yup. That fails because the expected health isn't correct. That should be simple to fix:

```
(ns wator.shark . . .)

(defmethod animal/reproduce ::shark [shark loc world]
  (if (< (health shark) config/shark-reproduction-health)
    nil
    (if-let [reproduction (animal/do-reproduce shark loc world)]
```

```
(let [[from to] reproduction
      from-loc (-> from keys first)
      to-loc (-> to keys first)
      daughter-health (quot (health shark) 2)
      from-shark (-> from vals first
                     (set-health daughter-health))
      to-shark (-> to vals first
                   (set-health daughter-health))]
  [{from-loc from-shark} {to-loc to-shark}])
nil)))
```

And with that, I think the model is complete. Let's see if we can put a GUI on top of it:

```
(ns wator-gui.main
  (:require [quil.core :as q]
            [quil.middleware :as m]
            [wator
             [world :as world]
             [water :as water]
             [fish :as fish]
             [shark :as shark]
             [world-imp]
             [water-imp]
             [fish-imp]]]))

(defn setup []
  (q/frame-rate 60)
  (q/color-mode :rgb)
  (-> (world/make 80 80)
      (world/set-cell [40 40] (fish/make)))
  )

(defn update-state [world]
  (world/tick world))
```

```
(defn draw-state [world]
  (q/background 240)
  (let [cells (::world/cells world)]
    (doseq [loc (keys cells)]
      (let [[x y] loc
            cell (get cells loc)
            x (* 12 x)
            y (* 12 y)
            color (cond
                    (water/is? cell) [255 255 255]
                    (fish/is? cell) [0 0 255]
                    (shark/is? cell) [255 0 0])]
        (q/no-stroke)
        (apply q/fill color)
        (q/rect x y 11 11)))))

(declare wator)

(defn ^:export -main [& args]
  (q/defsketch wator
               :title "Wator"
               :size [960 960]
               :setup setup
               :update update-state
               :draw draw-state
               :features [:keep-on-top]
               :middleware [m/fun-mode])
  args)
```

Yeah, that wasn't too hard. Figure 17.7 is a screenshot of the game in progress.

It's not super-fast; but that's not a big surprise. There are a bunch of things we could do to speed it up. But never mind that. Look at that GUI code. It depends on the model, yet the model knows nothing of the GUI. And that satisfies our original architectural goal.

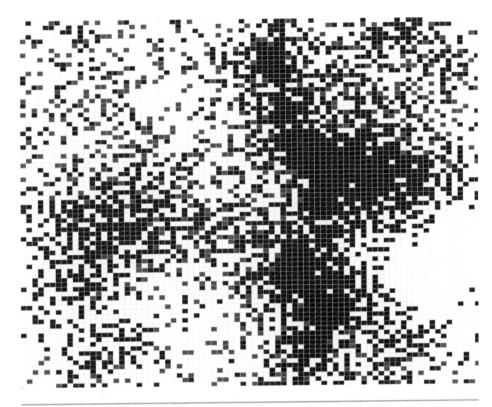

Figure 17.7. Screenshot of Wa-Tor in progress

CONCLUSION

Wa-Tor is a program that is "functional"[19] and object oriented; complete with several OO design patterns right out of the GOF book. Indeed, it was the OO partitioning that helped the design congeal so nicely.

The OO partitioning separates and isolates the various data types very nicely, and it provides pleasant locations for the related functions. Any OO programmer would be very comfortable with this.

---

19. Why the quotes? Because random numbers aren't referentially transparent, so this program is not purely functional.

However, at its heart, this is a data flow model. The world flows through the behaviors in the various objects, without any mutation. The plumbing model of functional programming still holds.

Is this a hybrid approach? Have we created an unholy alliance. . . a Frankenstein's Monster of a program?

I think not. Indeed, I think this combination of approaches is entirely natural and very beneficial. Data is encapsulated and immutable. Behavior is associated with the data it operates on. And yet the data elements flow through the behaviors as opposed to the behaviors iterating over the data.

In the end, I think this is the way software was meant to be.

By the way, you can find all the source code at https://github.com/unclebob/wator.

AFTERWORD

In March 2022, I attended a friend's birthday party where I overheard a couple of guys bantering about code. I introduced myself—I was in the market for some coding friends. Once we'd gotten the obvious exchanges of small talk out of the way, one of them dropped a bomb of a question on me.

He asked, "So, what's your preferred stack?"

All the little bits in my brain frantically searched for an answer while I was simultaneously trying to understand what he was asking me, until finally I very unconfidently answered, "Clojure?"

With a step back and obvious surprise, he exclaimed, "Really?! Like full-stack?"

[Confetti drops in my brain—nailed it!]

In shock, he continued . . . "Front end and back end all in Clojure? I've never heard of that before. How does that work? Clojure is a Lisp language, right? It's functional."

Yes, it is, but *Oh no! Another question . . . "How does that work?"*

Well, if you're reading this, then I assume you've read the preceding pages and thus have already received a much better and more elaborate explanation than I could offer you here, so let's address the elephant in the room: Why was asking me my preferred stack a bomb of a question?

Almost exactly 11 years prior to this birthday party, I began my career as a chemical engineer and a union scab in Metropolis, IL, where I was trained to operate processes and equipment in the manufacturing of uranium hexafluoride. Over the next ten years, I progressed my career into production leadership of various chemical manufacturing plants.

Across that decade, I learned a lot about procedures, state, people, corporate culture, and broken processes for which I lacked the skills to fix. Then, in March 2020, as I was balancing demands based on said broken processes with overwhelming life changes, the world as we knew it shut down. For eight weeks, I suddenly found myself in the near-constant presence of someone whom I knew not only had the skills I lacked, but had developed the rules for mastering those skills.

So I asked my dad, or as you might know him, "Uncle Bob," what it would take to learn software to the depths necessary to fix those problems I so desperately wanted to fix.

That evening he showed me one of his current projects—an automated daily chart on COVID-19 infections and deaths by county. When I didn't recognize the syntax, he took the opportunity to tell me about Clojure.

I immediately had questions because I'd only ever known the basics of languages like Java and Python. He explained the basic differences of OO procedural languages and functional languages and why he liked Clojure. In one example, he showed me why functional languages are "safer" and less complicated than those that rely heavily on mutable states by depicting a race condition for me that was almost identical to that of the phone call between Bob and Alice found in Chapter 15.

Then we dove into the code, and he allowed me an opportunity that I do not take lightly: to work with him on his COVID chart. I mostly just wrote a few basic arithmetic functions (after we wrote tests for those, of course).

He walked me through Quil too, and how even it was mostly functional and how instead of changing a state, it simply recurred a new state at each iteration. This went a little over my head at the time, but I fell back on this conversation a lot over the next year—I even have in front of me right now the printout of the source code we'd written that night as inspiration for writing this.

A little over a year later, I "graduated" from my software apprenticeship and became a full-time developer for Clean Coders Studio.

So, back to the elephant: As of March 2022, I was still pretty new to software; due to COVID-19, there hadn't been many large-group events that had taken place yet; and because Baton Rouge, LA, has some opportunity for growth in the software sector, I had been pretty isolated as a developer and had experienced little exposure to common industry lingo.

That birthday party offered me my first live interaction with a fellow developer outside of Clean Coders, and when I was asked my preferred stack, I had only enough knowledge to translate and puzzle together the question. And it was a bomb of a question because I wasn't confident that I had all the pieces.

With that out of the way, I'll leave you with two final tidbits.

1. The real-life moment Clojure blew my mind was when we were working on a project that built off a Java project that used Angular for the front end. When implementing anything in Angular, we of course had to test and create almost identical methods in Angular and Java (and sometimes in Clojure, as we were migrating a legacy system). Double work everywhere!

Then they asked for a mobile application using all the same functionality as our Clojure features. We extracted much of the core functionality into a `cljc` library, and from there we were able to build the mobile app with little to no code duplication or rewrites.

We used common functions for the `cljs` mobile application, as we did for the back end, by utilizing Clojure common namespaces.

In how many languages can you say you've done that—had the back end and, potentially, multiple front ends all functioning on the same, simultaneously tested code?

2. This got me, as I've seen it get others, and if you're used to OO it will probably get you. `for` in Clojure is not a loop. It is a list comprehension macro, and it does not force side effects. Instead, use `doseq`, which returns `nil` but will accomplish what you are incorrectly trying to achieve with `for`.

Good luck!

—Gina Martiny, Clean Coders

INDEX

Page numbers with "n" indicate footnotes.

Register Your Product at informit.com/register

Access additional benefits and save up to 65%* on your next purchase

- Automatically receive a coupon for 35% off books, eBooks, and web editions and 65% off video courses, valid for 30 days. Look for your code in your InformIT cart or the Manage Codes section of your account page.
- Download available product updates.
- Access bonus material if available.**
- Check the box to hear from us and receive exclusive offers on new editions and related products.

InformIT—The Trusted Technology Learning Source

InformIT is the online home of information technology brands at Pearson, the world's leading learning company. At informit.com, you can

- Shop our books, eBooks, and video training. Most eBooks are DRM-Free and include PDF and EPUB files.
- Take advantage of our special offers and promotions (informit.com/promotions).
- Sign up for special offers and content newsletter (informit.com/newsletters).
- Access thousands of free chapters and video lessons.
- Enjoy free ground shipping on U.S. orders.*

* Offers subject to change.
** Registration benefits vary by product. Benefits will be listed on your account page under Registered Products.

Connect with InformIT—Visit informit.com/community

 twitter.com/informit

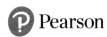 Pearson

Addison-Wesley • Adobe Press • Cisco Press • Microsoft Press • Oracle Press • Peachpit Press • Pearson IT Certification • Que